RUN
with the
CHAMPIONS

OTHER BOOKS BY MARC BLOOM

Cross Country Running
The Marathon
Olympic Gold
The Runner's Bible
The Know Your Game Series
The Miler

RUN with the CHAMPIONS

TRAINING PROGRAMS AND SECRETS OF AMERICA'S 50 GREATEST RUNNERS

BY **MARC BLOOM**, SENIOR WRITER, **RUNNER'S** *WORLD* MAGAZINE

RODALE

© 2001 by Marc Bloom
Cover Photograph © by Tim Davis/Stone

The training information in "Training: Buddy Edelen" on page 82 is from *A Cold Clear Day: The Athletic Biography of Buddy Edelen* and is reprinted with the permission of the author.

Runner's World is a registered trademark of Rodale Inc.

Printed in the United States of America
Rodale Inc. makes every effort to use acid-free ∞, recycled paper ♻.

Cover and Interior Designer: Christopher Rhoads
Cover Photographer: Tim Davis/Stone

Library of Congress Cataloging-in-Publication Data

Bloom, Marc, date.
    Run with the champions : training programs and secrets of America's 50 greatest runners / by Marc Bloom.
        p.   cm.
    Includes index.
    ISBN 1–57954–290–5   paperback
    1. Runners (Sports)—Rating of—United States.   2. Running—Training.
I.Title.
GV1061.14 .B59   2001
613.7'172—dc21   00–012787

Distributed to the book trade by St. Martin's Press

2   4   6   8   10   9   7   5   3   1   paperback

Visit us on the Web at www.rodalesportsandfitness.com, or call us toll-free at (800) 848-4735.

WE **INSPIRE** AND **ENABLE** PEOPLE TO IMPROVE
THEIR LIVES AND THE WORLD AROUND THEM

For my parents

Acknowledgments

Thanks to friends and colleagues for help with statistics and hard-to-find information: Hal Bateman of USA Track and Field for his "Century of Stars" compilation of U.S. international athletes; Scott Davis for his U.S. outdoor record progressions and various American annuals; Ed Gordon, editor of the USA indoor record book, for his world indoor record progressions; Ryan Lamppa of USA Track and Field Road Running Information Center for U.S. road record progressions and national champions; Walt Murphy, editor of *Eastern Track*, for his American Annuals of the 1970s and the few issues of *Track and Field News* that I'm missing; and Stan Saplin, track historian, for his U.S. indoor record progressions. Also thanks to Pat Tyson for discussing the training of Steve Prefontaine, his college roommate at Oregon; coach Roy Benson for reviewing the training chapter; and Doris Hale for her hospitality and reminiscenses of her father, 1908 Olympic marathon champion Johnny Hayes. A final citation to the interview with Abel Kiviat by Professor William Simon in the winter 1986 issue of the *Journal of Sport History*, an excellent reference. And a special thanks to all of the athletes interviewed for their candor and insight in recalling the special moments of their lives.

Contents

A Running Start

Top 30 Men

Top 20 Women

Train the Champions' Way

A Running
Start

Introduction

I started running high school track and cross-country in the early 1960s because of Jim Beatty. In neighborhood games, I was always the last one to be caught, and I had few peers in schoolyard sprints. Even then, I understood that running had a certain grace and heroism and could bestow a hard worker with nobility. The work itself was a crown.

When Beatty, a regular-looking guy with a sweet Carolina drawl and polite manner, became the first runner to break the 4-minute mile indoors in Los Angeles in 1962, I was enthralled. I attended indoor meets like the Millrose Games and went to see Beatty run at Madison Square Garden. When he broke 4 minutes again, I knew that running was the sport for me.

I didn't want to be a miler; I much preferred running down chubby boys on the 100-yard stretch we marked off in crayon on my block in the Sheepshead Bay section of Brooklyn. But the mile seemed glorious, and one after another, the great ones came: Tom O'Hara, Jim Grelle, Dyrol Burleson. People on the street knew who they were.

We were great then, we Americans. We had dazzling milers and wily 5-and-10 men—rugged men with coaches from the old country—and we had a marathoner named Buddy Edelen who broke the world record in England with a knotted handkerchief on his head.

Soon, life got even better. Jim Ryun appeared.

When I was a high school senior in 1964, Ryun was a junior and ran his first sub-4:00 mile. I saw it right there in black and white on television. He ran with a child's fumbling gait and with precious gifts that I don't think we understand even now. Every time Ryun destroyed some record by about 98 seconds, I traded calls with my track team buddies and we all gasped. I had the audacity to write Ryun's coach, Bob Timmons, to ask how Ryun trained. Timmons sent back a six-page handwritten letter telling me the whole story. I wish I still had it. But I remember sharing the letter with the track guys. Some kids snuck *Playboy* magazine into the house; we handled Ryun's workout plans with the same discreet excitement.

That's what this book is about: Jim Beatty and Jim Ryun and America's greatest distance runners—the 50 best, from milers to marathoners, and how they achieved their successes and thrilled the public. America has a rich distance history, perhaps the richest of any nation, and we need to remember that. Running a beautiful mile or marathon reflects on our national character. We were great, once, and we can be great again. It's my hope that the examples of these 50 runners will help today's athletes grow and excel and aspire to run with the world's best.

The lessons of the success of these 50 athletes are also valuable for everyday runners. By examining the innovative training approaches of the stars, you're bound to find motivation and a clever workout idea to inspire you, no matter what your pace or experience. This is the first time that our all-time greatest runners' training programs have been collected in one place. The individual styles—Nina Kuscsik's marathon segments or Billy Mills's tee-to-greens, for instance—offer a mouthwatering look into the ways that the athletes adapted to their environments.

I turned out to be only a marginal high school runner. But I found my niche as a fan early on when in 1964, I collected 25 cents from each of the 40 guys on our track team and made a $10 contribution to the United States Olympic Committee. For our donation, we received a small plaque that still stands in the school trophy case. Later that year, I was walking down the street and heard a radio report from the Tokyo Olympics ringing out from a shop. It announced that Billy Mills had won the 10,000 meters. I was sure the 10 bucks we had donated must have helped.

As a journalist, I've come to know Mills and many of the others among the 50 fairly well over the years. Just about everyone I called to interview was delighted to go back into their mind's archives. Most were enjoying prosperous lives: They were healthy, had families, and were content their present work. Many still ran or did some exercise regularly. A few sounded like they still regretted some near-miss at the Nationals or Olympics and wished they could have a certain race back—just one—to run over again.

The hardest athlete to track down was Sydney Maree, the only athlete living abroad, in his native South Africa. I had his e-mail address but it wasn't working; finally, after weeks of pursuit, I talked to him on the phone. He expressed the same dignity and fight that I'd seen in him years before. That could be said of the group as a whole: They spoke like champions, revealing, even in their sixties and seventies, an edge, a sense of irony, a notion that you do whatever you must to succeed. As runners, this is the promise we all make to ourselves.

I started on this project determining who the top 50 would be. I felt that 30 men and 20 women would be a fair breakdown, since organized women's distance running began only in the 1970s. As I did my research and compiled the final list, it was heartbreaking to leave out a deserving few. That gave me the idea to do an additional, alphabetical 31-to-100 list for men and 21-to-50 list for women: The Rest of the Best: Top 31–100 Men can be found on page 139; The Rest of the Best: Top 21–50 Women is on page 223.

Compiling the actual rankings and deciding who would be number 1 was a formidable challenge. I came up with a Lifetime Honors Point System to help guide me. As you'll see, I awarded points for a variety of titles and achievements. But this system was only a guideline. As explained on page 14, there's too much variation in the athletes' different eras for the point system to serve as an all-encompassing assessment of an individual career. That would be unfair.

All along, I sensed that Frank Shorter and Joan Samuelson would be the number 1 man and woman. Their historic, run-away Olympic Marathon victories against magnificent fields were of surpassing greatness—and heralded turning points in American running—and each had an arm's-length collection of additional, lustrous titles to go along. I imagine that the rankings, from number 1 on down, will generate some debate.

Feel free to chip in with your opinions by e-mailing me at mbloomedit@yahoo.com.

American runners have taken knocks for a long time now. The downturn since the early 1980s has been difficult to swallow, especially for those of us who reveled in the glorious period of the 1960s and 1970s. I've written my share of criticism on the subject. It's time to take steps to fix the problem, and I offer some ideas in The Glory of Our Times: U.S. Greatness Restored on page 7.

I hope that this book serves as a tribute to our 50 greatest runners, and to the underlying, uniquely American spirit that moved them. I remember sitting with Joan Samuelson in June 1984 under a tree in the shadows of the Los Angeles Coliseum. I interviewed her for background on the first women's Olympic Marathon, which I would be covering that summer. She told me a story that I would use to end my article on the event.

Speaking of the childhood grooming that had given her strength, she recalled her first love, skiing. "There came a time," she said, "when I wasn't able to ride the T-bar between my father's legs, and I was off on my own. The Maine winters were cold, and if I wanted to ski and couldn't find somebody to ride the T-bar with, I had to ride it myself."

That's the spirit.

The Glory of Our Times: U.S. Greatness Restored

After years of frustration over weakening American distance performances, a national mission has been mobilized to rejuvenate U.S. running and put us back among the world's best. The efforts are coming from corporations, organizations, coaches, and the athletes themselves.

The Fila company has started a Discovery USA program to mirror its hugely successful system for developing talent in Kenya. Under the supervision of Dr. Gabriele Rosa, who has coached numerous Kenyan stars, Fila has begun screening and testing postcollegiate runners to be nurtured for long-term progress.

USA Track and Field, the sport's national governing body, has also announced its Team USA Distance Running program. Under this plan, training centers will be established nationwide with hopes of attracting 60 athletes by 2003. The runners will be given coaching, financial support, and medical resources. New York City Marathon officials have pledged $20,000 to help get the program going. Frank Shorter, Bill Rodgers, and Joan Samuelson have lent their names for support.

The vigorous, enterprising efforts of a few coaches have created satellite training centers that have been a magnet for young American talent. At Stanford University, coach Vin Lananna has developed a collegiate powerhouse, and three of his athletes—Brad Hauser, Gabe Jennings, and Michael Stember—made the 2000 Olympic team. At the University of Colorado, coach Mark Wetmore has produced Olympians Alan Culpepper and Adam Goucher, who is our best hope for world distance supremacy in 2 decades. Coach Joe Vigil's program in the mountains of

Alamosa, Colorado, vaulted Deena Drossin into the world-class ranks. Near Stanford, Bob Kennedy and steeplechaser Pascal Dobert train under the auspices of Kim McDonald, the agent-coach from England who works with many Kenyans.

So we have companies and groups that want to help, coaches who know what they're doing, and at least some athletes who are willing to sacrifice and make a commitment to long-term success. It's a good start, but these initiatives do not address the fundamental problem: that our culture's predominant values, attitudes, and messages turn many of our best young athletes away from running.

We must get talented teenage athletes into running, and we must nurture them properly for the future. That should be a primary mission. If we can't do that, the wisest coaches, organizational pledges, or corporate sponsorships will not be enough. We just won't be that good.

It's clear that the number of kids running high school track and cross-country has increased to healthy levels. We also have outstanding coaches in the high school ranks. But the evidence, at least anecdotally, is that as slam-dunk pro sports have been endlessly marketed and community soccer has grown, many of the very good athletes have been diverted away from running (who wants to wait 2 to 3 years to cash in?) and into whatever they perceive will give them status and immediate gratification.

Alberto Salazar and I have spoken about this. With his own sons, he has seen the grip soccer can have on kids. Salazar's wife, Molly, ran for Oregon; their youngsters surely have the bloodlines to excel in running. But instead, they're into soccer and other sports.

Kicking a soccer ball has commanding appeal. It's a game, it's fun, you can score on the first day of practice, you can howl and hit one another like they do on TV, and everybody you know will be tickled that you're on the soccer team. Besides, if you're any kind of athlete at all, you've probably been playing soccer for years, and your parents have been schlepping you all over the map in what is not only a soccer-mom trend but a total family lifestyle.

I know; I did it with my two daughters. They were both fine athletes and loved soccer. Our family was a soccer family. We saw a lot of fanatical parents and coaches going overboard. My wife and I stayed in the background, but we rooted hard nonetheless. Both of my girls were pretty fair runners and I urged them— pleaded with them—to run in high school. After some balking, both realized it was best for them and did.

But I'm not the average parent when it comes to running. As coach of a high school boys' cross-country team in New Jersey for 5 years, I've been on the front lines of this issue of sport choice and society. The average parent is like the father of a boy on the cross-country team I coach. This boy played on the soccer team in the fall and ran track in the spring. He was a beautiful runner to watch and won the state 3200-meter title 2 years straight in our parochial-school division. Anyone could tell that the boy would be a marvelous cross-country runner— and a much better trackman as a year-round runner—but even in his senior year, the boy refused to run cross-country. He preferred to play soccer, even though he was just an average player. Who's to say this kid could not have been another Marty Liquori, also a native of New Jersey, who started out playing basketball?

When I told the boy's father how much potential his son had, the man was indifferent. His answer was that the boy had been playing soccer since he was 7 years old. And that was that.

So how do we get the best athletes out for running? I had another youngster, a freshman who had run grammar school track and did some summer cross-country workouts with our team. When fall came, he went out for soccer. His mother told me that if he was cut from soccer or wasn't in the starting lineup, he'd probably come back to cross-country.

Terrific! We get the castoffs. This is a pattern observed by coach Jack Daniels, one of our most astute distance authorities. "I tend to think that track and cross-country increasingly attract castoffs from other sports. When an athlete gets cut from the soccer team for being too slow or too small or too anything else that rings of inadequacy, he is told to try cross-country because 'that only takes dedication and perseverance,'" he notes.

Dedication and perseverance are certainly prized in running. The problem is that they're no longer prized in our culture. Whether it's the Internet, instant techno-wealth, or the basketball game on TV, the quick, bombastic hit is like a drug, and anything else just isn't worth it. In the 1960s and 1970s, when the United States led the world's distance runners, there was a climate—so quaint does it seem now—of planting roots and working patiently toward a faraway goal. That's what Shorter and Mills and Samuelson did.

Shorter, it should be noted, biked to school as a youth. Several others in the 50 Greatest did the same. A few walked or even ran to school. Who does that anymore? A recent study by the Centers for Disease Control and Prevention found a significant reduction in the number of children traveling to school on their own two feet.

Which brings us to the Kenyans. Our own distance malaise wouldn't look so bad if not for the rise of the Kenyans, who not only rule worldwide distance running but also dominate just about every major road race in America. It may be a cliché, but it's true that many Kenyans run 5 to 10 miles back and forth to school and engage in rigorous farm work (like Craig Virgin did on his family farm). That's one reason for Kenyan success.

There's no point in arguing that we should be like the Kenyans because on the whole, we're not. Their culture encourages running; our culture produces quarterbacks. But we can pick up a few tricks and start to move in on them. Bob Kennedy stared the Kenyans in the face, trained with them, lived with them, learned from them, and became great. Adam Goucher has adopted the same attitude. He refuses to be intimidated by the Kenyans.

This attitude finally has begun to trickle down to our youth—and let's hope it will become contagious. In 2000, there were four high school boys who as a group were as outstanding as any since the days of Jim Ryun and Gerry Lindgren, the Lennon and McCartney of high school track. They were Don Sage of Illinois, Dathan Ritzenhein of Michigan, Alan Webb of Virginia, and Ryan Hall of California. Sage, a senior who ran a 4:00.29 mile (the fastest high school time in 33 years), went on to Stanford University. The other three were juniors and promised sensational things in 2001 and beyond.

It's not easy to find a common thread among the quartet. They do train harder than other kids and have more confidence. But they seem to share something more—a hungry, incontrovertible running mindset that says, "One day, I'm going to be great. There's nothing that can stop me." Before he started college, I happened to speak with Sage, who told me that Goucher and others made an impression on him. "We have people to look at who are not only Kenyans," he said. "When you see someone from America who grew up in the same environment as you, you no longer make excuses for yourself."

To develop more people like Goucher and Sage—or why not 10 Bob Kennedys, as people like to say—we should take advantage of our abundant resources. Here are some specific measures that would help advance the crusade.

• Hire a full-time national distance coach and set him up in a running center with support staff and housing to work year-round with our best talent. I would bet that a lot of postcollegians would be drawn to a setup like this. For coach, my vote goes to Vin Lananna. His ability is proven. He relates well to athletes, knows how to get the best out of them, and can handle an abundance of top talent, male and female, all at once. He's in the prime of his own career, has achieved a great deal at Stanford, and could devote many years to this position. The center could be in the Stanford area, where the training and facilities are great, or at the Olympic Training Center in the San Diego area. A satellite retreat should be established in the mountains for high-altitude training. Mammoth, in California, where Lananna takes his college athletes, sounds right. Where do we get the money? This is a marketing bonanza for any corporate sponsor.

• We need to create the same position for high schools—a national distance coach to spread the gospel on the best way to develop young talent. Here, it should be a panel of three people. For character, experience, and know-how, three of the best candidates are Joe Newton of York High School in Elmhurst, Illinois, Pat Tyson of Mead High School in Spokane, Washington, and Bob Latham of Bend High School in Bend, Oregon. Newton and Tyson coach boys. Latham coaches boys and girls. Between them, they've produced 40 state championship squads and countless individual stars. But it's not just their résumés, it's how they relate to young people that's important. Start with a summer conclave where the trio presides over a gathering of coaches, athletes, and parents from across the United States. Stage a cross-country race. Make it a big deal, then send Newton, Tyson, and Latham to select meets during the year to spread the word. They could be available year-round as consultants, reachable by a toll-free number or e-mail. (By the way, high school track and cross-country runners should be let in free to any major track meet in America by showing a national I.D. card. There's no problem if seats run short—the kids can stand.)

• Age-group running, with its carrot of the national Junior Olympics, puts too much emphasis on competition and not enough on development. Is it really a good thing to have a bunch of 9-year-olds traveling around the country in pursuit of a trophy? I've seen some scary coaches and parents in this arena— people who go nuts over a 10-year-old setting an age record. But very few of these little Olympians stick with running in the long-term. Better to make running pure fun and give awards for practices attended or for helping a teammate. Hold pressure-free races and forget team scoring. If we're fair to kids, they will prosper as runners, and so will we as a nation.

• When it comes to natural resources, who better to talk about success than our Olympic gold medalists of recent vintage: Frank Shorter, Billy Mills, Bob Schul, and Joan Samuelson. None of the four were college superstars by any means. Send them out to speak to college athletes. They can explain how they went from being good (but not great) in college to being the world's best. What 20-year-old runner—not to mention his coach—wouldn't soak this up?

• Let's address the average youth: all of those soccer players as well as sedentary kids, plus the ones who run an impressive mile in gym class but wouldn't think of running cross-country because to them it has all the prestige of badminton. Every day, we hear about our troubled youth and their boredom, their lack of direction, their lack of faith, and their desperation to find something to latch on to. We remember too well the ghastly school shootings and we debate how to prevent them from happening again. If we get kids moving, sweating, in-volved—believing in something—at least we can begin to ef-fect change. And we'll also pick up some good runners in the process.

Here's a four-pronged campaign to start us off.

1. Create a national Walk to School program. Get kids walking a mile or two before classes start, and they'll feel better and learn better. Offer the walkers breakfast or a sports drink or energy bar for a late snack. Give out certificates for each day and awards for the most days walked. Design maps so kids know the best and safest routes to take. Recognize the walkers at school assemblies. Before you know it, some kids will want to walk home, too. (Some may even want to run or bike.)

2. Help physical education teachers integrate running into their lessons. There are some wonderful examples of this around the country, but they're few and far between. Publish a booklet with national guidelines and distribute it to all schools. Share how some schools already get kids moving successfully. Connect with local running stores and arrange for them to send personnel to the schools as advisors and to provide shoes and other gear as prizes or at a discount.

3. Set up the High School Mile Challenge, in which all incoming freshmen run a mile the first week of school. Find out who the good runners are and direct them to the track and cross-country programs. You can't force kids to join a team. But when youngsters realize their talent, it's powerful motivation to do something with it. So far, most good young runners have no idea that they possess a special gift.

4. To help show that running is cool, have Olympic stars visit schools in their home states. We take pride in our own, those who grew up next door. Send Suzy Favor-Hamilton to schools in Wisconsin, Bill Rodgers to schools in Connecticut, Mary Slaney to schools in California, and Vicki Huber to schools in Delaware. Show the kids footage of the athletes' greatest moments. Give out posters for the stars to autograph.

These ideas address youth, high school, college, and post-collegiate athletes. They require commitment, creativity, personnel, and money. They can be done. Let's not waste time. We are indeed a land of plenty; we have the intellect, the energy, and the know-how. All we have to do is care. Let's return distance-running glory to America.

Lifetime Honors Point System

The 50 Greatest distance runners were chosen and ranked according to a wide range of criteria: records set, titles won, superiority among U.S. and international peers, Olympic and world championship successes, consistency, durability, versatility, and trailblazing.

Not every factor could be applied to every athlete; a runner of the 1930s did not compete under the same circumstances as a runner of the 1980s. Each runner named had a dominant quality that marked his or her career as special for its time. I tried to regard all distances with equal prominence and name the truly distinguished among the hundreds of candidates of the 20th century.

The rankings, along with the point system, should spark a vigorous debate. The point system is a guideline, offering some concrete yet inconclusive evidence of a runner's overall success. It could not possibly include every one of the sport's honors, and track fans will note, understandably, that the all-important smorgasbord of Grand Prix meets (the European circuit) is not included on the points list. There are too many meets to be included. Those events, however, and a multitude of others not listed, plus various intangibles, have been considered in the final analysis and ranking.

In the end, any such ranking is subjective. With my long experience in the sport, I hope I've been fair to everyone and given due recognition to our very best.

Here are examples of how point totals were computed for one male and one female runner.

Lifetime Honors Point System

Olympic gold medal 2,500

Olympic silver medal 1,500

Olympic bronze medal 1,000

World outdoor championship gold medal 1,500

World outdoor championship silver medal 1,000

World outdoor championship bronze medal 750

World indoor championship gold medal 500

World indoor championship silver medal 300

World indoor championship bronze medal 200

World cross-country gold medal 1,500

World cross-country silver medal .1,000

World cross-country bronze medal .750

Pan American Games gold medal 500

Pan American Games silver medal 300

Pan American Games bronze medal .200

World outdoor record (including marathon) 1,500

World indoor record 1,000

American outdoor record (including marathon) 1,000

American indoor record 500

Olympic Trials title 500

U.S. outdoor title 350

U.S. indoor title 250

U.S. cross-country title 350

NCAA outdoor title 200

NCAA indoor title 100

NCAA cross-country title 200

NAIA track or cross-country title 100

Olympic team member 200

World champion outdoor team member 200

New York City or Boston Marathon—1st place 1,000

New York City or Boston Marathon—2nd place 750

New York City or Boston Marathon—3rd place 500

Avon, Chicago, Fukuoka, Honolulu, London,

    Los Angeles, or Yonkers Marathons—1st place 750

U.S. national road title 200

World road record (excluding marathon) 500

American road record (excluding marathon) 250

NOTE: Relays not counted for track medals.

Billy Mills (number 6 man): One Olympic gold medal (2,500); one world outdoor record (1,500); four American outdoor records (4,000); one U.S. national outdoor title (350); one U.S. national indoor title (250); member of one Olympic team (200). **Total points: 8,800**

Mills is rated above others with higher point totals because as an amateur runner he had a relatively short career, and his Olympic victory, the only 10,000 meters ever won by an American, is of monumental significance.

Lynn Jennings (number 3 woman): One Olympic bronze medal (1,000); one world indoor championship silver medal (300); one world indoor championship bronze medal (200); three world cross-country gold medals (4,500); one world cross-country silver medal (1,000); one world cross-country bronze medal (750); two world indoor records (2,000); one American outdoor record (1,000); three American indoor records (1,500); two Olympic Trials victories (1,000); 38 U.S. national titles— 9 outdoor, 5 indoor, 9 cross-country, 15 road (10,550); member of three Olympic teams (600); member of four world championship teams (800); six American road records (1,500). **Total points: 26,700**

Top 30
Men

Lifetime Honors Point Total: 23,750

Best Times

2-mile—8:26.2 (indoors)
February 19, 1971, San Diego
(Indoor Games)

3-mile—12:52.0
June 8, 1974, Eugene, Oregon
(Haywood Field Restoration)

5000 meters—13:26.6
August 24, 1977, Zurich, Switzerland (Weltklasse)

10,000 meters—27:45.91
August 29, 1975, London,
England (Coca-Cola Meet)

Marathon—2:10:30
December 3, 1972, Fukuoka,
Japan (Fukuoka Marathon)

Born: October 31, 1947, Munich, West Germany
Current Residence: Boulder, Colorado
Education: Mount Hermon Academy, Northfield, Massachusetts (1965); Yale University (1969)
Affiliations: Florida Track Club, Frank Shorter Racing Team
Professions: Professional runner, businessman, TV commentator, drug-enforcement administrator
Career Highlights: Olympic Marathon gold and silver medalist and seminal figure in the running boom; U.S. record holder at 2 miles, 10,000 meters, and marathon; four-time Fukuoka Marathon world titlist; won 18 national titles; the premier distance runner in American history

Frank Shorter 1
10,000 Meters, Marathon

The Ultimate Pacesetter

Frank Shorter was the Frank Sinatra of American distance running. He was supreme, and he did it his way. Shorter's running, defiant and calibrated, was a lyrical testament to his willful disregard for convention. You could throw the whole of a contrary American society at him—hooting motorists and intransigent track officials—and Shorter was going to rise above the heap . . . and go on running.

From the start, Shorter operated outside the margins. He attended an Episcopalian boarding school in New York City, then Mount Hermon Academy in Massachusetts, then Yale. His father was a country doctor, his mother an artist. He grew up in Middletown, New York, north of the city, in a family of 11 children. Shorter learned to fend for himself, saw early on you had to make your own luck, and didn't cotton to the idea of going off to work in a dress shirt and tie. At Yale, Shorter's running was no great

19

shakes until his senior year in 1969, when he finally won the NCAA title in the 6-mile. But his independent nature was properly nurtured by the coach, Bob Giegengack, who saw to it that Shorter could eventually train himself and, if necessary, buck the system. After college, Shorter decided to take on the world. In 1970, he took the first step, winning the 10,000 meters in the closely watched U.S.– Soviet dual meet. *Sports Illustrated* put him on its cover.

"I want my time spent running to serve as a reward. I don't want it to take over every aspect of my life."

While training full-time, Shorter scraped by as a kind of migrant runner. He lived in Florida in the winter and Colorado in the summer. He briefly attended medical school, quitting when his money ran out; besides, who had the time? He attended law school, skipping semesters that interfered with competition. Shorter picked up a few bucks from the track circuit, but even those scant earnings would come back to haunt him in an ostensibly amateur sport. When Shorter testified before the President's Commission on Olympic Sports, saying "We're all professionals," track officials threatened to expel him.

Actually, Shorter was content with little. Wanting calloused him. For years on end, Shorter proceeded to win almost every important race he ran. Track, cross-country, the marathon, everything. When the 1972 Munich Olympics rolled around, Shorter already had four marathons under his belt, including the first of four straight victories in Japan's Fukuoka race, which drew the world's top field at the time.

In Munich, where Shorter was born (his father was doing army duty nearby), he first ran the 10,000 meters, setting American records in both the heat (27:58.2) and final (27:51.4), in which he placed fifth. A week later, Shorter ran the Marathon.

purely for fun

Nowadays, in addition to his drug enforcement work, looking after his sports marketing company, and doing TV commentary at marathons, Shorter runs about 60 miles a week. "I'm running for pure enjoyment with no competitive goals," he says. "I'm finding out how much I like running truly for its own sake."

The favorites were defending champion Mamo Wolde of Ethiopia, world record holder Derek Clayton of Australia, and Britain's Ron Hill, the 1970 Boston Marathon champion. Shorter was rated a long shot.

Television's role in sports was gaining momentum. When Shorter broke away after 9 miles, TV fixed on his grace and power, aided by the commentary of a Yale professor and runner who knew Shorter: *Love Story* author Erich Segal. Shorter won by more than 2 minutes in 2:12:20, becoming the first American in 64 years to capture the Olympic Marathon. His singular performance unlocked in average people a desire to run, and soon running grew from a hippie eccentricity to legitimate self-expression leading to better health and well-being.

As runners multiplied and Shorter became an icon, he prepared for the 1976 Olympics in Montreal, seeking a repeat triumph. He got into his best shape ever and wound up with the silver medal in 2:10:46. Running to the finish in Olympic Stadium, Shorter gestured as though offering an apology to expectant American fans.

An apology was hardly necessary. Shorter found out later that he was running with a broken bone in his foot. Two decades later, initial suspicions of the gold medalist's transgressions were confirmed: Waldemar Cierpinski of East Germany was implicated in his nation's admission of widespread strength-enhancing drug use.

Shorter enjoyed another 6 years of top-flight running, especially in road races like 10-Ks and 15-Ks, but his marathoning was never the same after Montreal. Since then, he's been an outspoken critic of drug use, and in 2000, Shorter was named chairman of the new U.S. Anti-Doping Agency. Perfect work for an elder statesman who sang the song in every aspect of the running movement.

Last to Be Caught

In his youth, Shorter had an eclectic sports background. He was home run champion in Little League. He showed early endurance by swimming farther than most kids his age, and in tag games he was always the last to be caught. In junior high, he gladly ran laps in gym class while others played football. For a time, he biked to school—2 miles each way. Shorter developed an interest in skiing and joined the ski team in high school before devoting himself entirely to running.

An Acute Sense of Pace

In one physiological test, Shorter was found to be an extremely efficient runner, expending little energy at top speed. Shorter could train beyond the level of most runners and not get hurt. From 1970 through 1979, he averaged 17 miles a day (about 120 miles a week). Much of it was at high altitude and with hundreds of races thrown in. It was a program that would have flattened almost anyone else.

Shorter loved running to the brink, then backing off just a touch and doing it again. He had a sharp sense of pace and how hard he could push. His routine was highly structured. He trained twice a day, Monday through Saturday, doing his first workout at 11:00 A.M. and the second before dinner. Nothing short of a world war could change that.

On Sunday, Shorter ran once, putting in 20 miles. He started at a 6:30-per-mile pace and worked down to race pace, 5 minutes a mile. He was a great believer in negative splits—running the second half faster than the first. Monday was a recovery day. He ran 7 miles in the morning and 10 in the afternoon, but not that fast. He needed his rest.

Tuesday was a speed day. After a 7-mile morning run, Shorter's afternoon speedwork consisted of, say, 4 × 1320, in 3:12 to 3:06, on a track, with a 660-yard jog in between. One time in Europe, before setting a career-best in the 10,000 meters, he ran 16 × 440 in 63 seconds—with a mere 50-yard jog for rest between runs. Another time, before his 1972 Olympic Marathon victory, he ran 4 × 880 in 2:03, 2:02, 2:01, and 2:00, prompting coach Bob Giegengack to exclaim, "Jeez, you're in shape!"

Wednesday was the same as Monday, and Thursday was more speedwork, like 440s in close to 60 seconds. Friday was a recovery day. Saturday was either a race or a mix of average-paced mileage with an accelerated pace. That was Shorter for 10 years running.

harder than anyone

During one period, Shorter pushed the envelope as never before. In the spring of 1972, he trained three times a day at an altitude of 8,000 feet in the Colorado mountains. His mileage reached 170 a week, equivalent to 200-plus at sea level. "I was convinced," said Shorter, "that nobody else in the world could have been training that hard."

Jim Ryun

800 Meters, 1500 Meters, Mile

**Lifetime Honors Point Total:
23,750**

Best Times

800 meters—1:44.9
June 10, 1966, Terre Haute,
Indiana (USTFF)

1500 meters—3:33.1
July 8, 1967, Los Angeles (U.S.
versus British Commonwealth)

Mile—3:51.1
June 23, 1967, Bakersfield, California (AAU Nationals)

2-mile—8:25.2
May 13, 1966, Los Angeles
(Coliseum Relays)

Born: April 29, 1947, Wichita,
Kansas
Current Residence: Lawrence,
Kansas, and Washington, D.C.
Education: East High School, Wichita, Kansas (1965); University
of Kansas, Lawrence (1970)
Affiliations: Club West
Professions: Professional runner,
U.S. congressman
Career Highlights: Set six world
records; held world mile record for
9 years and U.S. mile record for
14 years; set high school mile
record while defeating Olympic
champion Peter Snell; Olympic
silver medalist

Sweeping Talent

It might seem unfair to say that Jim Ryun
was running's greatest talent. That could
imply that his accomplishments came more
from natural gifts than hard work. Ryun *was*
a surpassing talent: all legs, precocious speed,
searingly tough—a high school runner who
could defeat the world's best. But no runner
ever worked harder. Take both—the talent
and the work—and the result was a miler
who swept us off our feet.

Track was booming in the 1960s. Why?
Ryun. We would watch the young Ryun on
TV, waiting for his sure and lethal kick; his
head-bobbing, schoolyard gait; his inevitable
victory. In his early years, he was a child
among men, a clean-faced kid with a crew
cut from Kansas up against grizzled veterans.

A shy, awkward youth, Ryun didn't fit in
easily with the teenage crowd. He wanted desperately to make friends as an athlete. He tried
track as a last resort and ran a pretty good
quarter-mile in junior high. When Ryun
joined the East High cross-country squad as a

sophomore in 1962, he found a pursuit that favored excess. He could pound the stuffing out of himself and in the process gain pride. "Maybe I can get a girlfriend," he thought.

In the spring of 1964, Ryun became the first high school runner to break the 4-minute mile. Only a decade earlier, Roger Bannister had run the first sub-4:00 ever. The best high school kids were lucky to break 4:20. That season, Ryun also ran the 1500-meter in 3:39.0, equivalent to a 3:56-plus mile.

"When I became a Christian, I realized God loved me because of me, not because of my athletics. Even at 25, you can be confused and wonder, Do people really like me?"

Ryun became a towering figure, a Tiger Woods in track shorts. Word leaked out about the punishing workouts given by his coaches, Bob Timmons and J. D. Edmiston; for example, 40 quarter-mile runs in succession with a short rest between. Nobody could believe it. The toughest athletes did half that. For Ryun, those quarters were not punishment but reward.

Timmons told Ryun, "You don't make progress without pushing back the pain barrier." Edmiston concurred. "The name of the game is pain, and Jim could take it with the best of them."

In 1965, finishing his high school career, Ryun took the line at the AAU Nationals in San Diego against Peter Snell, the New Zealander who a year earlier had swept the 800 and the 1500 at the Tokyo Olympics. Foreign runners were then allowed in the U.S. championships. Ryun, Mr. Pain, was prepared to "suffer." As an Olympic team member at 17, Ryun had seen Snell in Tokyo.

In his virgin-white WICHITA uniform, Ryun roared from behind to an astounding victory. Talent plus work—the deadly com-

a final fling at 40

After turning 40 in 1987, Ryun was motivated to renew some serious training and compete in the *Runner's World* Masters Mile, a series of track races for men age 40 and up. At the 1988 Millrose Games in Madison Square Garden, Ryun defeated Peter Snell again. Ryun took fifth in 4:29.60; Snell, 49, placed eighth (last) in 4:53.63. Frank Shorter, the other big name, was third in 4:21.95. Victory went to the unheralded Web Loudat in 4:20.04.

bination was paying off. Ryun's anguished look across the line told the story. His time was 3:55.3, an American record. Only Snell, Michel Jazy of France, and Herb Elliott of Australia had run faster.

That day, Ryun told himself he would be a world record holder, too. And he would, setting four world outdoor marks within 13 months from June 1966 to July 1967 while at the University of Kansas. One came in the 880 (1:44.9), one in the 1500 (3:33.1), and two in the mile (3:51.3 and 3:51.1). Those mile records—"They felt so easy," says Ryun now—were on slow, cinder tracks; synthetic surfaces were still new and rare. The most ballyhooed of the four races was the 1500 against Kip Keino, the Kenyan star, in the Los Angeles Coliseum. Ryun triumphed by nearly 30 meters.

Ryun's victory over Keino was the high point of his career. After that, he entered a turbulent period. His college nemesis, Marty Liquori at Villanova University, started to beat him. Ryun walked off the track in despair at an NCAA race. His allergies affected his running. He got mononucleosis. He retired from running, then came back. He lost the 1971 "Dream Mile" to Liquori. Did the "intense scrutiny," as he put it, become too much for Ryun? Or had all the pain-conquering crushed his desire?

Friends Forever
Ryun's early inspiration was Oregonian Jim Grelle, whose U.S. mile record he broke in 1965. "Jim's sense of inclusiveness allowed me to participate at a level I never dreamed of. He had every reason to dislike me, because I beat him at the 1964 Olympic Trials, but our relationship flourished."

Ryun's two Olympic 1500 efforts, in 1968 and 1972, reflected his precarious fate. Both times, he was the favorite. In 1968, undercut by the 7,350-foot elevation of Mexico City, Ryun took the silver medal while being soundly defeated by Keino, who lived at high altitude. In 1972, in the afterglow of an Olympic Trials victory—the proudest run of his life, he says—Ryun was tripped by another runner in the Olympic qualifying round at Munich. U.S. officials appealed, but to no avail. Ryun was eliminated.

By this time, Ryun had become a born-again Christian. Ryun joined the pro track tour and his running sputtered to an end in the mid-1970s. Married with four children, he eventually went into politics, becoming a U.S. congressman from Kansas.

Jim Ryun's Training Secret ▸▸

Forty Quarters! Is He for Real?

Ryun did 85 to 100 miles a week as a high school senior in 1965. His coach, Bob Timmons, had become the coach at the Univeristy of Kansas. That season, J. D. Edmiston worked with him, raising the high bar Timmons had set.

Ryun woke up with 4 to 5 miles every morning at 6:00 A.M. But the heart of his training was a relentless succession of sprints. Just before his 1965 AAU mile victory, Ryun ran 20 × 440, averaging 62 seconds, and the way Edmiston handled the rest was innovative for its time. He told Ryun he'd have exactly 2 minutes for each fast 440 and resting jog between. If Ryun dogged it and ran a slowish (for him) 65 seconds, the jog would be cut to 55 seconds to equal 2 minutes. If Ryun ran what he was supposed to—60, 61, or 62—he'd have 58 to 60 seconds rest. At that level, every second counts. The training design drove Ryun to his best.

Looking back, Ryun wonders if it was too much. "That's an awful lot of volume that late in the season for a high schooler," he says. But the one workout that stunned the running grapevine was 40 × 400 done in 69 seconds. Here, Ryun had a 3-minute interval, meaning his jog-rest was a little less than 2 minutes (1:51) for each 440.

In college and after, working with Timmons, Ryun maintained the same program only at greater intensity. He ran 120 miles a week, even close to the 1972 Olympic Trials when he needed to be fresh. Once, he ran 20 × 440 in a 60.5 average, with about a minute's rest. This was done in a 2-man "relay" with a teammate, John Lawson. Ryun and Lawson alternated fast laps, resting when the other ran. "That was a rough workout," says Ryun.

running for office

Serving as a Republican congressman from Kansas's 2nd District, Ryun runs 4 to 5 miles 4 to 6 days a week and takes part in the annual Capital Challenge, a 3-mile race for Washington's politicos. One year, Ryun ran with three of his adult children in a team called the Flyun Ryuns. In fall 2000, Ryun was still running—for reelection—and he won a third term.

Bill Rodgers 3
Marathon

Lifetime Honors Point Total:
23,200

Best Times Track:
10,000 meters—28:04.42
June 22, 1976, Eugene, Oregon
(Olympic Trials)

15,000 meters—43:39.8
August 9, 1977, Boston (en route
1-hour record attempt)

20,000 meters—58:25.0
August 9, 1977, Boston (en route
1-hour record attempt)

25,000 meters—1:14:12
February 21, 1979, Saratoga, California (en route 30-K record attempt)

30,000 meters—1:31:49
February 21, 1979, Saratoga, California (30-K record attempt).

Best Times Road:
10-K—28:15
January 15, 1983, Miami, Florida
(Miami 10-K)

15-K—43:25
June 28, 1981, Portland, Oregon
(Cascade Run Off)

20-K—58:42
September 6, 1982, New Haven,
Connecticut (Race of the Amer-
icas)

Half-marathon—1:04:46
February 5, 1978, Coamo, Puerto
Rico (San Blas Half-Marathon)

25-K—1:17:24
May 12, 1978, Grand Rapids,
Michigan (Old Kent River Run)

30-K—1:29:04
March 28, 1976, Albany, New York
(AAU Championship)

Marathon—2:09:27
April 16, 1979, Boston (Boston
Marathon)

King of the Road

Bill Rodgers was the world's greatest road racer—ever. With his weekly victories in the big ones, the little ones, and the in-between ones, Rodgers dominated this new American athletic form, symbolizing an exciting, populist era that joined professional marathons with jogger-next-door appeal to create one huge traveling party of running faithful.

Rodgers—who won four Boston Marathons and four New York City Marathons in 5 years—helped spread the running gospel

Born: December 23, 1947, Hartford, Connecticut
Current Residence: Sherborn, Massachusetts
Education: Newington High School, Newington, Con-
necticut (1966); Wesleyan University, Middletown, Con-
necticut (1970)
Affiliations: Boston Athletic Association, Greater Boston
Track Club, Asics, Puma, Brooks, Etonic
Professions: Professional runner, businessman, public
speaker
Career Highlights: Four-time Boston Marathon champion;
four-time New York City Marathon champion; world's
number-one ranked marathoner three times; World Cross-
Country bronze medalist; set 15 American records

not only with his victories but also with his unselfconscious, regular-guy demeanor. No champion was ever more humble, more sincere, more genuine. Bill practically asked you for *your* autograph. Who could seem more average?

He'd quit running after college only to pick it up after losing his job. Rodgers was a conscientious objector during the Vietnam war, during which time he worked at a Boston hospital transporting patients and blood samples.

"In high school, I was the fastest kid in gym class. That was very exciting for me, a perpetual high for 3 years."

"When I was fired," Rodgers says now, "I felt like I had nothing left in life."

So he ran. And it was a rebirth. He stopped smoking, started winning, then entered marathons. Who could forget Rodgers's first victory at Boston, in 1975, when he broke Frank Shorter's American record in 2:09:55 after stopping to tie his shoes? Who could forget Rodgers's first victory at New York, in 1976, when he defeated Shorter by 2 minutes following the Montreal Olympics in the city's first supercharged run through the five boroughs?

Rodgers was injured at Montreal and finished 40th, the only gap in his career. When the United States led the 1980 boycott of the Moscow Games, Rodgers saw his Olympic medal chances dashed and delivered a protest of his own. He took a courageous public stand against President Jimmy Carter's pronouncement, one of the few high-profile athletes to do so, and did not run the U.S. Marathon Trial, won by Tony Sandoval.

If Rodgers's tough action seemed incongruous with his soft-touch personality, it was like that in racing, too. His pure spirit appeared at odds with his running ferocity. Maybe it was that spirit, uncomplicated by nuance, that was Rodgers's genius. When it

lucky shoes

Early on, Rodgers had to scratch around for good running shoes. In 1975, he wrote to Nike for a pair. Just in time for the Boston Marathon, Rodgers received a pair from Nike-sponsored runner Steve Prefontaine. The track star also wrote Bill an encouraging letter. Rodgers wore the shoes at Boston and won; Prefontaine died a month later in a car accident. Rodgers has those shoes on display in the window of his running store in Boston.

came right down to it, the man just ran. He didn't need bluster or calculation. He ran like an angel.

At his best, no one could touch him. Rodgers added Rio de Janeiro, Stockholm, Toronto, Melbourne, Amsterdam, and Fukuoka, Japan, to his international marathon victory march. Fukuoka came in 1977, when Rodgers was in the midst of capturing 50 of 55 major road races. Rodgers could destroy an Olympic-level marathon field one week, then invite joggers to hang with him after a 10-K the next.

Everyone was gunning for him, but that did not affect him. If he won, he won; if not, it was no sweat. He lowered his American record to 2:09:27 at Boston in 1979 and 6 months later won his fourth straight New York, the eighth and final ring of his Boston–New York collection. Rodgers's marathoning grew less frequent in the 1980s, and he finished eighth at the 1984 Olympic Trials.

Rodgers kept running the short stuff, and after turning 40 in late 1987, he began collecting masters records, which he continues now with great pleasure in his fifties. Rodgers currently runs 10 miles a day also and does some weight training and light swimming. His weight is 135 pounds, compared to the 128 of his heyday. Rodgers is a member of the USA Track and Field and Distance Running Halls of Fame. In 2000, he joined basketball's Larry Bird and Red Auerbach in the Faneuil Sports Hall of Fame in Boston.

Rodgers is often linked with Frank Shorter, though their best years did not coincide. He outran Shorter, 20–14 (with one intentional tie), in head-to-head races through July 1981. In one arresting photo of the two men competing in a 10-K that year, they are eerily in sync, from their furrowed brows to their stride angles to the way their hair meets the wind.

Shorter won that one, but you can bet that Rodgers had a ball just the same.

Hard, Easy Day

Rodgers said the race "that felt the easiest in my life" at a world-class level was his bronze-medal run at the 1975 World Cross-Country Championships in Rabat, Morocco. Rodgers was so fit that he went right back to hard 2-hour training runs soon after the meet. "That race changed everything for me," Rodgers recalls. "People like Frank [Shorter] were telling me, 'You're there now.'" One month later, Rodgers won his first Boston Marathon.

Miles and More Miles

Rodgers's program was based on year-round high mileage, usually 20 to 25 miles a day. He rarely did speedwork, except for some long repetitions. Here's a rundown of his highest week ever—202 miles—done in January 1975, prior to his first Boston Marathon victory. Rodgers had extra time to train because he was on a semester break from graduate school at Boston College, where he received a master's degree in special education.

SATURDAY: A.M.—14 miles, including 3 miles at the Boston College indoor track in 4:48, 4:54, and 4:48, with a half-mile jog between runs; P.M.—16 miles

SUNDAY: A.M.—20 miles on hills; P.M.—10 miles easy

MONDAY: A.M.—17 miles; P.M.—13 miles.

TUESDAY: A.M.—16 miles; P.M.—13 miles.

WEDNESDAY: A.M.—16 miles; P.M.—13 miles.

THURSDAY: A.M.—16 miles; P.M.—15 miles.

FRIDAY: A.M.—23 miles on the Boston Marathon course

Four years later, before his fourth Boston title, Rodgers did less mileage, 120 to 130 a week, but at a faster pace, often 5:40 per mile. During this period, Rodgers also set world track records for 25-K and 30-K in the same race. He actually went for the 25-K, running 1:14:12, then jogged the last 5-K in 17:37 for 1:31:49, a record 30-K.

MONDAY: A.M. **(bad weather)**—3 miles on an indoor track

TUESDAY: A.M.—9 miles; P.M.—9 miles

WEDNESDAY: A.M.—6 miles; P.M.—10 miles

THURSDAY: A.M.—10 miles; P.M.—10 miles

FRIDAY: A.M.—10 miles; P.M.—10 miles

SATURDAY: A.M.—10 miles, plus 6 × 800 in 2:20 on a dirt path with 2-minute recovery jogs

SUNDAY: A.M.—12 miles; P.M.—10 miles

pizza and pancakes

Rodgers insists that his reputation for junk food—cold pizza with mayonnaise for breakfast—was exaggerated. So what *did* he eat? Pancakes before his first marathon, bacon and eggs before another. Good nutrition or dietary sin? Call it a tie.

Glenn Cunningham 4
1500 Meters, Mile

Lifetime Honors Point Total:
26,900

Best Times

800 meters—1:49.7
August 20, 1936, Stockholm,
Sweden (international meet)

1500 meters—3:48.0
June 30, 1940, Fresno, California
(AAU Nationals)

Mile (outdoors)—4:06.8
June 16, 1934, Princeton, New
Jersey (Princeton Invitational)

Mile (indoors)—4:04.4
March 3, 1938, Hanover, New
Hampshire (Dartmouth Meet)

Born: August 4, 1909, Atlanta
Died: March 10, 1988
Education: Elkhart High School,
Elkhart, Kansas (1930); University
of Kansas, Lawrence (1934)
Affiliations: New York Curb Ex-
change Athletic Association
Professions: Rancher, youth
advisor
Career Highlights: Set nine world
records and 14 American records;
won 10 U.S. national titles; cap-
tured six Wanamaker Miles; took
Olympic silver medal in the 1500

Rising from the Ashes

Glenn Cunningham could have done a milk commercial. He abstained from alcohol, was as straitlaced as they come, and drank only milk and water. His reputation as a model citizen and as a man of valor was peerless. After his running heroics made him a national figure, Cunningham—who became labeled "Mr. Clean"—passed on an offer of $100,000 a year to do public speaking. Instead, he started Cunningham Youth Ranches to teach needy youngsters how to live a spiritual, righteous life.

But more than anything, Cunningham, whose appearances packed Madison Square Garden and other temples of track, would be known for surviving "the Fire." He grew up on the Kansas prairie, and in 1917, when Cunningham was 7, a fire broke out in the small school he attended with his four older brothers and sisters 2 miles from home. It was a cold winter day and the potbellied stove used to heat the room sparked a flame that enveloped the building. Young Cunningham was overcome with smoke but came to the aid of a brother trapped inside. The brother died and Cunningham barely made it out alive.

He suffered severe leg burns and spent 6 months in the hospital while skin was grafted onto his legs. Doctors thought that amputation might be necessary, but somehow, Cunningham's scarred tissues healed and Cunningham learned to walk again. To improve blood circulation and strengthen his limbs, he took up running. He abided by his father's philosophy: "Never quit. Always go out there and try to overcome, no matter what."

> *"In track, it is man against himself, the cruelest of opponents. The other runners are not the real enemies. His adversary lies deep within him."*

Cunningham started competing in high school and was an NCAA 1500 and mile champion at the University of Kansas. He was given the Sullivan Award as the nation's leading amateur athlete in 1933, after sweeping the AAU national 800 and 1500, a rare feat. Cunningham toured Europe that year and was undefeated in 20 races. But Cunningham's best was yet to come.

He had charisma to go with his virtue, and people thrilled to see the broad-shouldered star rally on the last lap, shoot for records, and engage in match races with athletes hand-picked by meet promoters. One rival in the mile was Gene Venzke of the University of Pennsylvania. Cunningham beat him. Another rival was Princeton's Bill Bonthron. Cunningham beat him. Almost every big race produced a new record. Cunningham set a

he fooled them all

In 1936, Cunningham won the famous "typographical error" mile at the Knights of Columbus indoor games in New York. Cunningham had been beaten that season and decided to sit back and let others do the pacesetting. But no one wanted to lead, and the pace dawdled to a near walk. Finally, Cunningham sprinted to victory in 4:46.8. People who saw the exceedingly slow time in the papers assumed it was a typo.

total of 23 world and American records and won 10 national titles.

Though his métier was the mile, Cunningham would run just about anything. Matched against a star of the 880 in Stockholm, Cunningham still won in world record time. Matched against the best 2-milers, Cunningham took that one, too.

He was at his best indoors, hugging the tight tracks and winning six Wanamaker Miles at the Millrose Games. It took 48 years for someone (Ireland's Eamonn Coghlan) to go one better. When the 49th Street Garden was torn down for a new facility, Cunningham was voted the outstanding track and field performer in its 42-year history. Seven times, he set world indoor records for the 1500 and the mile.

Consistent Speed

In *Cunningham's era, a 4:10 mile was considered top-drawer. He ran 4:10 or better 16 times, 4:15 or better 41 times. Cunningham also had terrific speed and was capable of running the 100-yard dash in 10.2 seconds.*

Cunningham's most celebrated victory may have been his 1934 rubber-match mile with Bonthron. After they'd split their first two previous meetings that season, Cunningham raced Bonthron on his home track at Princeton, New Jersey. Cunningham won in 4:06.8, to break the world record of New Zealand's John Lovelock.

But it was Lovelock who in 1936 won the Olympic gold medal in the 1500 at Berlin; Cunningham took the silver. (At the 1932 Olympics in Los Angeles, Cunningham had been ill and placed fourth in the 1500.)

Cunningham, who won 26 races in 26 months from January 1937 to March 1939, would have been at his peak around 1940. But World War II prevented a 1940 Games, and during the war, Cunningham served as a naval officer, teaching physical fitness.

Cunningham had advanced academic degrees, including a Ph.D., but he ultimately chose to stay on his Kansas ranch and open his doors to needy children.

No Wasted Miles

Cunningham was said to have run more than 10,000 miles in his decade-long career. That's about 20 miles a week. Even as a low estimate, it's fair to say Cunningham emphasized short mileage and speedwork. He raced often, evidently using competition to develop strength and sharpen his instincts.

One reason for Cunningham's low volume was the lingering effects of the childhood fire that had burned his legs. As his University of Kansas coach Brutus Hamilton wrote in the early 1930s, "He does not have normal circulation in the leg muscles or normal muscular protection over the shin bones. This necessitates a program of training quite different from that of the average boy. He does much long walking, many exercises of the bicycling type, and confines himself to very little running on the track." Cunningham, the first cross-trainer!

And when he did venture onto the track, he did not wear spikes, which were said to be too "severe on his scarred legs." Instead, Cunningham trained in basketball shoes.

hot ticket

Millrose Games meet director Fred Schmertz would use Cunningham's status to impress people he favored with extra tickets. If someone came to Schmertz's office pleading for a couple of seats, he reached into a drawer and told the suitor he was giving him tickets from those precious few saved for Cunningham's group. Suffice it to say, Cunningham never had a problem with tickets.

Alberto Salazar
5000 Meters, 10,000 Meters, Marathon

5

Lifetime Honors Point Total:
16,350

Best Times

5000 meters—13:11.93
July 6, 1982, Stockholm, Sweden
(Galan Games)

10,000 meters—27:25.61
June 26, 1982, Oslo, Norway
(Bislett Games)

Marathon—2:08:13
October 25, 1981, New York
(New York City Marathon)

Born: August 7, 1958, Havana, Cuba
Current Residence: Portland, Oregon
Education: Wayland High School, Wayland, Massachusetts (1976); University of Oregon, Eugene (1981)
Affiliations: Athletics West, Nike
Professions: Professional runner, sports marketing consultant
Career Highlights: Won Boston Marathon and three straight New York City Marathons; set world marathon record and eight U.S. records, including the 5000 and the 10,000 on the track; won Comrades Marathon (53.8 miles) in South Africa

Tough Love

The tougher the circumstances, the better Alberto Salazar liked it. Whether it was the course, the weather, the opposition, or the record that Salazar said he would break, the Cuban who came to the United States as a child and excelled from his first strides in high school loved a tough fight.

"My attitude," says Salazar now, "was that I was going to push myself harder than anybody else."

While in college, Salazar went head-to-head with Kenyan star Henry Rono. He dove into the European track circuit in search of fast times in seasoned fields. He ran to the limit in the severe heat of the Falmouth Road Race on Cape Cod, Massachusetts, and had to be given last rites afterward. He challenged Suleiman Nyambui of Tanzania in a 5000-meter race at the Millrose Games without any experience on the Madison Square Garden track. He ran his first marathon at New York in 1980, dismissing the 26.2-mile distance and predicting that he would set records as "the Rookie."

And in 1994, at age 36, when he was long retired and experiencing difficulties with anxiety and depression, Salazar decided to run the world's most grueling race—the 53.8-mile Comrades Marathon in South Africa.

"There are a lot of guys out there now who know they are not working as hard as other people. I can't fathom how they think."

Was he insane? For years, Salazar had been merely jogging. Considered the Super Bowl of South Africa, this marathon was run along an uphill course. It would be hot, and everyone (including Salazar himself) knew that he had trouble running in the heat.

In a field of 12,700, Salazar went out and won. He broke the race open with a surge at 15 miles and ran unchallenged with a 4-minute lead and triumphed in 5:38:39. "More than anything," Salazar told *Runner's World* magazine afterward, "I'm happy to have my health and my running strength. I prayed more during this race than I've prayed in a year."

Finally, Salazar rested on his laurels. He deserved the rest. He did not proceed into other big races, but used his renewal in a continuing spiritual reawakening. He knew he could no longer live up to the pressure he put on himself when he rushed through life on a merry-go-round of victories in the early 1980s.

In 1980, Salazar won the first of three straight New York City Marathons in 2:09:41, a world-record debut at the time. In the 1981 New York City Marathon, he set his world record of 2:08:13. In 1982, Salazar was at his run-through-walls best, outrunning Rodolfo Gomez of Mexico at New York, literally in a

junior sensation

Salazar says that the turning point in his career came in his junior year at Wayland High School in 1975. Already a legend in the East, Salazar made the U.S. junior team (men age 20 and under), tying the national age-16 record with a 5000 meters done in 14:14.6. Then, he won the 5000 in a junior dual-meet against the Soviet Union. As a high school senior, Salazar improved his time to 14:04.8 and was victorious in the U.S.–West Germany junior meet.

cloud of dust in 2:09:29. That same year, he held off Dick Beardsley at the Boston Marathon in their spectacular "duel in the sun," 2:08:52 to 2:08:54, a course record.

While Salazar is known for his marathoning, he was a gem on the track, his preferred environment, setting American records in the 5000 (13:11.93) and the 10,000 (27:25.61) in the summer of 1982. He is the only man other than Steve Prefontaine to hold those marks simultaneously. Earlier that year, Salazar captured the world cross-country silver medal in Rome.

In 1981, Salazar raced Nyambui in an epic indoor 5000. Nyambui, the two-time defender attending the University of Texas at El Paso, was the 1980 Olympic silver medalist. Midway, they raced side-by-side in the 34-lap race. Salazar was no kicker, however, and when Nyambui bolted ahead with 2 laps to go, that was it. Nyambui set a world record of 13:20.3. Salazar was second in a U.S. record of 13:23.1. Both marks still stand.

After that, Salazar lost his edge. In 1983, he ran fifth at both the Rotterdam and Fukuoka marathons, and last in the 17-man world championship 10,000 final in Helsinki, as the 1984 Olympic year loomed. In the hot-and-humid Los Angeles Games, Salazar, who has an unusually high and debilitating sweat rate of 3 liters per hour in the heat, placed 15th in the marathon in 2:14:19. Victory went to 37-year-old Carlos Lopes of Portugal.

Salazar soon withdrew from the marathon wars and became an advisor for Nike. Following the Comrades Marathon, he settled into running 5 to 7 miles a day.

He helped coach Mary Slaney for a while and now coaches a high school cross-country team in Portland. These kids will learn toughness from the master.

Record Row

Salazar's 2:08:13 world-record victory in the New York City Marathon in 1981 was discredited by U.S. road-racing officials who claimed that the course was 148 yards short. The marathon officials, including the course measurer, Ted Corbitt, insist that the route was accurate and continue to list the 2:08:13 on the list of world and American records. To add to the confusion, U.S. officials no longer count records on "point-to-point" courses like New York, which means that performances on "circuit" courses like the much easier London and Chicago routes are given preference.

No Time to Relax

Salazar went to Oregon to train with Bill Dellinger, who coached him throughout his career. Salazar believes that his consistently high level of running year-round, with no breaks between seasons, was a key factor in his success. "Some people may have done certain workouts faster," says Salazar, "but I piled them on month after month."

Before his world-record 2:08:13 marathon at New York in 1981, Salazar ran 120 to 130 miles a week and trained twice a day. On Sundays, when he did 20 miles, he ran only once. Three days a week, he ran fast—1 day on the track; 1 day on the wood-chip trails that Eugene, Oregon, is known for; and 1 day combining trail work and roadwork.

His track work, for example, consisted of repeat 300s in 47 to 48 seconds, with a 100-yard jog between runs. "Nothing intense," he says, "just for leg turnover." His trail work was more intense—a 9-mile continuous run, alternating 5 fast miles of 4:32 to 4:35 each with 4 "rest" miles of 5:05. "And that was a pretty slow trail," Salazar notes.

Salazar also did an 11-mile run on a regular basis. He ran at 4:53 to 5:00 a mile, his goal pace for the marathon, while throwing in three fast ¾-mile surges. That callousing workout, as Dellinger called it, enabled Salazar to run a 4:33 split for his breakaway 17th mile at New York.

A year later (before he set his American 5000-meter and 10,000-meter records on the track), Salazar's mileage was slightly less. He ran 100 to 110 miles a week, with most of it at or below race pace. For example, he did 6 × mile in 4:20; or 4 × 1200 in 3:05 to 3:06; or 12 × 200 in 29 to 30—all with short rests.

keep it up longer

For the 53.8-mile Comrades Marathon in 1994—effectively, two marathons in one—Salazar had to do ultralong runs. In the 12 weeks leading up to the race, he did a weekly long run of 25 to 40 miles. Three days after a long run, he would do mile repeats in 5:10 to 5:15. "Just fast enough so that a 6-minute pace would feel easy," he says. It was hot and humid at Comrades, and Salazar's winning time computed to 6:18 per mile.

Billy Mills

10,000 Meters

6

Lifetime Honors Point Total: 8,800

Best Times

2-mile—8:41.4 (indoors)
February 26, 1965, San Francisco (Golden Gate Invitational)

5000 meters—13:41.4
July 15, 1965, Oslo, Norway (international meet)

6-mile—27:11.6
June 27, 1965, San Diego (AAU Nationals)

10,000 meters—28:17.6
August 12, 1965, Augsburg, Germany (United States versus West Germany)

Marathon—2:22:56
October 12, 1964, Tokyo, Japan (Olympic Games)

Born: June 30, 1938, Pine Ridge, South Dakota
Current Residence: Fair Oaks, California
Education: Haskell Indian School, Lawrence, Kansas (1957); University of Kansas, Lawrence (1962)
Affiliations: U.S. Marine Corps
Professions: Public speaking; humanitarian and Native American causes
Career Highlights: 1964 Olympic 10,000-meter gold medalist (only American winner); set world record for 6 miles and two American marks in the 10,000; international victories include U.S. duals with England and Germany

25 Laps of Honor

The track world was shocked when unheralded Billy Mills captured the 1964 Olympic 10,000 meters in Tokyo, becoming the only American ever to win the event. Mills himself, however, expected the victory, but nobody would listen.

To that point, nobody had ever listened to Mills, who as a Native American was put down at every stage in his running odyssey.

Growing up on the Oglala Sioux Indian reservation in South Dakota, Mills was taught by his father to stand up to the "dominant white society." His father would read him quotes from Socrates: "With achievement comes honor, with honor comes responsibility." Mills found little success in boxing, basketball, and football, but when he turned to track he became a high school state champion.

Mills received 18 scholarship offers and ultimately chose the University of Kansas,

39

where students, teammates, and even coach Bill Easton treated him with cruel dismissal. As a result, Mills grew angry and hostile, but he learned to use those emotions to build himself up and strike back where he could profit most—on the track. "Compete against yourself" became his mantra.

"Running was my passion. Passion leads you down a path of destiny. Destiny is God-given."

Mills graduated from Kansas in 1962 with a teaching degree and joined the Marines. In 1963, he competed at West Point in a qualifying meet for the NATO countries' interservice championship in Brussels. Though Mills won the 3-mile at West Point, he was not named to the U.S. squad. The colonel in charge left Mills out, so Max Truex, beaten by Mills, withdrew from the 10,000, opening a spot for Mills.

In Brussels, Mills ran his second 10,000 ever in 30:08. He had the lead with 500 meters to go, but lacked a kick and was roundly defeated. The winner was Mohamed Gammoudi of Tunisia, who told Mills he needed to work on his speed. Mills went back to Camp Pendleton in California and ran sprint after sprint, writing in his training log: "Must work hard. Tokyo '64 10,000 gold."

After placing second to 18-year-old Gerry Lindgren at the 1964 Olympic Trials, Mills returned to the interservice meet and won, but his times were not that fast, and in Tokyo he was barely noticed. There was more interest in the phenomenon Lindgren, who some experts named to place in the top six. The heavy favorite was Ron Clarke, the world record holder from Australia.

Mills was held in such low regard that when he tried to pick

daddy's girl

After the 1964 Olympics, Mills's daughter, Christy, took his gold medal to school for show-and-tell. "I told her what to say, that this is the gold medal only the best in the world win, that your daddy won in the 10,000-meter run," Mills recalls. Later that night, he asked his daughter how it went at school, and Christy replied, "I said, 'Boys and girls, this is the gold medal only the best in the world win. This is the gold medal Peggy Fleming won.'"

up a pair of running shoes from the company rep with the American team, he was told, "We only have shoes for potential medal winners." Mills said quietly, "But I think I'm going to win." To which the rep replied, "That's a bunch of bull."

Mills finally got his shoes, but he could have run the 10,000 in his Marine uniform, boots and all. He had visualized victory for a year and had finally grown comfortable with his "otherness" as a Native American. He'd trained on 110-meter sprints until his legs burned; a 23.4 practice 220 revealed his potential kick.

As expected, Clarke pushed the pace at the front of the large field of 38 runners as the 10,000 took shape. By midway, Clarke led a breakaway pack of 5 through 5000 in 14:04.6. Mills was in there, but wondered if he could hold the pace and briefly panicked.

He regrouped, focusing on one lap at a time. With only one lap to go, four men remained in contention: Clarke, Gammoudi, Mamo Wolde of Ethiopia, and Mills.

Gammoudi broke loose with his familiar head-bobbing sprint. Clarke chased. Mills fell back. The track was cluttered with lapped runners. At one point, Mills was driven wide by a Clarke elbow and looked dazed and out of it. But Mills found untapped reserves, lifted himself around the final turn, and raced madly down the home stretch. "All I could hear was the throbbing of my heart," he would say.

Mills ran down Clarke and Gammoudi for the gold medal in 28:24.4, an Olympic record. It was called the greatest Olympic distance upset ever. But Mills knew better. (A week later, Mills placed 14th in the Olympic marathon.) The next year, Mills set a world 6-mile record, running 27:11.6 in a tie with Lindgren at the AAU Nationals in San Diego.

Mills left competition soon after to motivate others to realize that they, too, could fulfill their dreams.

Crusading for Others

Today, Mills is on the road 300 days a year, giving speeches and nurturing various humanitarian causes. He's involved with aid to Africa and has helped Olympic champion Kip Keino with his orphanage in Kenya. Mills works with Running Strong for American Indian Youth, providing food and medical care. He's also on the board of Wings of America, which promotes Native American running.

Going the Distance on 110s

Mills essentially coached himself as he prepared for the 1964 Olympic Games while a marine lieutenant at Camp Pendleton in California. He ran twice daily, logged 90 miles a week, and concentrated on speed. That spring, Mills's training diary looked like this.

MONDAY: A.M.—2-mile warmup; 4-mile "tee-to-greens" on golf course, consisting of 18 340-yard runs covering every hole with 150-yard rest between; 2-mile cooldown. P.M.—2-mile warmup; 2 miles of repeat 110s; 1-mile cooldown. Total: 14 miles

TUESDAY: A.M.—2-mile warmup; 1 mile of repeat 110s; 2-mile cooldown. P.M.—1-mile warmup; 2 miles of sprint 150, float 70 in 8:50; 4-mile cooldown. Total: 12 miles

WEDNESDAY: A.M.—3-mile warmup; 1 mile of repeat 110s; 1-mile easy; 4 × 880 in 1:59 to 2:00 with 330-yard rest between; 2-mile cooldown. P.M.—4-mile warmup; cross-country run on sand with 1.5 miles easy and 1.5 miles at race pace; 2-mile cooldown. Total: 20 miles

THURSDAY: A.M.—3-mile warmup; 2 miles of easy 110s. P.M.—whirlpool and rest. Total: 5 miles

FRIDAY: A.M.—1-mile warmup, then whirlpool. P.M.—14 miles easy. Total: 15 miles

SATURDAY: A.M.—3-mile warmup; 1 mile of repeat 110s; 6 × 1,000 yards (slower than race pace), with 330-yard rest between; 1-mile cooldown. P.M.—4 miles easy; 4 miles hard; 1 mile easy 110s; 1-mile cooldown. Total: 18 miles

SUNDAY: A.M.—2-mile warmup; 1 mile easy 110s; 1 mile hard 110s; 1 mile easy 110s; 1-mile cooldown. Total: 6 miles

Total for week: 90 miles

In 1965, leading up to his world record 6-mile in June, Mills averaged 82 miles a week for 8 weeks. He knew that he was in great shape when he ran personal bests for the mile and 3-mile during weeks when he didn't taper off.

4-day meal plan

Mills ate a diet in the tradition of his Lakota tribe that was based on a 4-day cycle. One day, he ate something from "on the ground" (buffalo or deer in the old days, now lamb or beef); the next day "from the water" (fish); the next "from the air" (birds, now chicken or turkey); the next day from "in the ground" (vegetables). Each day, the diet also required foods of five colors: red, green, yellow, brown, and white; and they had to be "live" foods like fruit and grain.

Bob Schul

5000 Meters

7

Lifetime Honors Point Total:
11,050

Best Times
5000 meters—13:38.0
June 5, 1964, Compton, California
(Compton Invitational)

Born: September 28, 1937, West Milton, Ohio
Current Residence: Dayton, Ohio
Education: Milton Union High School, Dayton, Ohio (1955); Miami University, Oxford, Ohio (1966)
Affiliations: Los Angeles Track Club, Dayton Athletic Club
Professions: Teacher, coach
Career Highlights: 1964 Olympic champion in the 5000 meters (only American winner); set five American records and a world record in the 2-mile

Deep-Breathing Exercises

Bob Schul says that a little luck played a role in his 1964 gold medal run in the 5000 at Tokyo—the only Olympic 5000 won by an American.

Schul could have used some luck. As a child, he suffered from asthma and was never properly treated for it. His activity was limited, and at times he had to be rushed to the hospital. More than once, he almost died. Naturally, the young Schul, who grew up on a 100-acre farm, was forbidden to run.

But run Schul did, and a talent slowly blossomed. He became a modest 4:34 miler in high school and was a walk-on at Miami University in Oxford, Ohio. His breathing difficulties continued throughout his running, with smoggy air quality during the all-important summer track seasons presenting his greatest challenge.

Schul met the challenge with push-the-envelope training under the watch of Mihaly Igloi, the Hungarian expatriate who coached many U.S. distance stars. "I was so much fitter than anyone else on the American scene," says Schul of his Olympic season. "I could run at 80 percent and still win."

"You have to run consistently day after day to excel, but overall mileage is insignificant. It's speed that counts. If you run faster than race pace in a workout, you'll be able to relax more in a race."

Tokyo in the fall was a blessing, a veritable pollution-free zone. "Very clear air," Schul recalls. "Probably the only Olympic city I could have competed in." And when it rained on the day of the 5000 final, the air was cleansed that much more, enabling Schul to devour enough oxygen. "The rain made everybody equal."

When Schul took the Olympic starting line with the likes of Ron Clarke, Kip Keino, Michel Jazy, and Bill Baillie, he was more than equal; Schul was the favorite. He'd defeated the up-and-coming Clarke a couple of times the past winter. That spring, Schul had run 13:38.0 to break the American 5000 record by 7 seconds. Over the summer, he took the 5000 in the U.S.–Russian dual meet. Seven weeks before Tokyo, Schul set a world record for the 2-mile (8:26.4), defeating Tokyo 10,000 titlist Billy Mills and erasing the record held by Jazy. A week later, he broke 4 minutes in the mile for the second time.

Tokyo's welcoming air was not the only touch of fate to mark Schul's career. Poverty helped. Schul had left college after 2 years for lack of money and enlisted in the Air Force. Stationed at Oxnard, California, in 1961, Schul's commanding officer was Max Truex, a top 10,000 runner. Truex connected Schul with

two firsts for fast feet
Schul wore a pair of sprinter's shoes, the Adidas 9.9, to run the Olympic 5000. Because of frequent lower-leg trouble, Schul found a shoemaker in Los Angeles to put a heel lift in his 9.9s. Thus, his Olympic 5000 victory was not the only first for an American: Schul claims he was the first man to wear a heel lift in a track shoe.

Igloi, whose distance group was nearby. "Igloi killed me," says Schul, who was so famished after his initial workouts that he snacked on 2 pints of ice cream and a bag of peanuts.

In time, Schul came to thrive on Igloi's grueling program. He made the U.S. team and toured Europe that summer, running the 5000 and the steeple. Schul didn't win anything, but he learned enough from Igloi to train himself when he returned to college in 1963.

That year, Schul picked up his first international medal, the 5000 bronze at the Pan American Games in São Paulo, even though the air was bad and he ran with a calf injury. Schul's best was yet to come; he waited for the day when conditions would be just right.

Hello, Tokyo. The Olympic 5000 pace was slow, with the opening 800 going in 2:18.5. Then Clarke, who had won the 10,000 bronze 4 days before, strung out the field with several surges. But he would always retreat, and with 600 to go, nine men were still in contention. On the final lap, Schul buzzed by his American teammate, Bill Dellinger, for the lead, and turned on his sprint—the same closing sprint he had run during practice back in Ohio while his wife timed him.

Tale of the Tape

Schul says his toughest victory did not come in the 1964 Olympics but in the next year's AAU national championship 3-mile in San Diego. "I was always pulling my calf muscle, and came into the meet with an injury and my leg taped," says Schul. He faced a deep field that included the consistent Ron Larrieu, another Igloi protégé. Schul's leg held up fine and he ran an American record 13:10.4.

Schul's last quarter in Tokyo was 54.8, and he covered the final 300 in 38.70—and that was in the rain, on a muddy cinder track. His winning time was 13:48.8 as Dellinger won the bronze medal behind runner-up Harald Norporth of West Germany. Jazy wound up fourth, the newcomer Keino fifth, and Baillie, world record holder for the 1-hour run, sixth.

Schul's victory might have been the greatest come-through run ever. He'd actually told the media he would win the gold, adding to the pressure.

Why do something like that? "Telling someone made it real," he says. "Then I *had* to do it."

Bob Schul's Training Secret ▶▶

Slowpokes Not Allowed

Most runners like to do their hardest efforts—usually speedwork—in the afternoon or the evening, when they're limbered up from the day's activity or a morning distance run. Not so if you ran with coach Mihaly Igloi. You rolled out of bed, brushed your teeth, and got ready to burn speed on the track as early as 5:30 in the morning.

In 1961, when Schul started with Igloi, the group trained in the San Jose area. Later that year, the entourage moved to southern California and formed the L.A. Track Club. Schul ran twice a day, every day, except Sunday. He ran hard 4 days a week. Morning speedwork consisted of about 5 miles of fast work, like sprinting the straightaways and jogging the turns for 20 laps of the track. The afternoon of a hard day involved repeat 150s, 200s, 300s, 400s. If 400s, Schul would do 16 repeats in 63 seconds, with a brief 30-second rest between runs. Speed sessions could require as much as 10 miles' worth of hard running.

Schul's longest single run, on an easy day, was an hour. "We could go as slow as we wanted," he says. "But I hated it. I was so tired from the track work." Schul totaled 80 to 90 miles a week. He estimates that it was 70 percent high anaerobic, emphasizing that "intensity led to success."

Schul carried that approach into his banner year of 1964, when he tuned up for the Tokyo Olympics at the Miami-Ohio track. He trained alone on a cinder track with his wife timing him. His pivotal workout was 20 × 400, in which he ran 60, 60, 60, and 58 and continued that pattern. He took a next-to-nothing 120-yard jog rest between each run. And, simulating his expectations for the Olympic final, Schul always blasted the final 400 all out in 54 seconds and change. That just happened to be his exact split for the last lap in Tokyo.

no gain

Assessing recent American men's distance performances, Schul feels that there must be something wrong with current training systems. Given the slow cinder tracks of Schul's day, 5000 times—other than those of Bob Kennedy, the lone exception—are about "equal" 36 years later. He blames aimless mileage. "It's so easy for someone to go out for a 15-mile run, but it doesn't do a damn bit of good."

Steve Prefontaine 8
5000 Meters, 10,000 Meters

Lifetime Honors Point Total:
15,050

Best Times

1500 meters—3:38.1
June 28, 1973, Helsinki, Finland
(World Games)

Mile—3:54.6
June 20, 1973, Eugene, Oregon
(Hayward Field Restoration)

2-mile—8:18.29
July 18, 1974, Stockholm,
Sweden (July Games)

3-mile—12:51.4
June 8, 1974, Eugene, Oregon
(Hayward Field Restoration)

5000 meters—13:21.87
June 26, 1974, Helsinki, Finland
(World Games)

10,000 meters—27:43.6
April 27, 1974, Eugene, Oregon
(Twilight Meet)

Born: January 25, 1951, Coos
Bay, Oregon
Died: May 30, 1975
Education: Marshfield High
School, Coos Bay, Oregon (1969);
University of Oregon, Eugene
(1973)
Affiliations: Oregon Track Club,
Nike
Profession: Professional runner
Career Highlights: Set 15 Amer-
ican records; held every U.S. dis-
tance mark from 2 miles through
the 10,000; seven-time national
champion; fourth in 1972 Olympic
5000; won 119 of 151 outdoor
track races (including high school)
in an aborted career

An Athlete Dying Young

In a sense, we have been mourning the loss of Steve Prefontaine since his death in an automobile accident in 1975. He was 24, entering the prime of his running life, and a dynamic figure who could spit in the eye of the stodgy AAU and rally track fans to appreciate the beauty of the sport. Time and again since, as running has confronted the tough issues of professional growth, have we imagined how Pre would have provided steady and vigorous leadership.

With his 15 American records, daring, front-running style, and arms-wide embrace of the crowd, Pre was a runner with sex appeal, an ambassador abroad, a hero who touched people of all ages.

His pricking of recalcitrant track officials added to his populist appeal. Pre took on the establishment, and with flair. In his native Oregon, where running was seen as a proud challenge to convention, Pre was adored.

"Go, Pre!" became the mantra at Hayward Field in Eugene, Pre's home track at the University of Oregon. At college and later on, Pre won 35 of 38 races on that track. It's where he ran his last race, a 5000, on May 29, 1975, a mere 3 hours before his 1973 MGB plowed into an embankment late at night and crushed the life out of him. Pre won that final race in 13:23.8, missing his U.S. record by 1.9 seconds.

"If the AAU doesn't give me permission to run where I want in Europe this summer, I won't run in the AAU meets."

From the time he starting winning high school events in Coos Bay, Oregon, a tough, logging town where sports was a proving ground, Pre ran with fire in his heart. In college, he had the legendary Bill Bowerman as head coach to nurture his spirit, and the more subdued Bill Dellinger, then assistant coach in charge of distance runners, to shape his training. Bowerman predicted that Pre would become the world's greatest.

He might have been.

Pre won the NCAA 5000 title as a freshman, sophomore, junior, and senior, becoming the first college track–and–field athlete to win the same event all 4 years. He had the instincts of a veteran, and he thrilled to burn off an opponent. You just couldn't stop him, on or off the track.

Pre saw Europe and its summer circuit as an untapped frontier for American runners. He first ran abroad when he was just out of high school and returned every summer, finding glory in the marquee meets of Scandinavia. Pre set American records in Oslo, Stockholm, and Helsinki. He made

star of track and screen

Few Hollywood movies are made about runners, but there are two about Pre: *Prefontaine*, a $9-million production from Disney in 1997, and *Without Limits*, a $25-million effort from Warner Brothers in 1998. *Without Limits* is by far the better film. Directed by Robert Towne and written by Towne and former *Sports Illustrated* writer Kenny Moore (a two-time Olympic Marathoner), *Time* magazine praised it for "the uncompromising spirit it sweetly celebrates."

friends with the Finns and brought them to Eugene to compete. He also brought back his lust for the cushiony wood-chip running trails of Scandinavia; today, sustaining his memory, a 5-mile "Pre's Trail" in Eugene gives thousands of runners the same lift.

Pre's first trip to Norway came shortly before the 1972 Munich Olympics. He had won the Olympic Trials 5000 in 13:22.8, an American record and personal best by almost 7 seconds as well as the third fastest ever worldwide. In Oslo, Pre won the 3000 in 7:44.2 to shatter the U.S. mark by 10 seconds and reaffirm his medal contention for Munich.

Only 21, Pre was the youngest contender in the Olympic 5000. The early pace was slow, not to Pre's liking. The tempo accelerated as runners tested one another, setting up the final push. With two laps to go, Pre was in a lead group of five men, all with a chance to win; but of course only three would get

Great Start
Prefontaine's running talent was discovered in high school P.E. class by the Marshfield track coach, Walt McClure. He was undefeated his junior and senior years, setting a national high school 2-mile record of 8:41.5 in 1969.

medals. Pre held third into the homestretch but was passed at the finish by Britain's Ian Stewart and wound up fourth in 13:28.4.

Pre took the loss hard but was inspired. At the time, Pre was living in a $60-a-month trailer, surviving on his $101-a-month college scholarship and using food stamps. Pre turned down a six-figure offer to join the quirky pro track tour because he felt that it lacked authenticity. In 1973, he raised $40,000 for a new grandstand at the university by running a mile against Dave Wottle, the 1972 Olympic 800-meter champion.

Prefontaine won all six of his spring races in 1975, the year of his death. The night of the crash, Pre had been at a party. He liked his beer, but it was unclear if alcohol was a factor in the accident. At his funeral in Coos Bay, the pallbearers were fellow runners who dressed in their warmup suits. Another gathering was held in Eugene, where 4,000 people turned out to pay tribute.

Steve Prefontaine's Training Secret ▶▶

He Knew the Drill

In college, Pre ran every day—usually twice—covering 80 miles and more a week. His longest runs were 10 to 12 miles, with a pace that often went well under 6 minutes a mile. Pre was more interested in running fast than long.

In the mornings, he ran 4 to 6 miles. In the afternoons, he either ran more distance or did speedwork. On Tuesday and Thursday afternoons and Saturday mornings, Pre did his quality work on the track.

The school distance coach, Bill Dellinger (who succeeded Bill Bowerman as head coach in 1973), created a menu of innovative workouts that have become Oregon standards. One was the 30/40s. You run a 200 in 30 seconds followed by a 200 in 40 seconds continuously until you can no longer hold the pace. "Most guys stop at 8 laps," says Dellinger. "Alberto Salazar did 16 laps. Pre still holds the record at 18."

Another classic was 4 × 1200 with a 400 jog between, then 2 × mile with a 400 jog. Before the 1972 Olympics, Pre ran one set of 1200s in 3:12, 3:09, 3:06, and 3:00. An even tougher workout using 1200s also mixed in 200s like this: run one 1200 hitting 80, 70, and 60 for the three laps, jog a lap, then run 4 × 200 in 30 with a 30-second jog between. Repeat for a total of four sets.

Dellinger's meat-and-potatoes workout, which he has been refining over the years, was called the 30th Street Drill—a nonstop 10-miler with several surges in which each segment was timed. Here's how it went for Pre and company.

1. Start with a 1200 on the track, hitting 60, 65, and 70 for the three laps.
2. Go out to the road at 6-minute-mile pace.
3. After 2 or 3 miles, throw in a fast 1200 on the road in 3:00 to 3:10.
4. Resume a 6-minute pace and after about 8 miles on the road, return to the track.
5. Finish with another 1200 in 70, 65, and 60.

Pre liked to stay up late, but when the 30th Street Drill was scheduled for Saturday morning, he'd go to bed at 10 o'clock on a Friday night, according to a college roommate and teammate, Pat Tyson.

breath test

In a landmark 1975 study of elite distance runners conducted at the Institute for Aerobics Research in Dallas, Prefontaine scored the highest in the measure for max VO_2; that is, oxygen consumption. This test determines the amount of oxygen an athlete can take in and process, a critical factor in performance. Pre scored 84.4, while the average for his group was 78.8.

Marty Liquori 9
1500 Meters, Mile, 5000 Meters

Lifetime Honors Point Total:
10,100

Best Times

1500 meters—3:36.0
July 1, 1971, Milan, Italy
(international meet)

Mile—3:52.2
May 17, 1975, Kingston, Jamaica
(King Games)

2000 meters—5:02.2
July 7, 1971, Louvain, Belgium
(international meet)

2-mile—8:17.2
July 17, 1975, Stockholm,
Sweden (international meet)

5000 meters—13:15.06
September 4, 1977, Düsseldorf,
West Germany (World Cup)

Born: September 11, 1949, Mont
clair, New Jersey
Current Residence: Gainesville,
Florida
Education: Essex Catholic High
School, Newark, New Jersey
(1967); Villanova University, Vil-
lanova, Pennsylvania (1971)
Affiliations: New York Athletic
Club, Florida Track Club, Athletic
Attic
Professions: Professional runner,
TV producer and commentator,
business executive
Career Highlights: Ranked
number one in the world three
times; set four American records;
won 14 national titles; captured
three straight Wanamaker Miles;
defeated Jim Ryun in "Dream
Mile"

Dream Miler

Before he made a commitment to running, Marty Liquori was more interested in joining the Rolling Stones than the U.S. Olympic Team. But after being given an ultimatum by his coach, Liquori traded his sheet music for the lyricism of the track.

Liquori was a smash hit from the start. As a high school runner in 1967, he ran a 3:59.8 mile and had to enter events with older athletes to be challenged. At Villanova, he made the 1968 Olympic Team at 19, won the NCAA mile in 1969, 1970, and 1971, collected nine straight Penn Relays titles, defeated Jim Ryun in the ballyhooed "Dream Mile," and was twice named the world's number-one miler.

After college, Liquori set four American records, including two in the 5000 within 11 days in the summer of 1977, when he was ranked number one in the world in that event.

He won the first in Zurich in 13:16.0,

51

defeating the Ethiopian Miruts Yifter. Liquori later said that he almost regretted scoring the victory because it exposed him to Yifter, who won the second and more important match at the inaugural World Cup in Düsseldorf, West Germany. There, Liquori improved his U.S. standard to 13:15.06.

"Track racing is like playing Carnegie Hall, while road racing is just rock 'n' roll."

As a teenager, Liquori didn't strive to be the best runner but the best guitarist. Imagining himself a Julliard student, he played in a garage band, fancied himself a Keith Richards, and ran only to get in shape for playing basketball.

At Essex Catholic High School in Newark, the track coach, Fred Dwyer, saw talent in Liquori and appealed to his parents. As Liquori recalled, "Fred told them I had to stop playing gigs at night to be rested for meets." Or else. Liquori finally did decide to get his satisfaction on the track.

At Villanova, coach Jumbo Elliott taught Liquori that what was deep in a runner's heart counted more than the heart's pulse rate. A confident, streetwise kid, Liquori was a willing adherent to Elliott's wisdom.

He developed a tough, frank style, counting on a strong psyche to take him far. He always had flair, whether winning 14 straight mile races in Madison Square Garden or outrunning the reigning Olympic champion, Kip Keino, at the 1970 King Games in Jamaica.

All of Liquori's fire and panache would come into play at the next year's King Games, held at Philadelphia's Franklin Field and featuring the "Dream Mile." No American race ever had a greater buildup. No race was ever steeped in that much glamour. No race ever embodied as much of the track's allure. It was the

serving good health

In 1994, at age 45, Liquori was diagnosed with a mild form of leukemia called chronic lymphocytic leukemia. In a fateful coincidence, Liquori had already begun serving as a spokesperson for the Leukemia Society of America. He has continued efforts to raise funds for leukemia research and has not let the disease limit his own life. Liquori's condition is under control and he is in good health today.

defining moment for Liquori: the brash kid from the street versus Jim Ryun, the modest world record holder from Kansas.

On a raw, drizzly day before 20,000 fans, an 11-man field took the line on a track made famous by the Penn Relays. After a slow first half, Liquori made a big move with 700 to go. Ryun followed by a long stride until the final turn, when he drew even. The home crowd roared for Liquori, who grew up just an hour away. Waiting for Ryun's breath on his shoulder, Liquori accelerated, but Ryun stuck with him and they ran like that to the finish, dueling, with nothing but a lifetime's reputation at stake. Liquori won by inches as both runners were timed in 3:54.6.

Afterward, Liquori, treated like a hero, said, "I wanted us both sagging in the stretch, looking more like boxers, both dead, like we were running on sand."

That's Marty. He saw the track, the race, as an opportunity for gallantry, for beating the odds. He always believed that the best runners grew out of deprivation, a way he explained the sliding American performances of the affluent 1990s. Liquori himself never lacked for comfort, but he managed to adopt the work ethic of someone who desperately needed the affirmation of victory.

Voice of the Sport

Liquori has nearly overshadowed his running achievements with his other successes. He was cofounder and president of the Athletic Attic, a national sporting goods chain. He's been producer and host of ESPN's Saucony Running and Racing *program for more than a decade. With a silky voice and astute perspective, Liquori does network TV commentary, covering the New York City Marathon, the Olympics, and various track meets.*

Liquori couldn't find it in an Olympic year, however. After being the youngest Olympic 1500 finalist ever at the 1968 Games in Mexico City, Liquori was injured in 1972, 1976, and 1980. Amid the U.S. boycott of the Moscow Games, Liquori tossed his spikes into the stands at the 1980 Olympic Trials in Eugene and called it a career at age 30.

Liquori went on to develop his business interests and to work in television. Eventually, he resumed playing the guitar, but no longer in a garage. "My main gig," Liquori says now, "is backing up 12 old ladies at hospices in Florida."

Winning KISS

Liquori's Villanova coach Jumbo Elliott, who mentored many great milers, was well known for his KISS—an acronym for the system he designed to Keep It Simple, Stupid. "When I was on the track," said Liquori, "I ran hard. When I was on the road, I ran easy."

As Elliott dictated, training need not be fancy. In college, including the 1971 "Dream Mile" period, Liquori ran 90 to 100 miles a week during his buildup phase. He did speedwork 3 days a week and distance runs 2 days a week, usually racing on Saturdays and jogging a little the day before.

Liquori ran twice a day, except on race days. On most mornings, he ran 6 miles. On Wednesdays, his main run was a relaxed 10 miles. On Sundays, he ran 5 in the morning and 10 in the afternoon. Mondays, Tuesdays, and Thursdays were track days.

On Mondays, he did 16 × 400 in 58 to 59 seconds, with a 400 jog between runs. On Tuesdays, he did 8 to 12 × 200 in 25 to 27 seconds, with a 200 jog between runs. On Thursdays, he did a few very fast 400s, in 55, taking complete rest between runs.

When Liquori moved up to the 5000 in the late 1970s, he ran 100 miles a week, or a little more, with greater frequency. But when he experimented with other distance training, he found it too drawn out. "I ran hard on the roads and did long intervals. That didn't work psychologically for me as miler."

Liquori decided to train primarily like a miler, with some distance touches. He increased his 200 repetitions to 20, starting at 33 seconds and taking it down, a half-second a week, to 27. He did 8 to 15 × 400, working down to 60 seconds each. He did 5 × 800, working down to 2:02.

When coaching himself, Liquori mixed it up, drawing from different sources. He did a ladder workout of 200-400-600-400-200, with only 30 seconds rest. For his 800s, he picked up a trick from Britain's Brendan Foster. He'd run the first 600 in 1:28, rest for 30 seconds, then blast the final 200 in 27.

In May, fine-tuning for the big meets, Liquori was on the track every day. "When I would tell people that, the reaction was, 'Oh, my God!' But it was sharpening, not volume." One day, he did 4 × 400, another day 2 × 200, a third day a mile's worth of short sprints.

Like the man said, KISS.

it ain't rocket science

Influenced by coach Jumbo Elliott's muse, Liquori didn't give things like diet a thought. "He would tell us Ron Delany [Villanova's 1956 Olympic 1500 champion] ate a hot dog before winning the NCAA. Jumbo was trying to make you believe running was not scientific—that nothing mattered except getting on the track and being tough."

10

Jim Beatty
Mile, 5000 Meters

Lifetime Honors Point Total:
23,100

Best Times

1500 meters—3:39.4
August 9, 1962, Oslo, Norway
(International Games)

Mile—3:55.5
July 7, 1963, Compton, California
(Compton Invitational)

2-mile—8:29.8
June 8, 1962, Los Angeles (South
Pacific AAU)

5000 meters—13:45.0
August 24, 1962, Turku, Finland
(international meet)

Born: October 28, 1934, New
York, New York
Current Residence: Charlotte,
North Carolina
High School: Central High School,
Charlotte, North Carolina (1953);
North Carolina State University,
Raleigh (1957)
Affiliations: Santa Clara Valley
Youth Village, Los Angeles Track
Club
Professions: Business executive,
politician
Career Highlights: Ran world's
first sub-4:00 mile indoors; set 18
American and four world records;
only man to hold six U.S. distance
records at once; set five U.S.
marks in 16 days in Europe in
1962; Sullivan Award winner

Little Giant Runs Big Times

Jim Beatty, called the Little Giant by some, elevated the mile to a marquee event in American sports in an era when a sub-4-minute mile was big news.

At 5'6", the barrel-chested Beatty, a former boxer, led an early 1960s U.S. mile corps that also featured Dyrol Burleson, Jim Grelle, Cary Weisiger, and Tom O'Hara, all consistent sub-4 runners at a time when the world record, held by New Zealand's Peter Snell, was still in the 3:54 range.

While Burleson, compared head-to-head, may have been the superior miler, Beatty also excelled at the 2-mile and 5000 meters, and compiled an overall record as prolific as any in American distance annals. Beatty set 18 U.S. and 4 world records in the 1500 meters, mile, 3000 meters, 2-mile, 3-mile, and 5000 meters.

With his compact size, Beatty was a dynamo indoors, and that was where he first made his mark—in 1962, a year when he was practically unstoppable, running the first indoor sub-4:00 mile.

By the winter of 1962, Beatty had been training for more than 2 years under coach Mihaly Igloi in California and was still feeling the void of the 1960 Rome Olympics, where he sat in the stands with an injury. "My disappointment was so great," says Beatty. "I became angry. I'd decided to come back and attack the records."

"Set reasonable goals—intermediate goals that add up to the ultimate goal. You must do speed to improve. Interval training can be applied to any level."

Beatty was America's Bannister. The U.S. indoor circuit was thriving, and Igloi told Beatty the sub-4:00 attempt should come on February 10 at the *Los Angeles Times* meet. Beatty, wearing the colors of the Los Angeles Track Club, got pacing help from teammates Laszlo Tabori and Grelle, who led at three-quarters in 3:01.2. Beatty took over, implored by the crowd of 13,000 to make history, and charged home triumphant in 3:58.9.

Beatty had erased the world mark of 4:01.4 held by Ireland's Ron Delany. He was fulfilled for himself and his country. "I used to say, 'It was time to bring the record home,'" Beatty recalls.

With his spunky style and tidewater drawl, Beatty was a perfect ambassador for American track forces. He won the 1500 meters in the U.S.-Soviet dual meet in 1961 and 1962. In the latter event, he ran 3:39.9, becoming the first American under 3:40. Almost every time Beatty stepped on the track that year, he set a record.

or i'll punch your lights out

Beatty started out in sports as a 118-pound amateur boxer. He prided himself on his stamina and went out for high school track. After a week of practice, he asked the coach if he could run the mile in a meet. The coach told him no, he would get hurt. Beatty persisted, set a school record that day, and went on to win two state mile titles.

In his European tour that August, Beatty set five straight American records in 16 days while competing in England, France, Finland, and Sweden. If not for the cold, rainy weather and lack of competition, Beatty might have shattered some world records, too. Beatty's marks came in the 1500 meters (3:39.4), mile (3:56.5 and 3:56.3), 3000 meters (7:54.2), and 5000 meters (13:45.0), which was set in Turku, Finland, the home of legendary runner Paavo Nurmi.

Beatty was given the 1962 Sullivan Award as the nation's outstanding amateur athlete. Olympic years, however, were not kind to Beatty. In 1956, while an up-and-coming junior at North Carolina State University, he failed to make the Melbourne squad in the 5000.

In 1960, Beatty picked up an injury before Rome, ran the 5000 heats hurt and did not make the final. Although Beatty lowered his world indoor mile record in 1963 (3:58.6 in New York's Madison Square Garden), an injured foot requiring 22 stitches later that year took Beatty out of contention for Tokyo in 1964.

Beatty retired at 30 and went into the executive search business, heading his own firm. He also went into politics, serving as a state legislator in North Carolina but losing a 1972 bid to win a seat in the U.S. Senate.

Beatty chaired the organizing committee of the 1996 Olympic Marathon Trial for men held in Charlotte, and as a New Yorker by birth—he moved to the South at age 5—Beatty is on the committee to bring the summer Olympics to the Big Apple in 2012.

Beatty stays in shape today with tennis and walking.

Western Union Calling

Beatty was prepared to give up his track career after college, but two things brought him back. First, while in the army and stationed at Fort Jackson in South Carolina in 1957, he received telegrams inviting him to various meets. "I called it the Telegram Tour," Beatty says. Second, he went to watch the inspiring 1959 U.S.–Soviet dual meet in Philadelphia. That fall, he emptied his bank account, packed his bags, drove to California, and showed up at the track where coach Mihaly Igloi was training runners.

"Who's this fat man?" Igloi remarked as Beatty approached him.

"I'm Jim Beatty from North Carolina. I'd like you to train me for the Olympic team."

"You start tomorrow," Igloi told him.

Jim Beatty's Training Secret ▶▶

In the Swing of It

Beatty's training group with Igloi was first based in northern California and went by the name Santa Clara Valley Youth Village. In the fall of 1961, the club relocated to southern California and was known as the Los Angeles Track Club. Igloi was a Hungarian who studied coaching systems worldwide, became an American citizen in 1963, coached in Greece in the 1970s, and died at age 89 in 1998. His athletes broke 49 world records.

Igloi emphasized speed, customized workouts to the individual athlete, and demanded unwavering dedication. He rarely used a stopwatch, had keen instincts and a hard manner, and used few words. With just a glance from Igloi, you knew how to run or whether you were dogging it.

Beatty rarely ran more than 60 miles a week. His longest run was an hour. But he trained for 3 hours a day—1 hour in the morning and 2 hours in the evening. Igloi's system featured repeated short runs at a fast pace, so Beatty ran sets of 20 or more 150s and 200s back and forth across a football field. He trained hard 4 or 5 days a week, taking off only on Christmas, Easter, and New Year's.

The key was pace, and Igloi used his own language to direct Beatty and the others: "Easy speed," "Middle speed," or "Short speed." Or: "Easy swing tempo," "Middle swing tempo," or "Hard swing tempo." The athletes acquired a keen sense of their bodies' rhythms under stress as opposed to meeting arbitrary standards of hitting specific times.

Ironically, Beatty never trained indoors, not even for his historic sub-4:00 mile in 1962. It didn't matter; it was faith in the coach that apparently mattered the most.

playing around

Beatty's favorite place to run was not the track but the park trails near the Santa Monica beach in California. "I considered them play runs," says Beatty. "I used to love running there."

11

Mel Sheppard
800 Meters, 1500 Meters

Lifetime Honors Point Total:
20,250

Best Times

800 meters—1:52.0
July 8, 1912, Stockholm, Sweden
(Olympic Games)

1500 meters—4:03.4
July 14, 1908, London, England
(Olympic Games)

Born: September 15, 1883, Almonesson Lake, New Jersey
Died: January 4, 1942
Education: Brown Preparatory School, Philadelphia (1905)
Affiliations: Irish-American Athletic Club, Millrose Athletic Association
Professions: Worked as a clerk at Wanamaker's department store in New York, Millrose Athletic Association recreational director
Career Highlights: 1908 Olympic champion in the 800 and the 1500; 1912 silver medalist in the 800, with two golds in Olympic relays; nine-time AAU national titlist; set world indoor records for 600 and 1000 yards; winner of more than a thousand races

Beating Blisters for Olympic Gold

Mel Sheppard, the greatest American runner of the early 20th century, considered himself a country boy, and he even took pride in the unrefined conditions in which he often ran.

At the time, there were few decent tracks to speak of, scant few "niceties," as Sheppard described it, to give comfort to hardworking athletes with Olympic aspirations. "Our enthusiasm was not dampened by blisters sustained as a result of running on unsure footing," Sheppard once wrote.

Sheppard must have set a standard for blisters to go along with his numerous track records. He was said to have won more than a thousand races from 1904 through 1915—an average of more than 80 races a year for 12 years.

What, no injuries?

Sheppard said he had his share of "pulled tendons," which makes you wonder how he could have competed so often, especially given the primitive running shoes of the day.

Sheppard grew up in southern New Jersey and attended Brown Preparatory School in nearby Philadelphia. While at Brown in 1905, he ran the 2-mile in 9:57.4, which was considered a high school record, except that Sheppard was of college age (21) at the time.

"I have seen the start of such a race cause a silence in the old Garden to the point where it seemed one could hear a pin drop— a silence so complete it made me feel as I were poised in a great vacuum until the starter's pistol had sent us away from our marks."

If Sheppard was not quite precocious, he was surely prolific.

A year out of school, Sheppard won the AAU indoor 1000 yards and outdoor 880, the first of his nine national titles. At 5-feet, 8-and-a-half inches and 165 pounds, he cut a powerful figure, with leg muscles bulging and a thick chest.

He was known as "Peerless Mel," and when he'd come from behind with a long, sustained sprint, "There goes Shep" was heard in arenas throughout the country.

Sheppard favored indoor running. Who could blame him? Many of the outdoor tracks were awful, like the one used for the Nationals in Chicago. It had been built at an ash-and-garbage dump on the shores of Lake Michigan. The athletes, said Sheppard, looked like coal miners after they had competed there.

Indoors, Sheppard had tracks he could count on, like

a thousand victories . . . but who's counting?

In 1963, the track historian R. L. Quercetani of Italy, writing in *Track and Field News*, named Sheppard the top American track and field athlete of the 1901–1910 decade. Quercetani was impressed with Sheppard's Olympic achievements as well as his "durability." You win more than a thousand races, you're durable.

Madison Square Garden, where he twice set world records for 600 yards. The second, 1:13.8, in 1908 lasted 5 years. Sheppard's work on the tight boards sharpened his competitive instincts, and by the time of the 1908 Olympics in London, he was a master tactician.

Sheppard was not considered a miler, and he was rated a long shot in the Olympic 1500. He was positioned fourth into the home-stretch and used a well-timed sprint to out-kick Britain's Harold Wilson, the first man to run under 4 minutes (3:59.8), for the gold medal. Sheppard's time was 4:03.4 to Wilson's 4:03.6.

A week later, Sheppard shot out at 53 seconds for the opening lap of the 800. His pace slowed but he still triumphed convincingly in 1:52.8, a world record. Sheppard also ran the anchor 800 on the victorious U.S. sprint-medley relay and bagged a total of three gold medals.

Sheppard continued winning AAU titles, setting records, and collecting victories by the score. At the 1912 Stockholm Games, Sheppard knew he'd have a race on his hands from Ted Meredith, 20 years old and just out of Mercersburg Prep.

Sheppard tore the first lap in 52.4, but Meredith stayed on his heels and nipped him at the finish in a world record time of 1:51.9. Sheppard took the silver medal in 1:52.0, which lowered his U.S. record. Sheppard again added a relay gold, this time leading off the 4 × 400.

Failing the Fitness Test

You'd think that a man with five Olympic medals would be pretty fit. But Sheppard was rejected from the New York City police department because of anticipated heart problems. As the New York Times reported, the department secretary said, "Most athletes have weak hearts. . . . We don't want a man on the force whose heart might give way under a sudden strain."

Climbing the Ladder at Celtic Park

Sheppard trained 6 days a week and took 2 days' rest before a meet. Considering how many races he ran, Sheppard got a fair amount of rest. He ran once a day and typically did what we now call a ladder workout: a series of successive up-and-down distances like 440, 600, 700, 800, 440, 300.

Sheppard did most of his training at Celtic Park on Long Island, home of his team, the Irish-American Athletic Club. The site was no more than a leveled-off hillside, and not easy for Sheppard to get to, either. It took him 3 hours each way, using a combination of streetcars, subway, ferry, and even the horse and buggy.

When he first arrived at Celtic Park, Sheppard found a track that was fairly rough on his legs. "Instead of cinders," he wrote, "the surface was composed of sand and loam with plenty of cobblestones. It was not unusual for a runner, when attempting to take a turn, to step on a rock with his spikes and be thrown off his stride so forcibly that he couldn't make the turn at all."

a tree grows in harlem

The arduous conditions Sheppard confronted apparently put hair on his chest. In addition to Celtic Park, Sheppard also trained at Harlem River Park, which featured a tree positioned in the middle of the backstretch. More than once, Sheppard managed to smash into it. The runners tried to use the obstacle as a tactical advantage because after that, running on clear tracks, even in big meets like the Olympics, was a welcome treat.

Steve Scott
1500 Meters, Mile 12

Lifetime Honors Point Total: 20,050

Best Times

800 meters—1:45.05
July 4, 1982, Byrkjelo, Norway
(international meet)

1500 meters—3:31.76
July 16, 1985, Nice, France
(Nikaia Grand Prix)

Mile—3:47.69
July 7, 1982, Oslo, Norway
(Oslo Games)

2000 meters—4:54.71
August 31, 1982, Ingelheim, West
Germany (international meet)

3000 meters—7:36.69
September 1, 1981, Ingelheim,
West Germany (international meet)

5000 meters—13:30.39
June 6, 1987, Eugene, Oregon
Prefontaine Classic

Born: May 5, 1956, Upland,
California
Current Residence: Carlsbad, California
Education: Upland High School,
Upland, California (1974); University of California, Irvine (1978)
Affiliations: Sub-4 Track Club,
Tiger Track Club, Asics Track Club
Professions: Professional runner,
college coach
Career Highlights: World Championship silver medalist in the
1500; set 16 U.S. records; outdoor mile record stands since
1982; won 11 U.S. titles;
amassed all-time high 136 sub-4:00 miles; three-time Olympian

The Blue-Collar Miler

Steve Scott was the ultimate blue-collar miler. He survived a bruising college program and thought nothing of training until his fair skin baked red in the sizzling Arizona heat. He was part of the new breed of barnstorming professional runners touring Europe every summer.

As such, he fought hard as the lone American against the world and earned a reputation as a good-natured prankster trying to keep a lively spirit in lonely hotels.

Scott was not a pretty runner. But he did have power and a driving kick, and he knew how to win. Scott had a sure sense of fairness. He bristled when the media rallied behind Don Paige, the cleancut Jim Ryun look-alike and NCAA champion from Villanova University, to dethrone him as the nation's best miler in the late 1970s. Scott says his most satisfying race was his 1979 AAU 1500 victory over Paige.

At the University of California at Irvine, coach Len Miller ran Scott to exhaustion as he achieved the first of his record 136 sub-4:00 miles and the first of his eight straight U.S. number-one rankings.

Miller's upfront style rubbed off, and Scott carried his boldness abroad to take on all challengers. In contrast to the backroom maneuverings of some calculating opponents, Scott was honest to a fault.

"I'd like to be known as the miler who competed with honesty, ran sick or hurt, never quit on a field, and came back year after year with consistency, passion, and a heart full of desire."

Hardened by the United States Olympic boycott of 1980, Scott, hitting his prime, hungered for a chance to meet the world's best. In the early 1980s, he set 11 of his 16 American records, including personal bests in the mile indoors (3:51.8 in 1981) and outdoors (3:47.69 in 1982). Both records still stand; the duration of each record is a record in itself.

Scott was ranked number two in the world in 1982 and 1983. In 1982, when he ran three sub-3:50s in Europe (and won Oslo's "Dream Mile"), he probably should have been number one. But it was hard for Scott to overcome the British influence that elevated Sebastian Coe, Steve Ovett, and Steve Cram to peerless status.

In 1983, Scott had only himself to blame. He mistimed his kick in an unbearably slow world championship 1500 final at Helsinki, taking the silver medal by $^{26}/_{100}$ of a second to Cram.

As a southern California native, Scott, now living in Ari-

shooting for sub-fore

One record that Scott never got credit for took place in 1979 on a golf course in Anaheim, California. For a publicity stunt, he tried to get into the Guinness Book of World Records for the fastest round of golf. Scott played fast, ran from tee to tee and shot 18 holes in a record-breaking 29:30. But no one from Guinness showed up to confirm the performance, and Scott's effort went for naught.

zona, shouldered enormous Olympic pressure in the next year's Olympic 1500 in Los Angeles. Stung by the slow Helsinki race, Scott and Miller came up with a risky plan to beat Coe and company. To assure an honest pace, Scott would lead. But he was not totally confident in this race strategy and went into the Games a little shaky.

After the opening 400, Scott rushed to the lead as planned. He finished only 10th as Coe won his second straight Olympic title.

Scott fell into depression but rebounded to go after his 100th sub-4:00 in 1985. He got it at the Bruce Jenner meet, running an easy 3:56.5.

Scott regained the U.S. number-one ranking in 1986, winning the Grand Prix final in Rome, and went on to place fifth in the 1988 Olympic 1500 at Seoul. Moving up in distance, Scott set his last U.S. record indoors in the 3000, in a stirring 1989 duel with victorious Said Aouita of Morocco at the New Jersey Meadowlands.

Running after Cancer

Scott beat testicular cancer in 1994. He endured a successful 5-hour operation and was back running again 2 months later, laying the foundation for a sub-4:00-at-40-mile quest in 1996. Early in 1995, only 7 months after surgery, Scott ran a 4:24 mile. Gradually, he knocked that down to a series of sub-4:10s, but no faster.

After that, Scott's performances fell off, but he continued running sub-4:00s until 1993, when he ran his last one (3:59.8) at the Sunkist indoor meet in Los Angeles. Scott won 71 of his 136 sub-4:00s; and the total does not include his scores of equivalent times for 1500 meters. For his durability, Scott was often compared with baseball's Cal Ripken.

In 1994, at age 38, Scott was diagnosed with testicular cancer, which he conquered with his customary resolve, paving the way for yet one more sub-4:00 attempt. He came as close as 4:05 in 1996 before finally letting go of the mile.

After that, Scott took a coaching position with the new track and cross-country program at California State University, San Marcos.

Push Beyond Limits

At Cal-Irvine in the late 1970s, coach Len Miller used a tough love approach that practically brought Scott to his knees. But it worked. "Len was able to motivate me and challenge me to go beyond my perceived limits," says Scott. "Those workouts were like going to war. By doing them, I felt I could conquer anything."

Scott ran 90 miles a week like this.
- Most days, he did double-workouts starting with a 5-mile morning run.
- Every afternoon workout was preceded by more than 100 pushups and 100 situps plus 100-meter strides.
- Speedwork consisted of 20 × 400 in 60 seconds, with a 400 jog between runs; or 20 × 800 in 2:25, with a 400 jog; or 10 × mile in 4:45, with an 800 jog.
- Hill work consisted of running 4 miles to a 150-meter hill off campus, doing 40 repeats of the hill, then running 4 miles back.
- On easy days, Scott did a 10-mile run at 6:00-per-mile pace.
- His weekly long run was 15 miles at 6:00 per mile.
- One day a week, he did 40 110-meter sprints on grass.

After college, Scott moved to Arizona to work with Miller, who would leave Irvine to become coach at Arizona State. During his peak years in the early 1980s, Scott logged 90 to 100 miles a week and used the same system of quality work. He just ran faster and cut down the rest between runs. For example, Scott ran his 400s in 57 to 59, with a 200 jog, blasting his final lap in 52.

One of Miller's toughest workouts was three sets of 800-400-800. Scott ran the 800s in 1:56 and the 400s in 55. He took short jogs between runs, and full-recovery, 5-minute rests between sets. Everything was geared toward a world record mile. When Scott ran his best time of 3:47.69 in 1982, he just missed Sebastian Coe's world record of 3:47.33.

Scott also trained in New Zealand with John Walker, the 1976 Olympic 1500 champion. The two were good friends, and Scott absorbed Walker's commitment to high mileage as a factor in track success.

In 1992, Scott started working with coach Irv Ray of California Baptist University, who helped him resume training after cancer in 1994. Scott had plenty of strength stored up but needed to redevelop his speed to try for a sub-4 at age 40. He did 10-mile runs at 5:00 per mile and 100-meter sprints with full recovery. In a sense, he tried to become 98 percent of the old Scott. But the older Scott found his limits at about 97 percent.

wait for me, mom

The first running star in the Scott family was mother Mary, who startled her California neighbors by jogging 6 miles a day in shorts and a T-shirt in the late 1960s. Young Scott preferred baseball and, despite his mother's influence, avoided running at all cost. Finally, "the weird lady of Euclid Avenue," as his mom was known, convinced Scott to go out for the Upland High track and cross-country teams. He took second in the state 880 and got a college scholarship worth $624 a year.

Horace Ashenfelter

3000-Meter Steeplechase

13

Lifetime Honors Point Total:
16,100

Best Times

3000-meter steeplechase—
8:45.4
July 27, 1952, Helsinki, Finland
(Olympic Games)

Born: January 23, 1923,
Phoenixville, Pennsylvania
Current Residences: Glen Ridge,
New Jersey; and Stewart, Florida
Education: Collegeville High
School, Collegeville, Pennsylvania
(1941); Pennsylvania State University, University Park (1949)
Affiliations: Shanahan Catholic
Club, Penn Athletic Club, New York
Athletic Club
Profession: FBI agent for 9 years,
also in the precious-metals business
Career Highlights: 1952 Olympic
champion in the 3000-meter
steeplechase in world-record time,
11-time AAU national champion in
various events, set six American
records in the steeplechase, 2-
mile, and 3000 meters

Breaking Barriers

Horace "Nip" Ashenfelter III, one of only
two Americans to win the Olympic steeplechase (the other victory came in 1904), first
built endurance doing 5-mile runs in the Air
Force while serving as a World War II pilot
based at several installations in the South from
1942 to 1945. He had enrolled at Pennsylvania State University in 1942, and then went
back to college in 1946 after the war.

At Penn State, the military man had untapped reserves. Running on the university
golf course to stay in shape, Ashenfelter met
a couple of trackmen who told him that if he
went out for the team, he would get a free
locker and towel.

That incentive motivated Ashenfelter to
approach track coach Chick Werner, who
asked him, "Can you run?"

To which Ashenfelter replied, "A little."

Ashenfelter made patient progress, win-

67

ning the NCAA 2-mile as a senior in 1949. Around that time, he started running the steeplechase—which has 28 3-foot-high hurdles including 7 over a water jump—when a coach from a rival college observed his springy stride and suggested that Ashenfelter give the event a try.

"Every endurance athlete knows that he can fool the coach, but he can't fool himself. There are few distance runners who are born great. You have to work very hard very often."

Applying high school physics, Ashenfelter would develop an innovative style of negotiating the water jump. Instead of extending his lead foot over the hurdle, he tried to tuck it under his body to maintain momentum as he cleared the hurdle. You can see Ashenfelter's technique in action in pictures of the 1952 Olympic final.

The year before the Games, Ashenfelter won the first 2 of 11 AAU individual championships, capturing the cross-country and steeple crowns. But he was not yet considered much of a prospect for the Helsinki Olympics. Runners from Sweden and Finland had won 11 of the 15 steeple medals in the previous five Olympics, and continued European dominance was assumed. The Helsinki favorite was Vladimir Kazantsev of the Soviet Union, who lowered his world record to 8:48.6 just 6 weeks before the Games.

But Ashenfelter was on the move. That year, he had won the first of five straight AAU national indoor 3-mile titles, as well as the first of four Millrose Games indoor 2-milers. By then, he was working full-time for the FBI and was forced to do a lot of training at night and on weekends. He coached

worth their weight in gold

Like in a fairy tale, Ashenfelter's Olympic gold medal shoes were custom-made by a Belgium shoemaker. Ashenfelter sent drawings of his feet to the specialist, who constructed lightweight spikes of kangaroo leather. They cost him $50, an exceedingly high price in the 1950s. "My one splurge," he says. Ashenfelter still has the pair hanging in his basement.

himself, and he was already married with two children and a third on the way when the Games arrived.

In Helsinki, Ashenfelter set an American record of 8:51.0 in the qualifying round and was suddenly a contender for the Olympic gold medal. In the final, Kazantsev's countryman, Mikhail Saltykov, led the field through the first kilometer in 2:49.8, well under world record pace. Soon, Ashenfelter took over, Saltykov fell back, and Kazantsev moved up to challenge. The two men traded the lead, bumped arms, and were dead even as the bell signaled the final lap. As Kazantsev stumbled over the last water jump, Ashenfelter breezed over it and won convincingly in 8:45.4, a world record.

In that cold war period, American sports writers noted that it was the first time an FBI man had allowed himself to be followed by a Russian.

Ashenfelter won the 1952 Sullivan Award as the nation's top amateur athlete and continued his record-breaking pace for the next 4 years. He was rarely beaten and lowered his national-best 2-mile to 8:50.5 indoors at New York's Madison Square Garden in 1954, and 8:49.6 outdoors at the Compton Invitational in California in 1955. He also took the silver medal in the 5000 meters at the 1955 Pan American Games in Mexico City.

Ashenfelter would never better his steeple-chase time from Helsinki—no American would for another 6 years. Ashenfelter also made the 1956 Olympic team but did not get past the qualifying heats in Melbourne. He retired from competition after the 1957 season. Today, Ashenfelter stays in shape with 3 or 4 days of running per week and a regular golf game.

Oh, Brother

You don't find two brothers on the Olympic team very often, especially in the same event. But Horace's younger brother (by 21 months) Bill was also a steeplechaser and Penn State grad who competed in Helsinki, failing to finish his qualifying heat. Bill made up for that disappointment after the Games by running on a U.S. team that set a world record in the 2-mile relay. "We had a third brother; you didn't hear much about him," says Ashenfelter. This was Don, the youngest. All three Ashenfelters ran on a Penn State four-man team that won the Penn Relays 4-mile title in 1949.

Hard Times

As a serious student who got married in college and was already a father before graduation, Ashenfelter had little time to squander in his early development. He had to train efficiently and make the most of every workout.

At Penn State, he alternated distance runs, usually on a golf course, with speedwork on the track. For distance, he ran 5 to 9 miles, much of it at 80 percent of maximum effort. Sprints included 100s, 200s, and 400s. Once a week, he did something today's runners rarely do: He ran all-out. For example, he would do three or four × 880 "as hard as I could." Or, he would do 1½ miles at 4:22 mile pace, about the same tempo as his fastest 2-mile races. He needed some recovery time, and took Fridays off before a Saturday meet. His mileage never exceeded 40 per week.

As a working man preparing for the 1952 Olympics, Ashenfelter had even greater demands on his time. His system was simple and intense: "I ran as hard as I could as often as I could." He never used a watch to guide him; Ashenfelter had an acute sense of pace and what his body could do. He was never injured.

Ashenfelter's concession to comfort was an easy 30-minute run in the mornings before work. Three nights a week, starting as late as 10:00 P.M., he would run for up to an hour. He had no adequate college facility near his New Jersey home and had to improvise in order to practice hurdling for the steeplechase. When the U.S. team prepared to go abroad for the Games, they gathered at a training camp in Princeton, New Jersey, and Ashenfelter briefly had a regulation training setup.

Most of Ashenfelter's training was done alone. Occasionally, he ran with Curt Stone, a former Penn State teammate and two-time Olympian with 13 AAU national titles to his credit.

if you want to be good

If you don't have the best equipment, improvise. Some of the world's greatest runners never had a track to train on or even a decent pair of running shoes. Before the Helsinki Olympics, Ashenfelter had to do some of his steeplechase practice at a park near his home. He lined up park benches as hurdles and jumped over them until the point of collapse. "I just wanted to be good. That's me."

Craig Virgin
10,000 Meters, Cross-Country

Lifetime Honors Point Total: 10,800

Best Times

2-mile—8:22.0
July 17, 1979, Oslo, Norway (Oslo Games)

3000 meters—7:48.2
July 9, 1979, Berkeley, California (Brooks Invitational)

5000 meters—13:19.1
July 5, 1980, Oslo, Norway (Oslo Games)

10,000 meters—27:29.16
July 17, 1980, Paris, France (Sport 2000)

10-mile (road)—46:30
April 27, 1980, New York (Trevira Twosome)

Marathon—2:10:27
April 20, 1981, Boston (Boston Marathon)

Born: August 2, 1955, Belleville, Illinois
Current Residence: Lebanon, Illinois
Education: Lebanon High School, Lebanon, Illinois (1973); University of Illinois at Urbana—Champaign (1977)
Affiliations: Athletics West, St. Louis Track Club, Front Runner Racing Team
Professions: Sports marketing, broadcasting, politics
Career Highlights: Two-time world cross-country champion (only American man to win the event); three-time Olympian; world's fastest 10,000 runner of 1980, setting U.S. record; seven-time U.S. record holder in road and track

Renaissance Runner

Craig Virgin says that his goal was to be a "renaissance runner, to do everything well." He excelled in track, cross-country, road racing, and the marathon. Virgin honed a toughness that perhaps went unappreciated—but would be counted on years later when illnesses and accidents almost took his life—as he fought the international stars, first in college at Illinois and then in championship events the world over.

Virgin embodied the classic American tale of the farm boy who thrived on values dear to the national character, overcame hardship, and would not let up until the sun went down. Images of Virgin setting high school records in the early 1970s in his Greyhounds uniform symbolized the American vision that hard work could conquer all.

Virgin relished calling himself a "white Kenyan" for the physical labors he experienced as a youth working on his family's 900-acre spread. He was lucky to be alive because he was born with a congenital urological disease. Despite early surgeries, Virgin's ailment would plague him until his right kidney was ultimately removed in 1994. "The discomforts I suffered as a youngster taught me to disassociate from pain. I was willing to pay a price. I was willing to build my life around two workouts a day," says Virgin.

"Farm work made me tough and contributed to my tenacity. Desire and determination are still paramount for success, and having the right attitude will take you far."

At times, Virgin's demeanor was dead-on serious with a steely glare that could pierce skin. This was his countenance as he tackled the 1980 Olympic Trials 10,000 meters—a race that meant nothing because of the U.S. Olympic boycott.

Three months after becoming the first American men's winner of the world cross-country title, Virgin would not merely go through the motions. He ran hard from the gun, winning in a still-standing meet record 27:45.61, and showed that it would take more than an Olympic boycott to bury him.

At other times, Virgin showed a sense of irony and got a big laugh out of track. When the Ethiopian Miruts Yifter outkicked him in the 10,000 at the 1979 World Cup in Montreal, Virgin dubbed him "Yifter the Shifter," a name that stuck. At the height of his career, Virgin would go dancing on Thursday nights before a Saturday meet. "Disco limbered me up for competition," he says.

The dance routine began in 1980 and heralded a 2-year period in which Virgin left no challenge uncovered. That summer

public affairs

With his experience in public, Virgin twice ran for political office, losing both times to entrenched incumbents. In 1992, he ran for the Illinois state senate, and in 1998 for the St. Clair County Board. He hopes to seek public office again.

in Paris, he improved his American 10,000 record to 27:29.16, the fastest time in the world.

In 1981, Virgin repeated as world cross-country champion in Madrid in March, ran 2:10:16 for second place in the Boston Marathon in April, and repeated as Bay-to-Breakers 12-K road champion in San Francisco in May.

The Boston Marathon was perfect Virgin territory—a new adventure that tested his courage. In 1979, he'd set a world record for a marathon debut, running 2:14:46 at Mission Bay. But even so, Virgin seemed too frisky for the marathon and was not considered a serious challenger to Bill Rodgers, the Boston defender, and Japan's marathon warrior Toshihiko Seko. If Virgin could bend nails, Seko could eat them.

For Boston, Seko had done workouts of up to 50 miles in New Zealand. Virgin's nod to going long was an occasional 18-miler. But Virgin had enough will to outrun Rodgers and duel shoulder-to-shoulder with Seko until 23 miles. Then, Seko drew away powerfully to win by a minute.

Virgin's marathon career was short-lived, but he would glow on the roads, winning just about every major event, from the Peachtree 10-K in Atlanta to the Falmouth 7.1-miler on Cape Cod in Massachusetts, while setting five U.S. road records.

After recovering from his kidney removal, Virgin hoped to run masters events in his forties. But early in 1997, he was involved in a head-on collision with a wrong-way driver and almost died as a result of multiple injuries. He had to undergo eight operations in the next 2 years as well as continuous physical therapy.

With his health restored, Virgin is running again and hopes to get into college coaching. "I can still fit into my college uniform," he says with pride, then hedges, "Just barely."

High School Prodigy

Virgin was a unanimous choice as 1973 High School Athlete of the Year by a Track and Field News *magazine panel. Few high school runners break 9 minutes for 2 miles. Virgin did it first as a sophomore and collected 18 sub-9:00s (and 5 sub-8:50s) at Lebanon High, breaking Steve Prefontaine's national record with an 8:40.9. And Lebanon didn't even have a track.*

Early Lessons Endure

For most great runners, high school track was a prelude to the real work. For Virgin, it was a proving ground and a place for lessons learned early that carried his career. He learned that speed counted more than distance and avoided the 100-mile weeks of some young rivals. He learned that running twice a day kept him motivated, and he did easy morning runs before school. He learned that negative splits—running the second half faster than the first—were essential to victory. And he learned that you make the most of what you have.

Lebanon High had no track, so Virgin did his speedwork on a baseball field. Coach Hank Feldt marked off a 660-yard course around three backstops and a foul pole. Virgin ran a hard 440 and jogged a 220. It was perfect, if you didn't mind kicking up some dust. He would start out running 66 seconds and finish running 59s. "I would always run my last interval like it was the last lap of a race," he says.

At the University of Illinois under coach Gary Weineke, Virgin increased his mileage and reached 100 miles a week prior to winning the NCAA cross-country title in his junior year. That season, leading to Virgin's first Olympic team in 1976, he ran 4 to 6 miles in the morning and 10 to 15 miles twice a week for distance. The rest was intense: intervals, fartlek (speed training in which you alternate fast and slow running for a mix of distances), or hills.

After college, Virgin coached himself to a fine edge for the world cross-country. As a foundation for his two victories, he did two or three hard workouts a week to build strength and endurance. One was a 10-miler on the roads in which he ran 2 easy miles, did 6 miles of fartlek (with surges of 200 to 1200 meters using telephone poles and mailboxes for markers), then finished with 2 easy miles. Another was 12 × 440 uphill, going from 78 seconds to 68 for the last one. His long run was 15 miles or longer. On recovery days, Virgin ran 4 miles in the morning and 10 miles in the afternoon.

Closer to an event, Virgin tried to simulate competition with sets of 600s. He would run through the 400 in 63 seconds, and then accelerate with a 27-second 200 to finish. "No lollygagging," he says. "To race in Europe, you needed at least two gear changes." In March of 1981, 3 days before the world cross-country, Virgin's last workout was 12 × 400 on a cinder track with the last one done in 57.5 seconds.

For the Boston Marathon a few short weeks later, Virgin's concession to distance was to work harder on his 18-mile workout. One week before the race, Virgin did a time trial on the 18-mile course at 5:20 per mile; he also practiced taking drinks on the run.

home runs

Virgin's favorite place to run was at home near his family's farm in Lebanon. "I had various loops of 4 to 12 miles," he said. "I got as much of a training effect there as anywhere in the world."

Abel Kiviat 15
1500 Meters, Mile

Lifetime Honors Point Total:
15,350

Best Times

1500 meters—3:55.8
June 8, 1912, Cambridge, Massachusetts (Olympic Trials)

Mile—4:15.6
June 8, 1912, Cambridge, Massachusetts (Olympic Trials)

Born: June 23, 1892, New York, New York
Died: August 24, 1991
Education: Curtis High School, Staten Island, New York (1910)
Affiliations: Wanamaker's; Irish-American Athletic Club
Profession: Federal court clerk in New York City
Career Highlights: 1912 Olympic silver medalist in the 1500 meters; set three world records in the 1500 and seven American records at other distances; nine-time national champion; numerous cup victories, including the Baxter indoor mile four times

Prodigy Keeps Pace for a Century

It's hard to imagine Abel Kiviat as a teenage prodigy because his vigor as a late-in-life track official and symbol of bygone Olympic amateurism made him the sport's grand old man. Even in his eighties and nineties, Kiviat was a presence. He was a handsome man with a droll wit, a character called the George Burns of track and field.

Recognized in his nineties for being the oldest living Olympic medalist, Kiviat's zest for life began when he starred as a high school athlete on Staten Island. Being Jewish in an Italian section of New York's appended borough, Kiviat was the outsider, a theme that would mark his track career. Later, he competed for the Irish-American Athletic Club, noted for its burly shot putters and hammer throwers drawn from the ranks of New York's policemen, firemen, and sanitation workers. Kiviat marched with his teammates in the St. Patrick's Day parade.

Kiviat's family had fled the pogroms of Russia to come to the United States. His father was a big man, athletically inclined, who would swim 2 miles across the Narrows to Brooklyn, and back, for exercise. Kiviat went out for baseball and football at Curtis High School. At 5 feet and barely 100 pounds, he took a beating in football and had to quit.

"I was never sick a day in my life until I was 92. I used to smoke five or six cigars a day. Now I allow myself one, and sometimes I forget to smoke it."

But he was an outstanding shortstop—the "Jewish Honus Wagner," according to the *New York Evening World*—and showed his speed winning match races across the field. Before long, Kiviat was playing ball in the morning and running track in the afternoon. He was fast enough to win citywide titles with record-breaking high school times in the 880 and mile on the same day in 1909. His efforts caught the attention of Lawson Robertson, later an Olympic coach, and Kiviat joined the AAU.

Just 17, Kiviat won three AAU titles that summer and traveled the country with the Irish-American Athletic Club. His victories and 4:23 mile time pegged him as a runner to watch. In 1911, Kiviat won the Baxter and Hunter miles, among the premier indoor races, and took the 600 and 1000 yards at the AAU indoor nationals—a double victory unequaled to this day (except by Kiviat, who repeated the feat in 1913). His times were exceptional—4:03.4 for the 1500 and 4:19.6 for the mile.

Kiviat ran every distance from the 440 to the mile. He picked up some money doing sales work for Wanamaker's, but his needs were modest because he lived at home. At times, he had to pay his own expenses to meets. If he were awarded more than a medal

close to 100

Kiviat got married in 1914 to a woman who designed clothes for Broadway shows. They had one son but divorced when Kiviat returned home after World War I. He remarried and moved with his wife to a New Jersey retirement community in 1972. His second wife died in 1981. Kiviat lived another decade and planned to attend the 1992 Olympics in Barcelona at 100, but he died of prostate cancer.

for a victory, it would be something like shaving cream.

In 1912, when he was not yet 20, Kiviat broke the world 1500 record three times in the 13 days leading up to the Stockholm Olympics. First he defeated Mel Sheppard, the 1908 Olympic champion, in 3:59.2 on Long Island. A week later, on the same track, he lowered the mark to 3:56.8. Six days after that, at the Olympic Trials at Harvard before a crowd of 20,000, Kiviat ran 3:55.8, which would stand as a world mark for 6 years and an American record for 16.

As he crossed the finish line of that 1500, officials screamed for Kiviat to continue down the track another 100 meters or so for the mile record. Though Kiviat had lost his momentum and could not regain top speed, he raced ahead with his bowlegged stride and hit the mile in 4:15.6 to tie the world mark. (Since the event was a 1500, he didn't receive credit for the mile mark.)

In Stockholm, Kiviat was the gold medal favorite. He led with a lap to go, but Britain's Arnold Jackson jumped him on the far turn and went on to triumph in 3:56.8. Kiviat and his teammate Norman Taber finished together in 3:56.9, with Kiviat getting the silver medal by a hair. He did earn a gold medal in Stockholm as a member of the five-man squad that won the 3000-meter team race, which was set up as a cross-country run.

After that, Kiviat continued winning national titles for another 2 years, then went overseas during World War I as a member of the national guard. Following the war, he ran on and off, making 1924 his last season. At the 1924 Olympic Trials, officials said they were short of steeplechasers and insisted that Kiviat try it. He had never run the steeple and fell flat on his face over a hurdle, hurting his ankle and ending his career at age 32.

Life Begins at 90

Kiviat stayed close to track by serving as a press steward at Madison Square Garden meets and other events for more than 50 years until age 87. When he turned 90 in 1982, he was rediscovered by the media and feted by the New York Road Runners Club. Two years later, he appeared on The Johnny Carson Show and was asked to be a 1984 Olympic torchbearer during the ceremonial cross-country relay. He jogged 1 kilometer in Manhattan, being careful not to let the flame burn his mustache. A year before his death, Kiviat was still running—doing a 100-yard dash in 47.6 seconds in the 95-to-99 age division at the New Jersey Senior Games.

Abel Kiviat's Training Secret ▶▶

If You're Good, Take It Easy

Kiviat raced on weekends, often on both Saturday and Sunday, and trained a mere 1 or 2 days during the week. "The good athletes, the ones that won," he said, "didn't have to train as hard as the ones that finished second, third, or fourth."

His coach, Lawson Robertson, believed in conserving energy for competition and in getting the most out of few workouts. Sometimes, Kiviat trained on sprints. Other days, he would run 1½ miles in a little over 5-minute mile pace and then stop for the day. "Faster than a jog" is how he described it to writer William Simons in a 1986 issue of the *Journal of Sport History*. Kiviat also got weekly massages, which he called a European rubdown.

Kiviat did his training at Celtic Park on Long Island, the grounds used by his Irish-American team. Sometimes he would run in the woods near his home on Staten Island. He trained in heavy sneakers with thick soles that "cost 39 cents wholesale."

Kiviat's diet, influenced by his club, consisted of a lot of rare roast beef, vegetables, plenty of eggs, and pitchers of milk, but nothing fried. He grew to 5'3" and 120 pounds.

hold the horseradish

Kiviat's training table featured his mother's homemade gefilte fish, considered a Russian delicacy at the time. He ate it without the customary horseradish topping, however. This, he said, may have contributed to his good health and longevity.

Lifetime Honors Point Total:
13,400

Best Times

6-mile—28:00.8
July 12, 1963, London, England
(England Amateur Athletic Association)

10-mile (track)—48:28.0
April 13, 1963, London, England
(England AAA)

Marathon—2:14:28
June 15, 1963, Chiswick, England
(Polytechnic Marathon)

Born: September 22, 1937,
Harrodsburg, Kentucky
Died: February 19, 1997
Education: Washington High
School, Sioux Falls, South Dakota
(1955); University of Minnesota,
Minneapolis (1959)
Affiliations: Chelmsford (England)
Athletic Club, Hadleigh Olympiads
Profession: College teacher
Career Highlights: World record
holder in the marathon; winner of
7 of his 13 marathons, including
Kosice and Athens (breaking
Abebe Bikila's course record); set
at least 10 American records; won
numerous titles in the United
States and Europe

Buddy Edelen 16
Marathon

Buddy Who?
World Record Holder

If ever there was a groundbreaking American runner who excelled in obscurity, it was Leonard "Buddy" Edelen. Opportunities for U.S. marathoners were scarce in the 1960s. After graduating from the University of Minnesota with little notice—winning the Big 10 cross-country title was as far as he got— Edelen picked himself up and moved to England, where marathoning was cultivated.

Edelen got a job as a $120-a-month private school teacher, joined a running club, and lived in a one-room flat with no phone or refrigerator. He embodied the disenfranchised amateur runner whose life revolved around workouts and was satisfied with his lot. "I don't consider myself as making a lot of supreme sacrifices," he said. "I'll put in my mileage; that's a job to be done. It's just one of the many things that make up my life."

Edelen said he was indebted to the English for nurturing his development. Before his move across the Atlantic, he'd done few long runs. "Now," he said, "I knock up to 100 miles a week. If it wasn't for the English club setup and the competition I get regularly, I hate to think how I would be running back in the States."

With his endearing manner, humility, and hunger for excellence, Edelen became a popular figure in British running circles. By 1963, with marathons behind him in England, Wales, Czechoslovakia, and Japan, Edelen was approaching his peak and improved his American 10-mile record on the track to 48:28.0 in the British championship. With all his success, Edelen had yet to win a U.S. title.

"Without the experiences, there would be no memories. Always dare to be the very best."

The 10-mile race was held in April. In May, Edelen won the historic Athens Marathon on a hilly course starting in the village of Marathon. Edelen favored hilly terrain and ran 2:23:07 to break the course record of 1960 Olympic champion Abebe Bikila of Ethiopia by 37 seconds. Edelen had written his desired intermediate times on the backs of his hands for guidance. He defeated the international field by close to 4 minutes.

Only 3 weeks later, in June 1963, Edelen achieved his greatest run ever. He competed in the 50th Polytechnic Harriers Marathon, from Windsor to Chiswick in England. Marathoners usually need at least 3 *months'* recovery between marathons, but Edelen was in exceptional shape. Even his American coach, Fred Wilt, an FBI agent, was impressed. When Edelen told him that he'd done a 15-mile training run in 79 minutes (about 5:15 per mile), Wilt responded, "Terrific."

Edelen took 2 days off to rest before the race. Even he would say the mere 3 weeks' break was "ridiculous." But Edelen proceeded to vanquish the field, setting a world record of

getting his start
Edelen was born in Harrodsburg, Kentucky, and lived in Minnesota before moving to South Dakota prior to his senior year in high school. He went out for track and won the state mile in 4:28. Earlier, he had attended a Roman Catholic boarding school. Though not a Catholic, Edelen had considered becoming a priest.

2:14:28. Edelen won by 3½ minutes, broke the world record by 48 seconds, and was the first marathoner under 2:15. He improved his best time by over 4 minutes and set his sights on the next year's Tokyo Olympics.

However, Edelen had no money to fly to the United States for the Olympic Trials. Youngsters from Sioux Falls, South Dakota, where Edelen had spent part of his youth, came to his rescue. They raised $650 through car washes, dances, and basketball games. Edelen was on his way and trained in four sweatshirts to prepare for the heat.

In 91-degree temperature and high humidity, Edelen won the Yonkers Marathon, designated as one of two U.S. trials. Including a course-record victory at Kosice, Czechoslovakia, in late 1963, it was his fourth straight marathon title in 12 months. Now he had 5 months—an eternity—before Tokyo, where Edelen would be among the favorites.

Leading up to the Games, he trained well, combining a 30-mile run with fast 440s on the track. But Edelen had a back injury and was in pain. He grew nervous, which was unusual for him. Suddenly, in the glare of the Olympics, people knew who he was and expected big things. Edelen's back problem persisted and he placed sixth (2:18:13). Bikila won again by more than 4 minutes in world record (2:12:12) time.

Miracle Worker

In 1971, while taking a summer-school course in Missoula, Montana, Edelen was in a car accident. He had a broken pelvis, a broken shoulder, and a damaged diaphragm, among other injuries. He was not expected to survive but made a miraculous recovery. In August of that year, doctors told Edelen he'd be on crutches until Christmas. "I threw away my crutches in September and was running in October," he recalled.

Edelen ran four more marathons and wrapped up his career in 1967. He went for his master's degree and got a position teaching psychology at Adams State University in Alamosa, Colorado, which was becoming a high-altitude running hotbed. Edelen taught for 15 years and eventually moved to Tulsa, Oklahoma, where he worked for the state and lived his last years.

Still unknown to the nation's running millions, Edelen would sign letters with "Buddy Who?" and draw a happy face. He died of cancer at the age of 59.

Balancing Distance and Speed

Fred Wilt, Edelen's coach and a two-time Olympian himself, was an intuitive distance-running technician. It was he who urged Edelen to take advantage of running opportunities abroad. Once settled in the English countryside, Edelen did long runs along the Thames estuary or caught a train to London to meet up with other runners. The school in which he taught was 4.5 miles from his flat, and Edelen ran to or from work most days.

This was Edelen's day-by-day training in June 1963, leading up to his world record 2:14:28 in the Polytechnic Harriers Marathon, with some commentary, as described in Frank Murphy's biography of Edelen, *A Cold Clear Day.*

June 1: 3 sets of 10 × 110–120 yard sprints (30 in all), followed by a swim in the sea

June 2: 10–11 miles steady, followed by a swim

June 3: 22–23 miles in 2:03–2:04, followed by a swim

June 4: 3.5 miles; 7 × sprint series of 55-110-150-220; 3.5 miles

June 5: 10.5–11 miles in 54–55 minutes.

June 6: A.M.—6 miles hard; P.M.—4 sets of 5 × 440 in 64.8, with 220 to 440 jog recovery between: "Tremendous workout."

June 7: 20 × 440 in 70–71, with a 45-second jog recovery between

June 8: Club track meet: mile in 4:23; 880 in 2:07; 110 leg on sprint relay

June 9: 22–23 miles in 2:01, followed by swim: "I am less stiff after today's run than I have been in ages."

June 10: 4.5 miles from school, then swim

June 11: A.M.—4.5 miles to school fast; P.M.—25 × 440 in 67.4, with 60-second jog recovery

June 12: A.M.—4.5 miles to school fast; P.M.—11 miles in 55–56 minutes, then swim

June 13: No running

June 14: No running

June 15: Marathon

heat of the moment

Even though Edelen trained for the heat, the 1964 Olympic Trials marathon at Yonkers was dangerously hot. Coach Wilt followed Edelen in a car, making sure he drank plenty of water. At 20 miles, Edelen was on the verge of heatstroke, but he held on to win. Only 41 of the 128 starters finished.

Bill Dellinger
5000 Meters

17

Lifetime Honors Point Total:
13,450

Best Times

1500 meters—3:41.5
August 5, 1958, Budapest,
Hungary (international meet)

2-mile—8:43.8
September 4, 1960, London,
England (international meet)

5000 meters—13:49.8
October 18, 1964, Tokyo, Japan
(Olympic Games)

Born: March 23, 1934, Grants
Pass, Oregon
Current Residence: Eugene,
Oregon
Education: Springfield High
School, Springfield, Oregon
(1952); University of Oregon,
Eugene (1956)
Affiliations: Air Force, Emerald
Empire Athletic Association,
Oregon Track Club
Professions: Teacher, college
coach
Career Highlights: 1964 Olympic
bronze medalist in the 5000
meters; Pan American champion;
set eight American records and
two world indoor records; three-
time Olympian

Handball Player Scales the Wall

With his subdued demeanor and easygoing sense of excellence, Bill Dellinger was a quiet distance hero who knew little about running when he started competing for coach Bill Bowerman at Oregon. "I was too naive to know any of the great Oregon runners," he says.

Dellinger quickly became one of them, however. In 1954, as a sophomore, Dellinger was the first Duck to win the NCAA mile, coming from last place in the final 200. Dellinger never lost a collegiate cross-country race, but during that period, Bowerman did not take the squad to the NCAA meet for lack of funds.

Bowerman's heralded training system was not fully developed by then. "He was still learning," says Dellinger. "We were guinea pigs." In preparation for the 1956 Olympics, Dellinger didn't train every day.

83

Some days, his workouts involved 1 hour of running and 1 hour of playing handball. He was a good player and would teach handball at Oregon when he began coaching there.

Still, Dellinger lowered the American 5000 record three times in 1956 and won the 5000 meters at both the NCAA and Olympic Trials. He was not yet ready for international success, however, and dropped out of the Olympic final in Melbourne. His opposition made an impression on him. "I'd be sitting in the cafeteria and the 5000-meters guys would be coming in after their workouts," Dellinger recalls. "I thought, 'What are these guys doing, running *twice* a day?'"

"There's no secret to running. Use common sense, do it long enough, and you'll get to be pretty good at it."

Dellinger started running twice a day. "It made all the difference in the world," he says. As a serviceman in the Air Force in 1958, Dellinger set a U.S. 1500 record of 3:41.5 in Budapest, and in 1959 in Chicago, he won the Pan American 5000 title with a 60-second last quarter. That same year, Dellinger captured the AAU national indoor 3-mile and the first of two straight AAU outdoor 5000s.

He also set world indoor records of 8:49.9 for 2 miles in Boston and 13:37.0 for 3 miles in New York, a mark that lasted 5 years.

Dellinger, 26, was ready for a better Olympic effort in 1960. He ran second to Jim Beatty in the Olympic Trials 5000 meters, then competed well in Europe, winning miles in Glasgow and Dublin and running a U.S. record 3000 in Finland. But Dellinger

the road to recovery

In August 2000, Dellinger, 66, was stricken with a stroke. He was in New Jersey at the time, en route to a running camp in Rhode Island. Dellinger suffered some paralysis on the right side of his body and began a rehabilitation program at the Kessler Center in New Jersey. By fall, he was back home in Oregon and starting to coach again.

took ill with dysentery at the Rome Games and did not make it out of the heats.

You would think this disappointment would have caused Dellinger to make a big push for 1964, but laid-back Dellinger spent the next 3 years "doing some running and playing a lot of handball." In the fall of 1963—"not completely out of shape"—Dellinger began training in earnest for the Tokyo Olympics.

The man finally had a full-scale program: solid mileage, long runs, and long repetitions, with Bowerman as a continuing advisor. Some of Dellinger's practice times exceeded American records. In Tokyo, in the rain, nine men, including Dellinger and Bob Schul, were packed in the lead with 600 to go. Dellinger moved to the front and led as the bell sounded.

Michel Jazy of France quickly surged ahead and Dellinger slipped back. Schul rallied and won the gold medal while Dellinger, whose stretch run was the fastest of all, wound up third in a career-best 13:49.8 for the bronze medal.

"I was disappointed," Dellinger says. "I felt I should have won but waited too long to start kicking." That was Dellinger's last big year. He became Bowerman's assistant, then Oregon head coach in 1967, a position he held for 32 years.

Dellinger retired in 1999 while continuing to coach a few individuals like Mary Slaney and up-and-coming Nick Rogers, who made the 2000 Olympic team in—what else?—the 5000 meters.

Like a Duck in Water

Dellinger is one of the most successful U.S. distance coaches ever. In the 1970s, his teams at the University of Oregon won four NCAA cross-country titles and placed second four more times. He developed stars like Steve Prefontaine, Alberto Salazar, Rudy Chapa, and Matt Centrowitz, who combined to set 18 American records. Fourteen of his Ducks went on to earn Olympic berths. He also worked with Julie Brown and Mary Slaney in the latter part of their careers.

Motoring to School

Before his first Olympics in 1956, Dellinger did not know his training distance or even the amount of time he ran when he went out for roadwork. He ran courses by name, like "the pink house run." (Years later, when he found out people were running for time, he would go out for an hour run and keep checking his watch because "I didn't think I'd ever finish.") In the spring of 1956, he did 8 × 440 for speed. A particularly hard workout was 2 × 2000. He ran 6 days a week, resting on Sundays. His longest run was about 8 miles. He figures he did 30 to 40 miles a week.

Prior to his Olympic bronze medal run in 1964, Dellinger had a real system, training 90 miles a week. He was a high school P.E. teacher and every morning ran 7 miles to school, finishing with 12 × 100 on the football field. After school, he ran home. On Sundays, he no longer rested but logged 15 miles.

Dellinger liked to keep things simple. Once every 3 weeks, he ran 4 × 1200 and 3 × mile on the high school track. His goal for the 1200s was a world-record pace—a 13:35 5000. He ran them in 3:15 and faster. For the miles he ran "easy–hard–hardest." In his last workout before Tokyo, Dellinger ran 3:15, 3:13, 3:11, and 3:09, then 4:40, 4:30, and 4:20. "Tough," he says.

Occasionally, he would run time trials at the Oregon track with Bowerman's squad. Once, four 800 runners paced Dellinger to an 8:32 2-mile, which bettered the American record.

the finger method

In 1958, Dellinger was in the Air Force and spent all winter at a remote radar site on an Indian reservation in Neah Bay, Washington, 92 miles from the nearest track. Dellinger lived in a trailer house bordering the Pacific Ocean and loved running along the beach at low tide. Without any distance markers, Dellinger developed a training method he would use throughout his career.

He counted strides. Every 10 strides, he raised a finger. He calculated 12 fingers, or 120 strides, per ¼-mile. If he wanted to run 220s, he ran for 6 fingers, or 60 strides. One day, Dellinger drove to a track to assess his fitness. With his wife timing him, Dellinger ran 4:05. Then, he ran a 440 in 60 seconds and counted his strides. He said that it took him only 100 strides—10 fingers.

Bob Kennedy
5000 Meters

18

Lifetime Honors Point Total:
10,150

Best Times

1500 meters—3:38.32
June 25, 1991, Hengelo, Netherlands (Paulen Invitational)

Mile—3:56.21
June 4, 1994, Eugene, Oregon (Prefontaine Classic)

2-mile—8:11.59
July 19, 1997, Hechtel, Belgium (international meet)

3000 meters—7:30.84
August 8, 1998, Monaco (Herculis Grand Prix)

5000 meters—12:58.21
August 14, 1996, Zurich (Weltklasse Grand Prix)

10,000 meters—27:38.37
May 7, 1999, Stanford, California (Cardinal Invitational)

Born: August 18, 1970, Bloomington, Indiana
Current Residence: Bloomington, Indiana
Education: Westerville North High School, Westerville, Ohio (1988); Indiana University, Bloomington (1992)
Affiliations: Nike International
Profession: Professional runner
Career Highlights: U.S. 5000 record holder and first non-African under 13 minutes; has run 14 of the 15 fastest American 5000s; U.S. 2-mile and 3000-meter record holder; winner of 12 national titles; 15 number-one U.S. rankings in the 3000 and the 5000

The Lone Warrior

With men's distance running in disrepair, Bob Kennedy has been the lone American warrior for almost a decade as he took the line again and again against the best in the world: the Kenyans, Ethiopians, and Moroccans.

Whether at the Olympics or the World Championships, or in Zurich, Oslo, or Stockholm on the Grand Prix circuit, just about any major 5000 has had a lineup of Africans and one guy from Indiana who has bucked the U.S. trend: Kennedy.

Instead of going into road racing for the easy money, Kennedy stuck by his desire to excel on the track. He knew it would take years, if it happened at all, but Kennedy would wait. After winning four NCAA titles at Indiana University—two in track, two in cross-country—Kennedy remained in Bloomington to train with Hoosiers' coach Sam Bell and focused his energies on summer racing in Europe.

87

In 1993, a year out of college, Kennedy improved his 5000 best to 13:14.91, earning the first of seven straight U.S. number-one rankings. But every time Kennedy improved, the rest of the world improved, too. The Africans were in the 12:50s. Kennedy trained harder. He ran 13:02.93 in 1994, gaining a number-four world ranking, then finally dipped into the 12:50s himself. Twice in 1996, Kennedy broke 13 minutes—12:58.75 at Stockholm (breaking Sydney Maree's U.S. record) and 12:58.21 at Zurich. He also broke Maree's 3000 mark.

"One thing about racing is that it hurts. You better accept that from the beginning or you're not going anywhere."

An American 5000 man under 13! Hallelujah! However, the Africans were now in the 12:40s. What to do? What else—train harder. By this time, Kennedy had switched coaches and training locales, from Bell in Indiana to Kim McDonald and his corps of Kenyans in the London suburbs.

Under McDonald, who was also his agent, Kennedy increased his mileage to more than 100 a week and ran speed with the very people he needed to match—like Daniel Komen, who'd run 12:45.09 to defeat Kennedy at Zurich. "Seeing the Kenyans train really woke me up," said Kennedy. "You think you're running hard. But the Kenyans? Wow!"

Kennedy gained power and confidence and shot to a new level. "I'm doing my intervals faster than ever, and it feels easier," Kennedy said at the time. "My recovery runs are at 5:30 pace and it feels like I'm jogging."

Kennedy took his strength and savvy to the Atlanta Olympics, which fell between his two 12:58s, and he went for

family business

Kennedy's father ran for Indiana and always told his son, "Whatever you do, athletics or playing sax, make sure you do your best, otherwise it's not worth it." Kennedy also got an appreciation of hard work from his parents, who owned a business distributing exercise equipment and worked 14-hour days.

broke. In a sweeping and gutsy move before an American audience, Kennedy surged to the lead with two laps to go. If Kennedy has any weakness, it's pure speed. The pace had been slow, and Kennedy had to try and burn out the field.

He was able to hold the lead for almost a lap, but the big kickers were too much for him, and Kennedy wound up out of the medals. He finished sixth and proud.

"I felt I ran the race in a manner to be as good as I could on that day," Kennedy said later. "That's all I've ever asked of myself. I still hope that will lead to a medal."

With the world record now under 12:40, that's not getting any easier. Kennedy placed sixth again in the 1997 World Championships and ninth in the 1999 Worlds. He may be the only man to have run five world championship 5000s. In 1997, he set a U.S. record (8:11.59) in the rarely run 2-mile; in 1998 he lowered his 3000 mark to 7:30.84; and in 1999, as a test, he ran his first major 10,000—a victorious 27:38.37 in California.

At the 1999 USA Nationals in New Orleans, Kennedy suffered his first 5000 loss to an American in 6 years. The winner was Adam Goucher, who brought new blood to the event. For 2000, Kennedy, turning 30, had planned to focus on the 10,000.

However, Kennedy's plan was spoiled by a car accident 2 months before the Olympic Trials. He suffered injuries and lost critical training time and decided to stick with the 5000. In a courageous effort, Kennedy wound up sixth, missing a spot on the U.S. team for Sydney, and said, "I know I did the best I could." He'll be back.

Cross-Country Springboard

Cross-country was a springboard to Kennedy's track success. In high school, he was Foot Locker national champion in 1987 (also running a 4:06.62 mile). At Indiana, he won NCAA titles in his freshman (1988) and senior seasons (1992). "That was my last college race, and I won on my home course by 41 seconds. Everything came together. It was the easiest run of my life," said Kennedy. Five days later, Kennedy won the USA national title, the first NCAA–U.S. cross-country double in 32 years.

High Quality, Short Rest

In July 1996, a week after his first sub-13 5000 and shortly before the Atlanta Olympics, Kennedy was training with coach Kim McDonald's group in Peddington, England, outside London. "The place is incredible," said Kennedy. "You can go for 30 miles linking different parks."

While Kennedy did 100 to 105 miles a week for base mileage during the winter, his volume was 60 to 65 later in the season. He said that high-quality repetition work with short rests was the heart and soul of his program. This was Kennedy's week of workouts, lighter than usual with the Olympics days away.

MONDAY: A.M.—5 × 1000 on the track with Moses Kiptanui in 2:32, 2:32, 2:31, 2:31, 2:32, with 2-minute jog recovery; P.M.—5 miles

TUESDAY: A.M.—7 miles; P.M.—5 miles

WEDNESDAY: A.M.—Four sets of 4 × 400 in 58–59 with a group of Kenyans, with 50-second rests between 400s and 3-minute rests between sets

THURSDAY: A.M.—5 miles; P.M.—Travel to Olympics

FRIDAY: A.M.—7.5 miles; P.M.—3 miles

SATURDAY: A.M.—3 miles; P.M.—8 miles

SUNDAY: A.M.—Two sets of 4 × 400 in 58–59, with 50-second rests between 400s and 3-minute rest between sets (Another favorite was a ladder workout of 2000-1600-1200-800)

Experimenting with 10,000 preparation in 2000, Kennedy settled his base mileage at 115 a week. Running by himself in Bloomington during the winter with the Olympics 6 months away, Kennedy ran his longest run, 18 miles, on Sunday.

He did quality work twice a week. On Tuesdays, Kennedy ran 8 × 1000 in 2:40–2:42 (26:40 10,000 pace) on the Butler University track in Indianapolis with a mere 1:40 recovery jog. On Fridays, on a flat gravel canal path, he did 3 × 2 miles in 9:50, with a 3-minute recovery.

one mile at a time

Kennedy always matured into higher mileage. In high school, Kennedy trained 35 to 40 miles a week, much less than other athletes of his caliber. In college, he suffered initially when required to do 70 to 75 miles a week. After college, he went from 80 to 100 to a high of 120 to 140 miles for a 5-week period in 1998. He cut that distance by 10 percent for 2000.

Clarence DeMar
Marathon

19

**Lifetime Honors Point Total:
11,900**

Best Time
Marathon—2:18:10 (24.5 miles)
April 19, 1922, Boston (Boston Marathon)

Marathon—2:34:48 (full 26.2-mile course)
April 19, 1930, Boston (Boston Marathon)

Born: June 17, 1888, Madisonville, Ohio
Died: June 11, 1958
Education: Farm and Trades School, Boston (1907); University of Vermont, Burlington (1911)
Affiliations: Melrose American Legion, North Dorchester Athletic Association
Profession: Typesetter
Career Highlights: Won a record seven Boston Marathons spanning 19 years; three-time Olympian, winning bronze medal in 1924; won four straight AAU marathon titles

Boston's All-Time Winner

Clarence DeMar, warned against running because of a heart murmur, won the Boston Marathon a record seven times. The event's second greatest winner is Bill Rodgers with four titles.

While Rodgers's victories came within 6 years, DeMar won his first Boston in 1911 and last in 1930, a tribute to his durability. As late as 1938, at age 50, DeMar was able to crack the top 10.

DeMar grew up in New England and started running cross-country at the University of Vermont, Burlington. By 1910, he was winning 10-mile road races and collecting prizes like silver tea sets. He also ran his first marathon that year, placing third at Brockton, Massachusetts, and entered his first Boston, coming in second in 2:29:52 (the course was not a full 26 miles, 385 yards until 1927).

DeMar worked as an $18-a-week printer,

which was pretty good pay, and race prizes of value were not to be dismissed. He ran a 10-mile event in Worcester, Massachusetts, hoping to win the first prize of a $25 suit of clothes.

The best he could do was fifth, and for that he was given a medal. His mother told him at least the medal didn't take up as much room as a trophy.

"Not only in running but in much of life is a sense of balance and proportion necessary."

It was before his first Boston win in 1911 that doctors discovered his heart defect during a routine exam. Nevertheless, DeMar proceeded to triumph by almost 3 minutes. His fellow printers presented him with a stick pin with a diamond chip. One of the company executives urged him to get a Turkish bath for his overworked muscles.

The victory in Boston earned DeMar invitations to many races as well as a spot on the 1912 Olympic team for the Stockholm Games. DeMar's Olympic debut was a struggle. The day was extremely hot, and a Portugese marathoner, Francisco Lazaro, died of heat exhaustion—the only fatality ever in an Olympic Marathon.

DeMar placed 12th (2:50:47). At one point, he had to walk. In 65 career marathons, that was one of only two instances—the other was in Nova Scotia in 1927—when DeMar "broke stride" and walked.

DeMar would not run another Boston for 6 years. He took up Bible study and began teaching Sunday school. He was busy with University Extension courses, seeking an associate degree from Harvard. He placed third at Boston in 1917 but his racing was brought to a halt by World War I. DeMar served in Europe, where he entered races for servicemen.

telling it like it was

DeMar fancied himself a competent and engaging public speaker. He spoke at schools, churches, YMCAs, and even prisons. He had marvelous stories to tell, and people trusted his common-man touch. He spoke on "The Race of Life" and "The Greatest Difficulty in Marathon Running."

DeMar took another break from the Boston Marathon because of duties as a scoutmaster in the Boy Scouts. He lost his job when the printers' union went on strike. He said the grind of visiting 25 to 30 shops a day to find new work was harder than running marathons.

He entered the Boston Marathon again in 1922, and won for 3 straight years, the last one by more than 5 minutes. Again, he was rewarded with an Olympic berth for the Paris Games in 1924.

This time, conditions were ideal. The course was flat and the air was cool. DeMar placed third (2:48:14) for the bronze medal. That was the last American men's marathon medal at the Olympics until Frank Shorter's victory in 1972.

DeMar continued running Boston every spring for almost a decade. He collected three more titles in 1927, 1928, and in 1930, at age 42. In another big victory, DeMar won a 44-mile race from Providence, Rhode Island, to Boston. He finished more than 2 miles ahead of the field in record time.

DeMar was selected for one more Olympic team in Amsterdam in 1928. His race instructions included a warning against jumping into the canals to cool off. DeMar felt he was in a running rut and placed a poor 27th. But his 16-year span of Olympic Marathons is the longest of any athlete.

In 1930, DeMar's running came alive again, and he won four of six marathons. But his running waned soon after, and DeMar, who enjoyed working with young people, decided to go into education and got a job teaching industrial arts to girls.

Getting Punchy

Midway through the 1922 Boston Marathon, as DeMar ran through Wellesley, Massachusetts, a motorist made a quick turn and grazed him. Furious, DeMar took a punch at the driver but hit the passenger in the rear seat. The incident so stirred DeMar that "it was enough to make me run even faster for a couple of miles." He won and set a record for the old course of 24.5 miles.

Long Jaunts, Long Sleep

DeMar regularly did 20-mile "jaunts," as he put it, covering almost 100 miles per week in his peak training for the Boston Marathon. Typically, he ran back and forth to work and took pride in bettering a 6-minute mile pace in street clothes.

During the war years, before he served, DeMar and his scouting troop made a garden out of a vacant lot. "I used to get up at 4 o'clock many mornings and run the mile up to our garden, work over 2 hours and run back, take a splash and breakfast, then run to the train and afterwards from the train to work," he wrote in his 1937 autobiography *Marathon*. "Sometimes in addition I took a practice run around Spot Pond."

In the early 1920s, DeMar rode his bike to work. During a sleet storm, he switched to running, a 9-mile round-trip. "It didn't tire me at all," he said. DeMar emphasized the important of a good night's sleep, recommending 9 hours per night to "balance the wear and tear on the human machine."

DeMar was found to have an extraordinary machine for running. Tests following the 1924 Olympics showed that his leg muscles could withstand the buildup of lactic acid, which brings on fatigue. Following DeMar's death at age 70 in 1958, an autopsy showed that he had coronary arteries two to three times the normal size.

breakfast club

Coaxed by a doctor from Michigan who had contacted him, DeMar ate a careful diet at a time when steak and eggs was considered an ideal prerace meal. He cut out red meat (except for Thanksgiving), ate fresh fruits and vegetables, and counted calories. He tried the doctor's plan (clearly a work in progress) for breakfast on the day of a race: a dozen oranges, ¼ pound of pine nuts, and 1 pound of caramels. "After this marathon of eating," DeMar concluded, "I didn't feel especially full of pep but found I had plenty of endurance in the race."

Dyrol Burleson
Mile

20

Lifetime Honors Point Total:
9,550

Best Times

1500 meters—3:38.8
June 28, 1964, New Brunswick,
New Jersey (AAU Nationals)

Mile—3:55.6
June 7, 1963, Compton, California
(Compton Invitational)

2-mile—8:39.6
May 13, 1966, Los Angeles
(Coliseum Relays)

Born: April 27, 1940, Cottage
Grove, Oregon
Current Residence: Turner,
Oregon
Education: Cottage Grove High
School, Cottage Grove, Oregon
(1958); University of Oregon, Eu-
gene (1962)
Affiliations: Emerald Empire Ath-
letic Association
Profession: Parks director
Career Highlights: Three-time
NCAA champion; three-time U.S.
champion; two-time Olympic Trials
winner; set five U.S. records;
ranked number one in the world in
1961 and number one in the
United States four times in 5
years

A Classic Miler

Dyrol Burleson was a classic miler. He was long and lean and confident, and he had a wicked kick. He spearheaded a great era of miling in America and in his beloved Oregon.

Called "Burley," he had great respect for his coach Bill Bowerman, and together they made running history at the University of Oregon.

Burleson had set the national high school record of 4:13.2 in 1958 and received the first full track scholarship given at Oregon. In 1959, Burleson set a collegiate freshman mile record (4:06.7), but NCAA rules prevented first–year runners from competing in college varsity meets. Burleson had to hold back but showed his enormous promise by defeating "big brother" teammate Jim Grelle, the NCAA champion, in the 1959 AAU 1500 in Boulder.

Burley's greatest race at home on Eugene's Hayward Field track came in April 1960. More than 7,000 fans turned out, and Burleson, the sophomore, put on quite a show. Stanford's Ernie Cunliffe set the pace, and Burley kicked the last lap in 57.4 to win in 3:58.6, surpassing the American record and the first U.S. sub–4:00, 3:58.7, by Don Bowden in 1957.

"I'm a Duck all the way. I have a son-in-law who's a Beaver [Oregon State]. We decided to let him into our house and eat at our table."

Burleson went on to win three straight NCAA mile titles and was undefeated on the track in collegiate races. That same spring of 1960, he set two U.S. records in the 1500.

Burley saved his best stuff for Hayward Field, of course. There, he regained his U.S. mile record, running 3:57.6 in 1961, set a U.S. 2-mile record of 8:42.5 in 1962, and ran on a world-record Oregon 4-mile relay in 1962. Burleson recorded a 3:57.7 anchor as a Ducks quartet raced 16:09.0 to shatter by 14.8 seconds the mark set by a New Zealand foursome in 1961.

The New Zealanders had been anchored by Peter Snell, the three-time Olympic champion. In 1961, Burleson was ranked number one in the world and faced Snell head-on. That winter (summer Down Under), Burleson won five of six races in an 18-day New Zealand tour.

He defeated Snell twice, the second time in an amazing

birthday boy

After retiring from track, Burleson continued doing speedwork, and every year on his birthday he would run 5 miles in 25 minutes or better on the high school track in Albany, Oregon. He did this until turning 45, when his time was 25:19. "Then, I quit." Well, sort of. Burley's next goal became 10 miles in an hour. He did this until his knee hurt and he had to undergo arthroscopic surgery. His doctor told him to take up swimming. Burley figured that he was so thin he'd sink in the water, so he tried bicycling. But his glutes hurt. So, he returned to running—slowly—a few miles a day.

880 in 1:50 flat over all three medalists from the 1960 Rome Olympics: Snell, Roger Moens of Belgium, and George Kerr of the West Indies.

After college, Burleson trained for the 1964 Olympics in Tokyo. He'd finished sixth in the Olympic 1500 at Rome, and by 1963, Snell, now the world record holder, had succeeded Burleson as the world's top miler. Snell defeated Burleson twice in 1963, when they were ranked one and two, respectively, in the world. In his second loss, Burleson ran his career-best 3:55.6 behind Snell's 3:55.0.

That season, Burleson won his third AAU title and registered his second victory in the U.S.-Soviet dual meet.

Burleson was set for a run at Snell in Tokyo. Burley won the Olympic Trials and also his trial heat at the Games. But Snell, the 800 victor, was too much for the field and sprinted the last 400 in 52.7 for the gold medal. Burleson placed fifth.

"That was a sad race, really stupid on my part," he said. "I got boxed. I should have at least gotten the silver."

Working full-time, Burleson took second to Jim Ryun in the 1966 AAU mile in New York and hoped for one last Olympics shot in 1968.

Training at Willamette University in Salem, Oregon, he got himself into excellent shape but pulled a calf muscle and decided to call it a career.

Burleson went on to serve as director of parks, museums, and forestry for Lynn County, retiring in 1997 after 31 years. He runs—or "waddles," as he puts it—30 miles a week and enjoys the Oregon countryside.

Covering His Tracks

Burleson's early inspiration was Roger Bannister and Burley's brother Larry. When Burleson started running in 1954, Bannister ran the first sub-4:00 mile (3:59.4) and was on the cover of Sports Illustrated. *Burleson had a sibling rivalry with Larry, 18 months older and a football player, and wanted to get on the cover of* SI *to upstage his brother. Eventually, in 1958, Burley did.*

Car Chase

As a college sophomore in 1960, the year Burleson first broke 4:00 in the mile, he was training on coach Bill Bowerman's evolving hard day/easy day system. He mixed light days of jogging and wind sprints with workouts like four sets of 330-220-110 at race pace. "On occasion," Burley recalls, "we'd do what Bannister did—10 × 440 in 59–60 with a 220 jog." Burleson ran a few miles in the mornings, did one weekly long run of 11 to 14 miles, and totaled 60 to 80 miles a week.

Burleson kept much the same program for the 1964 Olympic year while increasing his mileage to 100 a week as he built a base the previous fall. He was out of college, training on his own, and married at the time. He ran sets of 220s in the 23s and 21 repeat 110s, doing the first seven "floating," the middle seven fast, and the last seven "floating." "I always ran on a cinder track," said Burleson. "I loved it."

He also did one long road run on Sundays that fall. With his wife setting the pace by driving at 10 miles per hour (a 6-minute mile) beside him, Burleson ran up to 20 miles. She had the radio going and water for him. Burley found the runs useful but tedious. "I never understood these cross-country runners," he says.

bad timing

Before a calf injury ended his career, Burleson got into his best shape ever in preparation for the 1968 Olympic Trials. He said the workout that proved his fitness was 440-880-440 in 57, 1:54 and 57. He feels that he could have medaled in Mexico City.

Sydney Maree

1500 Meters, Mile, 5000 Meters

Lifetime Honors Point Total: 6,400

Best Times

1500 meters—3:29.77
August 25, 1985, Cologne, Germany (Grand Prix meet)

Mile—3:48.83
September 9, 1981, Rieti, Italy (international meet)

2000 meters—4:54.20
September 4, 1985, Rieti, Italy (international meet)

3000 meters—7:33.37
July 17, 1982, London, England (international meet)

5000 meters—13:01.15
July 27, 1985, Oslo, Norway (Bislett Games)

Born: September 9, 1956, Pretoria, South Africa
Current Residence: Johannesburg, South Africa
Education: Vlakfontein High School, Pretoria, South Africa (1977); Villanova University, Villanova, Pennsylvania (1981)
Affiliations: Athletic Attic, Puma Track Club
Professions: Professional runner, financial consultant, TV commentator
Career Highlights: Overcame apartheid in South Africa to set world 1500 record; became a U.S. citizen and set American records for the 1500 (still stands) and the 5000; number-one U.S. 5000 runner 4 straight years; won first Fifth Avenue Mile in record 3:47.52

A Fight to the Start

Sydney Maree carried the burden of his native South Africa wherever he ran. When Maree found his immense talent in running, breaking the 4-minute mile in high school on little training, he was punished from all sides.

In South Africa, apartheid limited his opportunity. Because of the international sanctions against South Africa—intended to pressure the white regime to repeal apartheid—Maree could not compete outside his country and was ineligible for the Olympics.

"The world would not recognize me as a human being unless I changed my citizenship," says Maree. He saw himself as an emblem of hope for South Africans, especially the children, and he knew that he had to find a way to prove himself.

In a 7-year saga, Maree left his homeland for the United States in 1977, attended Vil-

99

lanova University, married in 1980, graduated in 1981, and competed amidst controversy for a while because of his ambiguous international status. He finally received U.S. citizenship on May 1, 1984.

Maree's new life stemmed from his first mile race in South Africa. In high school, Maree was a soccer player who ran on weekends, raced a couple of informal 1500s in the 3:47 range, equivalent to a 4:15 mile. In 1977, Maree, a senior, was invited to be the rabbit in a "dream mile" in Pretoria. He was so naive he asked how long this special "dream mile" was. His coach told him "dream" meant it was a sub–4:00 attempt.

"There were millions of South African children who wished they had the same opportunities I had. I was the one who was 'chosen.' I was not going to fail them."

In a setup for the favorite of the white crowd, Clive Dale, Maree led after the half-mile as planned. Maree was the only black athlete in the stadium; blacks were not allowed in the grandstand seating. It was raining, and as he ran Maree noticed five black children sitting forlornly in the open. "My race was really for those five kids," he says. Maree, 19, proceeded to triumph by 25 meters in 3:57.9. "That was my ticket to America," he says.

Once at Villanova, Maree trained so hard that he had to do his morning 10-milers by himself. "I preferred to train alone. I could visualize the opposition better," he says. Maree's background had taught him to be wary; he couldn't miss a step. As a sophomore, he won the NCAA 5000 meters; as a junior and senior he won the 1500, and his 1981 time of 3:35.30 still stands as the meet record.

Later that year, Maree ran "the one race that made me cry."

the main line connection
In June 1977, after he first gained stardom in South Africa, Maree came to the United States for a brief visit. He met a track official who introduced him to Villanova assistant coach Jack Pyrah. Would Maree be interested in attending Villanova? Maree returned home to finish high school and take a University entrance exam. In the fall, he entered Villanova.

By then, Maree had resident alien status and was allowed to compete for the United States for the first time at the World Cup in Rome.

"It was the first time in my life that I had the chance to identify with something," he recalls. Maree wept as spectators, acknowledging his long battle, chanted, "Go, USA . . ."

Overwhelmed, Maree placed only fifth. But a few weeks later, he tore down the streets of New York to win the inaugural Fifth Avenue Mile in 3:47.52, which exceeded the world record but did not count coming on the roads. Maree's talent was revealed as he defeated a field that included Mike Boit, Steve Cram, John Walker, Steve Scott, and Eamonn Coghlan in a ballyhooed, nationally televised event.

Soon enough, Maree would acquire a legitimate world record—a promise he had made to Villanova coach Jumbo Elliott, who had died earlier in 1981. In 1983, Maree ran 3:31.24 to shave .12 from the 1500 mark in Cologne, Germany.

Then, inspired by his U.S. citizenship, Maree made 1985 his best year ever. He became the first man after Jim Beatty to hold U.S. 1500 and 5000 records simultaneously.

Flight Plan

When Maree ran his sensational 3:57 high school mile in South Africa in 1977, he was unaware of the significance of his run until boarding a flight home. "The captain invited me to come into the cockpit," Maree recalls. "I realized what I'd done must be something big."

In Cologne again, aiming for Said Aouita's world record of 3:29.45, Maree ripped through the 400 in 53.2 and 800 in 1:50.4. It was too fast, and Maree, slowing, ran 3:29.77, the first American under 3:30. In the 5000, Maree faced Aouita in Oslo. Maree led at the bell, Aouita pulled even and they raced to the wire. Aouita nicked the world record by .01 in 13:00.40 as Maree ran 13:01.15, breaking Alberto Salazar's U.S. mark by 10 seconds.

Maree was the number-two ranked American that year in the 5000, behind a deserving Doug Padilla. Maree was number one from 1986 through 1989, his last major season. He went into the financial services field, and although he is no longer a South African citizen, he returned to South Africa in 1995 with his wife, Lisa, and their five children. Maree continues to run vigorously.

Sydney Maree's Training Secret ▶▶

Fast Pace, No Letup

Maree relied on a strong, fast base to give him the range to move from the 1500 to the 5000 with ease. At Villanova, Maree ran 10 miles every morning at 6:00 A.M. He says his pace was 4:30 to 4:50, world-record pace for 10 miles on the road. Maree insists that he ran that fast, which is why his teammates were loathe to join him.

Maree was still fresh for track work 3 to 4 times a week. He ran 8 to 12 × 400 in 58 to 60 seconds with a 400 jog between runs. Or he did 5 × 800 in 2:02 to 2:04 with a 400 jog. He finished every track session with 6 × 150.

On nontrack days, Maree added 6 to 8 miles to his morning roadwork. His longest runs, on Sundays, did not exceed 12 miles. Let's face it: How long can you run at 4:30 pace? Maree totaled 100 miles a week. He also did full-body weight training 3 times a week.

After Villanova, Maree was coached by Tom Donnelly of nearby Haverford College. Donnelly shortened Maree's recovery time between repetitions, feeding him one blistering workout that Frank Shorter was noted for. Maree ran a 5000 on the track by running hard for 800, jogging 100, and repeating that cycle with a final, all-out 400. His time (not counting the few jogs) was under 13 minutes. "The Kenyans would surge," says Maree. "Tom prepared me to surge."

Before Maree's U.S. record 13:01.15 5000 in 1985, he used hill work to bolster his strength. In the morning, he would run 8 to 10 × 800 uphill; in the afternoon, he would add more distance, continuing 100 miles a week. On occasion, Maree trained with Marcus O'Sullivan, who was also coached by Donnelly. One warning, says Maree: Never do track work and hills on the same day.

still motoring along

Every day in Johannesburg, Maree gets up at 4:30 in the morning and runs 13 miles at 5 minutes a mile before work. He says he's too busy to bother with masters racing but prides himself on still being fit and trim. "I wear pants from college," said Maree. "My kids make fun of me, but they still fit."

Henry Marsh
3000-Meter Steeplechase

22

Lifetime Honors Point Total: 13,150

Best Times

Mile—3:59.31
August 16, 1985, Bern, Switzerland (international meet)

3000-meter steeplechase—8:09.17
August 28, 1985, Koblenz, Germany (international meet)

Born: March 15, 1954, Boston, Massachusetts
Current Residence: Bountiful, Utah
Education: Punahou High School, Honolulu (1972); Brigham Young University, Provo, Utah (1978); University of Oregon School of Law, Eugene (1981)
Affiliations: Athletics West
Professions: Professional runner, attorney
Career Highlights: Ranked number one in the world three times; ranked number one in the United States 10 times; set the American steeple record four times and has held mark since 1985; four-time Olympian; nine-time U.S. champion

A Great Closer

When Henry Marsh ran the 3000-meter steeplechase, his style was to hang back, sometimes in last place. He would look awfully lonely at the rear of the field, and anxious fans would urge him to move up, and fast.

What was an athlete of his caliber—the best in the world, or close—doing by himself when all the action was up front?

Rest assured, Marsh was a crafty competitor who left little to chance. He knew how to train, race, and master an event as complex as the steeple. Inevitably, just when it looked hopeless, Marsh would rally, first with a gradual move, then with a last-gasp, heroic surge, rescuing the narrow victory.

All along, he had it figured out.

Marsh was a pure steepler. He trained over the barriers two or three times a week and took the water jump with finesse. He didn't like getting his feet wet during the event, so he helped design a water-resistant shoe.

Marsh learned the steeple at Brigham Young; his teacher was Patrick Shane, the current women's head coach who then coached in high school while also helping the BYU steeplers.

"It's interesting that I became a distance runner because as a 1-year-old I almost drowned in a backyard swimming pool and x-rays later showed I had scar tissue on my lungs."

Marsh—America's most noted steepler outside of 1952 Olympic champion Horace Ashenfelter—was a 4:18 high school miler from Honolulu who could not get a scholarship to BYU. His initial college steepling was tepid; then, as a Mormon, he left school to go on a 2-year religious mission in Brazil. Returning to BYU in the fall of 1975, Marsh barely made the varsity cross-country squad and almost quit running in frustration.

But the next spring, a miracle occurred: Marsh and the steeple became one. "God's reward," he said. "I really believe that." Marsh took second in the NCAA and second in the 1976 Olympic Trials, making the first of his four Olympic teams.

At 22, he placed 10th at the Montreal Games, the only American finalist, and earned the first of 10 number-one U.S. rankings for the year. Marsh improved his best time by a minute, hitting 8:23.99.

Marsh won his first U.S. national title as a BYU senior in 1978, then embarked on a decade of steeple dominance, not only in the United States but also internationally. He was ranked number one in the world three times—in 1981, 1982, and 1985—a feat achieved by only a handful of American dis-

one long day

Noted for his low mileage, Marsh hardly ever ran more than 10 miles, and his longest training run was 14 miles—once. In 1977, on a lark, he ran a marathon in Salt Lake City to keep his uncle company. His time was 3 hours or so. "Afterward," said Marsh, "I couldn't walk for a week."

tance runners in any event. He was also ranked number two and number three during that stretch.

In 1981, Marsh was undefeated in Europe leading to the World Cup in Rome, where, after winning, he was disqualified. Coming from behind in his signature attack, Marsh wove through traffic like an Italian taxi driver, drawing contact and forced to run inside the next-to-last water jump.

Marsh claimed he was pushed. Officials said otherwise.

Marsh's timing was never right for the major championships. After setting his second American record (8:15.68) at the 1980 Olympic Trials, Marsh missed the Moscow Games because of the U.S. boycott. He was sick before the 1984 Olympics in Los Angeles and placed fourth. At Seoul in 1988, Marsh, then 34, ran a surprising sixth in his farewell season. After that race, he knelt and kissed the track.

Marsh set four American records over an 8-year span. His last, 8:09.17 at Koblenz in 1985, still stands. In the early 1980s, Marsh rarely lost. He was unbeaten in 1982, but in two world championships, he ran eighth (1983) and sixth (1987).

During this time, Marsh, an attorney, served for 9 years as chairman of the U.S. Olympic Committee's Athletes Advisory Council. Currently, Marsh writes motivational books and lectures on health and stress management for a Salt Lake City firm.

He runs casually, plays tennis, and skis for recreation.

A Start in Texas

Before moving to Hawaii, Marsh lived in Dallas and played football and basketball and ran track in junior high. In the ¾-mile run, the longest distance, Marsh set a league record in ninth grade, defeating John Lodwick, who would become a national-class marathoner. The next year, at King High in Corpus Christi, Texas, Marsh ran a 4:27 mile to qualify for the state meet, a performance he ranks with anything he did in the steeple.

Toeing the Line

Marsh was a low-mileage runner who counted on precise running form, technically sound steepling, and frequent competition to mold himself into the world's best. He rarely ran more than 50 miles a week "I was always up on my toes, using the right muscles," Marsh said when at BYU. "My calves are never sore after a race because I work out like I race."

That point helps explain Marsh's great finish. He didn't have to make a transition from a flat-footed stride to kicking form. Up on his toes all along, Marsh had a head start in accelerating his pace. He also says now, "The real secret of my success was that I had the smallest differential of anyone between the steeple and the flat 3000." Marsh was so efficient over the barriers, they cost him little time. "I wasn't quick," he said, "but I was loose and strong."

Most steeplers run the 3000 meters 30 to 40 seconds faster than the full steeple. Marsh ran the 3000 in 7:53, and his best steeple was 8:09—a 16-second differential.

After graduating from BYU, Marsh moved to Eugene, Oregon, and trained under Harry Johnson and then Bill Bowerman as a member of Nike's Athletics West club. Marsh ran hard 4 days a week leading to his number-one world ranking.

On Mondays, after 4 miles in the morning, he ran a brisk 10 in the afternoon in under an hour. On Tuesdays, he did ladders—200, 400, 600, 800, 1200, 800, 600, 400, 200—at race pace. He ran every other lap over hurdles and the water jump. Doug Padilla, another BYU graduate, was a frequent training partner.

On Thursdays, Marsh did about 1½ miles of fast work, like 200s, 300s, and 400s, with less hurdling. On Saturdays, Marsh either raced or ran a hard 2000 over the steeple barriers. Wednesdays and Fridays were recovery days. He took Sundays off to rest.

Through the 1980s, Marsh did more short racing before big meets to sharpen up. His best 1500, a 3:42 victory, came before the 1988 Olympics.

the dry look

To solve the soaked-foot problem of the steeplechase water jump, Marsh collaborated with shoe innovator Bill Bowerman to create a Nike model that did not absorb water. "One step out of the water jump, and it was dry," said Marsh. "It was the prototype for the shoe everyone uses today."

Lifetime Honors Point Total:
12,200

Best Times

3000-meter steeplechase—
8:30.6
June 21, 1968, Sacramento, California (AAU Nationals)

2-mile—8:22.0
June 1, 1968, San Diego (Champions' Meet)

3-mile—13:09.8 (indoors)
January 3, 1969, Philadelphia
(*Philadelphia Inquirer* Games)

5000 meters—13:29.4
July 9, 1972, Eugene, Oregon
(Olympic Trials)

Marathon—2:30:48
August 18, 1969, Alamosa, Colorado (Olympic Marathon Trial)

Born: July 24, 1937, Roswell,
New Mexico
Current Residence: Casa Grande,
Arizona
Education: Western High School,
Silver City, New Mexico (1955);
University of Arizona, Tucson
(1959)
Affiliations: U.S. Army, Phoenix
Olympic Club
Professions: Teacher, coach, athletic director
Career Highlights: Olympic bronze
medalist in the steeplechase; first
American runner to make four
Olympic teams; four-time Olympic
Trials champion; two-time world indoor record holder; six-time U.S.
record holder

George Young 23
3000-Meter Steeplechase

No Barrier Too High

George Young, who competed in four straight Olympic Games beginning in 1960, was set to give up his so-so track career after finishing his college running at the University of Arizona in 1959.

Young's times of 4:13 for the mile and 9:12 for the 2-mile hardly put him in the company of stars like Jim Beatty, Jim Grelle, and Dyrol Burleson, who would be gathering in Boulder, Colorado, for the 1959 AAU Nationals.

Still, Arizona coach Carl Cooper encouraged Young to go to Boulder for the AAU meet and try his first steeplechase. Young, who'd never even seen a steeple, trained for the event by running over hay bales. But Young fought hard like he belonged, and managed to finish second in 9:36.7, earning berths on the U.S. team for that summer's U.S.-Soviet dual meet in

Philadelphia and Pan American Games in Chicago. Young's international career was born.

For the next dozen years, Young repeatedly excelled when the odds were against him. He'd gone into the army in 1959 and was considered a long shot for the 1960 Olympic team. Young won the Trials steeple in 8:50.6, improving his best time by 16 seconds. "I didn't give myself enough credit that I could run with these guys," he said.

"I have seen hundreds of runners who were physically in better condition than I was. Mentally, however, they were not, so consequently they couldn't win the race."

At the Rome Olympics, Young tripped over a hurdle in the heats and did not make the final. But he ran 8:31.0 in 1961, the first of his six American records. He improved to fifth place in the 1964 Games at Tokyo, and by the next Olympic year of 1968, when U.S. sprinters were all the rage, Young was on fire. He trained 100 miles a week, much of it at high altitude, and won his third AAU steeple title, lowering his U.S. record to a career-best 8:30.6 in Sacramento, California.

Young started to show prowess at "flat" running, and 3 weeks before the AAU meet set an American record for 2 miles, 8:22.0, in spectacular fashion against the world record holder, Australia's Ron Clarke, in San Diego. It was probably Young's finest moment.

Though Young had defeated Clarke indoors, Clarke was an athlete of stature, while Young pressed on with quiet strength. The race had been billed as another Clarke record attempt, but Young's 58-second last quarter put Clarke away, and his time was the second fastest ever, shattering the U.S. mark.

it's simple: train harder

"You can probably do more than you give yourself credit for," Young advises. "If you get beat, you can remedy that. Any time I got beat, I trained harder. In fact, any time I won, I trained harder."

Young went on to win his third straight Olympic Trials steeple. And when they contested the 1968 trials marathon in Alamosa, Colorado, Young, like others, ran it on a whim. It was his first marathon—and he won it in 2:30:48.

At the Mexico City Games, the undefeated Young tangled with two Kenyans, Ben Kogo and Amos Biwott. In the lung-searing 7,350-foot altitude, Young kicked for his life with 300 to go and led over the final water jump. But the two Kenyans charged ahead across the last hurdle as Biwott (8:51.0) captured the gold medal and Kogo (8:51.6) the silver. Young (8:51.8) held off Australian Kerry O'Brien for the bronze.

Four days later, Young ran the marathon, drinking little, and placed 16th in 2:31:15. That was Young's second and last marathon.

The next year, in 1969, Young set world indoor records for the 2-mile (8:27.2) and 3-mile (13:09.8). After virtually going into retirement, he came back to make the 1972 Olympic team behind Steve Prefontaine in the 5000. At the Munich Games, however, Young did not go beyond the heats.

In 1973, Young, who struggled to make ends meet, joined the pro track tour. He was paid $4,000 to sign. "The thing I remember about that," says Young now, "is that running for money did not motivate me. Something was lost."

Young departed the track circuit in 1974 and went into education full-time. He was track and cross-country coach as well as athletic director at Central Arizona Junior College in Coolidge, for more than 20 years.

Since leaving the college in 1996, Young has continued to run and walk daily while satisfying his passion for golf and fishing.

Down, But Not Out

At Young's first Olympics at Rome in 1960, he was running among the leaders with three laps to go in his steeplechase qualifying heat when he hit a hurdle and fell. He got up and raced back to the front but took fourth in 8:50.8, missing the finals by 0.8, as the first three qualified. "I was right there," he says now. "I think I could have been a factor in the final."

Learning to Beat the Best

Still called a novice by track writers in 1960, Young trained at medium intensity prior to the Rome Olympics. As a serviceman, he was doing only 60 to 70 miles a week at Fort Lee, Virginia, and Fort Meade, Maryland. His longest run was 8 miles. He did no more than 10 repetitions of 400, in 63 to 64 seconds, with a 2-minute rest between runs. He took 1 or 2 days off a week.

What Young did focus on was the technical aspect of his event. He did a lot of half-miles over steeplechase barriers, covering five hurdles per run and trying for times of 2:15, with a one-lap jog. He worked at maintaining momentum through the water jump. He developed an efficient style, making up for any lack of pure speed.

In the late 1960s, Young trained like an Olympic medal contender. His mileage hit 100 a week. He did morning runs such as 7-milers at 5:30 pace. He increased his weekly long run to 20 miles. And he did three interval workouts a week. Young ran 12 × 400 as fast as 59 seconds per lap, with a 1-minute jog between. He did 16 × 300 in 45 seconds with a 45-second jog, or 24 × 200 in 28 with a 30-second jog.

Young coached himself after college and ran mostly alone. "Eventually," he wrote in *Runner's World* magazine in 1972, "I didn't want anyone else around because when I was doing my workout, I was in a world all my own. I was running races. Every time I run one of those 12 quarters, I am running against somebody—maybe Ron Clarke, maybe the Russians, but always against somebody."

egg on your face

Young's prerace meal was a soft-boiled egg on toast with honey and a glass of milk. "I thought that was a healthy approach," he said.

Gerry Lindgren
5000 Meters, 10,000 Meters

24

**Lifetime Honors Point Total:
10,250**

Best Times

Mile—4:01.5
August 13, 1964, Kingston,
Jamaica (Carreras Invitational)

2-mile—8:31.6 (indoors)
February 4, 1967, Seattle (Seattle
Invitational)

3-mile—12:53.0
May 14, 1966, Seattle (Northern
Division)

5000 meters—13:33.8
May 25, 1968, Modesto, California
(California Relays)

6-mile—27:11.6
June 27, 1965, San Diego (AAU
Nationals)

10,000 meters—28:40.2
August 17, 1967, Düsseldorf,
West Germany (United States
versus West Germany)

Born: March 9, 1946, Spokane,
Washington
Current Residence: Honolulu
Education: Rogers High School,
Spokane, Washington (1964);
Washington State University,
Pullman (1970)
Affiliations: Spokane Athletic Club
Professions: Running store propri-
etor, odd jobs, coach
Career Highlights: Set one world
record, five American records, five
collegiate records, nine world ju-
nior records, and nine U.S. high
school records; won 11 NCAA ti-
tles; numerous international victo-
ries; Olympic 10,000-meter
finalist at age 18

Running Away

They made the movies about Steve Prefontaine, but when it came to drama and
pathos—and bizarre plot twists—one of Pre's
contemporaries from the Northwest, Gerry
Lindgren, might have made the best story of all.

He was a scrawny, elflike figure who was
the last kid in the world anyone would have
pegged as a great distance runner. To hear
Lindgren tell it now, "I couldn't make the junior high track team. I was so uncoordinated
I couldn't put one foot in front of another."

But Lindgren did try running at Rogers
High in Spokane, Washington. He had to get
out of the house. In his early cross-country
races, he took a battering of elbows. "I was so
wimpy, I was getting beaten up," Lindgren
recalls. "One race, I surged to avoid the elbows. By the time everybody caught me,
they were too tired to hit me."

The next day, the Rogers coach, Tracy
Walters, pulled him out of class. "He said I

could make our team better by running in front. He said the other guys would train harder to keep up," said Lindgren. "That was my burning bush. I could actually do something to help people. That's been the theme of my entire running."

Lindgren ran more than any track runner: 50-mile days, 300-mile weeks, three workouts a day. He ran morning, afternoon, and night. He got out of bed at 1 o'clock in the morning and ran. Either people didn't believe it or they thought he was nuts.

"Anybody can be the best there ever was. It's not physiological. You can beat the Kenyans. You can beat anybody—if you're willing to pay the price."

When Lindgren became one of the world's best distance runners as a teenager, track fans marveled at him. But he seemed troubled; it was more than a case of the idiosyncratic runner, more than the gangly kid finding his path. With all his success, Lindgren didn't seem happy.

In truth, Lindgren was wracked with the effects of parental abuse. Revelations came out later—much later, when Lindgren "disappeared"—that his alcoholic father beat him and suppressed his fundamental self-expression. If young Gerry sang a song at the dinner table, the father smacked him off his chair.

Lindgren, who went from Rogers to Washington State University and finally to Hawaii, where he had first lived under an assumed name, does not conceal his troubled youth now. "I had a real bad childhood. I hated myself real bad," he said. He could find affirmation only through running and was in desperate need to bring joy to others. "I thought the only thing I could do of worth was to make the other guy run faster."

In the summer of 1964, when he was 18 and just out of high school, Lindgren was so confused and downtrodden that he wept after his most celebrated victory—the 10,000 in the U.S.-Soviet dual

hawaiian eyes

When Lindgren left Washington in distress in 1980, he ended up in Hawaii and used the name Gale Young. For years, no one knew where he was. Word got around, and there were Lindgren sightings, as though he were a UFO. Eventually, he was identified, came out, and connected with people in the Honolulu running community.

meet. Who was this kid beating the Russian men?

"I had no intention of beating those guys," Lindgren says in reflection. "I just wanted to make them run better. I felt bad when I would win." Today, Lindgren seems to get a kick out of the startling remark. He is easily ironic and funny, pricking the goofy kid he once appeared to be. But he is also a man in his fifties, finally trying to understand the hard emotions that drove him.

That season of 1964, Lindgren earned an Olympic 10,000 berth for Tokyo. Despite an ankle injury, he made the final and had the audacity to lead at 3000. He wound up ninth. Every week brought a new and astonishing Lindgren performance. In 1964, he set eight of his nine high school records, four of his nine world junior marks. Most of his high school marks still stand. The best are his 13:44.0 in the 5000 and 8:40 in the indoor 2-mile. Both are considered "Beamonesque."

Lindgren went on to win 11 NCAA titles, breaking Jesse Owens's record total. As a college freshman, he set a world record in one of the great distance races ever. At the AAU Nationals in San Diego, Lindgren raced to a tie in the 6-mile with 1964 Olympic 10,000 champion Billy Mills. Their time was 27:11.6, breaking Ron Clarke's mark.

Flapping to Victory

Lindgren feels that his best race was not one of his records but a 5000 in Stuttgart, Germany, in the 1969 Americas versus Europe meet. Up against West German miler Jurgen May, known for his blistering kick, Lindgren led the first 1500 in a fast 3:58. Lindgren recalls, "I grunted and flapped my arms, and sure enough May came by me." But Lindgren ran him down with a 57.8 last quarter to win in 13:38.4.

A strained Achilles tendon kept Lindgren off the 1968 Olympic team. A knee injury kept him off the 1972 squad. That year, he joined the pro track tour, which lasted 4 years. Lindgren was married and needed the money. But he was unsettled and would go through a series of jobs and move his family several times.

Early in 1980, in despair, Lindgren vanished, leaving his wife and two children. He wound up in Honolulu, where he now manages a storage warehouse and coaches a club called Coconut Road Runners. Lindgren runs 50 miles a week and says that he can knock out a 17-minute 5-K. "I'm still trying to break 13," he said with a childlike laugh.

50 Miles a Day

As a high school senior in 1964, Lindgren ran three times a day. He ran 5 or 6 miles in the morning, another 8 to 14 miles with the track team in the afternoon, and after going to sleep, got up at 1:00 or 2:00 A.M. for 10 more miles in the middle of the night. With added mileage on weekends, Lindgren says that he collected over 200 miles a week.

On weekdays, Lindgren switched between distance and speed with the Rogers team. If he did 400s, he did 15 of them in 60 seconds with a 400 jog between. If he did 800s, he did 8 of them in 2:05 to 2:10 with a 400 jog. These were world-class workouts, but Lindgren was running world-class times.

At Washington State, Lindgren's schedule initially allowed for only two workouts a day. He did his morning 5 or 6 miles and another 10 with the team in the afternoon. His favorite run was a 10-mile course through wheat fields. Lindgren says that his best time was 46:05, faster than Ron Clarke's world record on the track.

During one period at college, in late summer of 1967, Lindgren decided to outdo himself. He said that a physiologist at the school warned him against running more than 90 miles a week or risk breaking down. "I wanted to prove him wrong," said Lindgren. He proceeded to run 50 miles a day, 350 a week, for 6 weeks. "I ran at least five workouts a day," said Lindgren. "I felt great." He had a vegetarian diet, eating several meals a day.

reaching the peak

Almost every weekend as a high school senior, and about once a month throughout his career, Lindgren ran 88 miles round-trip on Sunday to the top of Mt. Spokane. He'd start out at 5:00 in the morning and try to get back home by 4:00 P.M. Once, he got back around 2:30 P.M., better than 7 minutes a mile all the way. "Those last 5 miles were hell," he says.

John J. Kelley
Marathon

25

Lifetime Honors Point Total: 17,150

Best Times

Marathon—2:20:05
April 19, 1957, Boston (Boston Marathon)

Born: December 24, 1930, Norwich, Connecticut

Current Residence: Mystic, Connecticut

Education: Bulkeley High School, New London, Connecticut (1950); Boston University (1956)

Affiliations: Boston Athletic Association

Professions: Teacher, coach, newspaper columnist

Career Highlights: 1957 winner of the Boston Marathon; eight-time winner of the Yonkers Marathon; 1959 Pan American Games marathon champion; two-time American marathon record holder; winner of 20 AAU national road-racing titles

Weekend Warrior

John J. Kelley, one of America's greatest marathoners, loved to race and competed almost every week for 20 years. By his estimation, he ran more than a thousand races.

Feeling a need to validate his running, Kelley regarded every race, even the minor ones, as significant, putting pressure on himself. "He would rather die than lose," said Ted Corbitt, a frequent rival.

Though a modest talent in college, Kelley knew how to win as his running matured. He collected 20 AAU national titles on the roads, including a record eight straight Yonkers Marathon titles from 1956 through 1963. Yonkers was one of hilliest courses around and, held in May, was usually run in the heat. Kelley set an American record (2:24:53) in his first Yonkers and ran in the 2:20s in each of his victories.

Even with his Yonkers dominance, Kelley—not to be confused with the older and more famous John *A.* Kelley—was identified most by his Boston Marathon performances.

Kelley finished 34 Bostons; but his first, as an 18-year-old in 1949, was a DNF. He placed second five times, was the top American eight times, and won the 1957 race in 2:20:05, his career best and another U.S. record.

"I often wondered why runners could accomplish what they did. It's like analyzing love or passion. Why I had to run remains one of the mysteries of my life."

Kelley was an introspective soul who thrived on the purity of running but not the notoriety. With all the foreign stars at Boston, the competition frequently pitted "Kelley against the World," as the newspapers trumpeted it. He hated the hype, saying it added to the pressure. Before one Boston, Kelley was so uptight that he went sleepless for five nights and was, as he puts it, "a haggard wreck."

When he was out of the limelight, Kelley was more at ease. In addition to Yonkers, his national titles came in 15-K, 20-K, and 25-K events. He also won the Manchester (Connecticut) Thanksgiving Day Run (4.75 miles) five times and captured the Pan American Games marathon gold medal at Chicago in 1959.

But any event was tame compared to Boston's high-wire act. When Kelley won in 1957, he dropped his foreign opposition at 16 miles and became the first American titlist—by almost 4 minutes—in 12 years. The previous year, as runner-up, both Kelley and winner Antti Viskari of Finland probably would have bettered the world record if the course had not been found 1,183 yards short.

the next generation

Kelley is believed to be the only Boston Marathon winner ever to coach a Boston champion. At Fitch High in Groton, Connecticut, his protégé was Amby Burfoot, a third baseman in Babe Ruth League who switched to track and went on to take Boston in 1968. "If Amby wanted to run 10 miles, I ran with him, instead of running to school that day," recalls Kelley. "It helped us both."

However, when Kelley, coming off an injury, suffered a second DNF at Boston, in 1960, it cost him dearly. Olympic officials had designated Boston and Yonkers as trials for the Games that year in Rome. Kelley was clearly America's best, but without "points" at Boston, he was out of the money for Rome. Kelley was so disgusted that he vowed that day he would never run again.

A protest ensued, and people like the Boston Athletic Association's Jock Semple, a trainer advisor to Kelley, convinced the U.S. Olympic Committee to soften its rigid qualifying system. If Kelley could win Yonkers again, he'd make the team. He did win it, and Kelley was the first American at Rome, placing 19th in 2:24:58. Though disappointed, Kelley was well ahead of his U.S. teammates, Alex Breckenridge (30th in 2:29:38) and Gordon McKenzie (48th in 2:35:16), in the field of 62 finishers. Winner Abebe Bikila of Ethiopia, running barefoot, ran 2:15:17.

With a growing family and being busy with teaching and coaching, Kelley cut back his training in the mid-1960s but continued running Boston on and off through 1992. Now retired, Kelley writes a popular running column in the New London (Connecticut) *Day*, and runs and walks at least an hour a day in the secluded woods near his home.

"More and more," he says, "I've turned to trail running as an escape to what's left of the natural environment. "I've developed a romantic notion that the closer you are to 'wildness,' the better off you are."

Kid Stuff

John J. Kelley (known as Johnny the Younger) was often confused with John A. Kelley (Johnny the Elder), who finished 58 Boston Marathons, winning twice. The Elder was 84 when he ran his final Boston in 1992. The habitually anxious younger Kelley found a way to settle down before one Boston: Ol' John invited him to his house to relax on the eve of the 1957 race. That was the year "The Younger" won.

Speed and Distance Merge

Kelley's success was based on a fierce, unwavering determination. Oftentimes, Kelley mixed distance and speed in the same workout.

Before his 1957 Boston Marathon victory, Kelley ran 14 to 16 miles in the 4:30 A.M. darkness every day before work. After work, he ran on a golf course, mixing in short accelerations as part of a 6- to 8-miler. That's some workday.

To develop his speed, Kelley did what he called cycles. He would run 4 minutes hard (5:00-mile pace), then jog; 2 minutes hard (4:30-mile pace), then jog; 1 minute hard (about a 400), then jog; and 30 seconds hard (a 200), then jog. He repeated this set—what is today called a ladder workout—three times. He liked to do these sets in the course of a road run, 6 to 8 miles, as opposed to keeping his speedwork on the track.

Kelley used this same approach in his Sunday sessions, throwing in some 200s in a run of 10 to 12 miles. He usually raced on Saturdays; but on a rare off-day, he would use the break to run long—16 to 28 miles. If it was a Saturday, Kelley had to push it.

Even so, Kelley had his limits. "I experimented with higher mileages, 115 to 120 a week, but it didn't produce the results I'd expected. I required more rest, and so 90 to 100 was optimal."

By the time of his last Yonkers victory in 1963, Kelley was starting to compromise. "I was trying to balance running, coaching, teaching, and family," he says. "I never found an ideal way of doing it." To save time, he ran round-trip from home to school, a distance of 3.75 miles that he stretched out to log 10 to 12 miles a day. His speedwork suffered, and he realized that with so many responsibilities, his best running days were behind him.

stormy weather

When Kelley trained in the winter in the morning darkness, he encountered brutal weather that would have turned back most runners. "I pushed through some terrific extremes," he says. He ran along a bay, and one storm soaked him to his waist in icy water. "I was wearing army khakis, and they froze to my skin. But I just ran through it as part of the challenge."

26

Johnny Hayes
Marathon

Lifetime Honors Point Total: 7,000

Best Times

Marathon (24.5-mile course)—2:26:04 (equivalent to about 2:35 for full marathon)
April 20, 1908, Boston (Boston Marathon)

Marathon (full 26.2-mile course)—2:49:10
January 30, 1910, San Francisco (race versus Dorando Pietri)

Born: April 10, 1886, New York City
Died: August 23, 1965
Education: New York Evening School, New York City (1904)
Affiliations: Irish-American Athletic Club
Profession: Food broker
Career Highlights: Winner of the 1908 Olympic marathon in world record time; winner of the first Yonkers Marathon in 1907; second, third, and fifth in his three Boston Marathons

He Stayed On His Feet

Johnny Hayes was raised in the heart of New York City and started running on city streets (near where the United Nations stands today) only 4 years before winning the Olympic gold medal in the marathon. He joined St. Bartholomew's gym to work out and at first took a licking from gym members in neighborhood races. One night, finally in good shape, Hayes "cleaned up the cream of the club's cross-country team." What else could they do but elect Hayes captain?

Hayes, the oldest of six children, did not have a runner's build. He was 5-foot-4 and squat, but observers said he "could run like a rabbit." He used a variety of track, road, and cross-country races to groom himself for the marathon. After running his first marathon, Boston, in 1906, placing fifth, Hayes decided to commit himself to the long distances.

He returned to Boston in 1907 and 1908, placing third and second, respectively, and his times improved dramatically to

119

2:26:04 for the 24.5-mile course of the time. In 1907, Hayes would have done even better had he not been held up 4 miles out by a passing freight train while the other contenders raced ahead. His championship caliber was affirmed later that year when Hayes triumphed in the first Yonkers Marathon, held on Thanksgiving Day.

"The fact that a man runs 20 miles good and the last 5 miles bad is the very reason a good many men do not get any medals for running marathon races."

In 1908, Boston was one of two Olympic Trials races, and Hayes was put on the U.S. team for the London Games. The team sailed from New York on the mail steamer *Philadelphia,* and Hayes trained on the ship's deck.

At the behest of the Royal Family, the Olympic marathon started at Windsor Castle, and the route to the finish at White City Stadium was 26 miles, 385 yards, which became the official marathon distance from that time on. "It was a bright, sunshiny day, and the enormous crowds grouped around this most beautiful of English castles," Hayes wrote. "I do not think I will ever forget."

Nor would Hayes—or anyone—ever forget the race, featuring perhaps the wildest finish the marathon has known. The athlete involved in the notoriety, Dorando Pietri, a candy maker from Italy, almost got disqualified prior to the start. Pietri appeared in a sleeveless jersey, then disallowed, and the judges refused let him run. An American trainer, Mike Murphy, sent a

sandhog and singer

After high school, Hayes worked as a sandhog building the original New York City subway system. (When he was over 70, Hayes was mugged on the subway and had to be hospitalized.) Before becoming a food broker, Hayes worked briefly as a P.E. teacher in New Jersey, where he lived after getting married. During World War I, Hayes did not serve because he was color-blind. Hayes had a good voice, and after the 1908 Olympics he appeared in vaudeville shows, singing Irish tunes. His awards and mementos are preserved in a beautiful, ornate trophy case at the home of his only child, Doris Hale, who lives in New Jersey. Hayes's original race number from London—26, of course—hangs on her wall.

call for handkerchiefs and fashioned them as sleeves on Pietri's shirt. If only that were the end of Pietri's troubles.

There were 56 men in the field. Only 27 would finish. After 20 miles, the leader was Charles Hefferon of South Africa, about 4 minutes ahead of Pietri. Hayes was far back in third but could tell from the shouts of the crowd that the front-runners were tiring. With a mile to go, approaching the stadium, Hayes passed the exhausted Hefferon and went after Pietri. As Pietri entered the stadium for the finish, he was received by more than 100,000 spectators. Pietri had a good lead, and all he had to do was stay on his feet for the gold medal.

But Pietri became disoriented and collapsed at least four times within strides of the finish. It was a pitiful sight, and some in the crowd wept openly. Medical officials finally came to his aid, propped Pietri up, and he tottered across the line first. Hayes crossed the finish 32 seconds later as Pietri was carried off on a stretcher. American officials protested the help given Pietri—clearly in violation of the rules—and Pietri was disqualified. Hayes became the Olympic marathon champion. His time of 2:55:19 was established as the first world record for the 26.2-mile distance.

The unassuming Hayes was feted as a celebrity. His teammates carried him around the Olympic stadium on a table with the winning trophy presented to him by Queen Alexandra. A few days later, visiting his grandparents in Ireland, he was "carried on the shoulders of the immense throng to a coach from which the horses were taken and drawn through a city ablaze with torch lights and bonfires."

Once home, Hayes became a professional runner and took on Pietri in a rematch that fall in an indoor marathon at Madison Square Garden. Pietri won. Hayes competed another couple of years and was a part of the 1912 Olympic team as a trainer.

Presidential Timber

After his marathon victory, Hayes received a letter from President Theodore Roosevelt that read in part: "I am particularly glad that it should be won by an American who had been emphatically a good citizen, a man who had worked hard and done his duty and yet found time for the healthy play . . . Let me see you whenever you are in my neighborhood . . ."

Johnny Hayes's Training Secret ▶▶

Three Times a Week, That's Enough

Most of Hayes's training was done at the Irish-American Athletic Club grounds at Celtic Park on Long Island. He ran three mornings a week, doing 10 to 12 miles on Tuesdays and Thursdays and at least 13 miles on Sundays.

good running, great view

During his peak running, Hayes worked as a clerk at Bloomingdale's store in New York, where a rooftop track was constructed especially for his use.

27

Ted Corbitt
Marathon, Ultramarathon

Lifetime Honors Point Total:
4,750

Best Times

Marathon—2:26:44
January 5, 1958, Philadelphia
(Shanahan Marathon)

50-mile—5:34:01
October 25, 1970, Rocklin, California (AAU Championship)

100-mile (track)—13:33:06
October 25–26, 1969, Walton-on-Thames, England (RRCA Invitational)

24 hours (track)—134.7 miles
November 3–4, 1973, Walton-on-Thames, England (RRCA Invitational)

Born: January 31, 1919, Dunbarton, South Carolina
Current Residence: Bronx, New York
Education: Woodmere High School, Cincinnati (1938); University of Cincinnati (1942)
Affiliations: New York Pioneer Club
Professions: Physical therapist, road running administrator
Career Highlights: 1952 Olympian who collected 30 victories in almost 200 marathons and ultramarathons; AAU 50-mile champion; set many ultra-distance records

He Invented Distance

With his whispering speech and matter-of-fact distance breakthroughs, Ted Corbitt was an unsung pacesetter on and off the course. While training upwards of 30 miles a day, competing in several marathons and ultras a year, and working full-time as a physical therapist, Corbitt founded the New York Road Runners Club, was named the first president of the Road Runners Clubs of America, and practically invented the system of course measurement for road races in use today.

When the New York City Marathon became a citywide event in 1976, sparking the worldwide marathon boom, officials argued over whose idea it was. But one thing was certain: It was Corbitt who had laid out and measured the five-borough route.

But the man preferred to remain deep in the shadows. "We called him the phantom of the opera," said Norb Sander, 1974 New York City Marathon winner. Ironically, the phantom, barely audible in interviews, acquired an aura of priestly mystery. But every mile he ran—and by career's end he'd covered 250,000 of them—was based on a simple proposition. "I had an urge to run," Corbitt says now. "During the day, my body would remind me, 'Get out and run.'"

"When someone on our college campus spoke up about racism, he was expelled from school for being a communist."

Corbitt, named after President Theodore Roosevelt, first felt the urge in his youth in Cincinnati where he saw 1936 Olympic star Jesse Owens in a race against players from baseball's Negro Leagues. Corbitt ran for the University of Cincinnati track team but faced racism at every turn. The squad could not compete at certain schools, like Kentucky, which barred blacks from campus. On bus trips, the athletes were denied access to hotels and restaurants. At one cross-country meet in Ohio, Corbitt ended up sleeping on a cot in a school gym.

After college, Corbitt was not allowed into Cincinnati area track meets, so he turned to road racing, which was less restrictive. Corbitt joined the aptly named New York Pioneer Club, run by a mortician named Joe Yancey.

In his first marathon, at Boston in 1951, Corbitt placed 15th. The next year, Corbitt's 3rd-place at Yonkers put him on the Olympic marathon squad for Helsinki, where, suffering from stomach distress, he placed 44th. In 1954, he won three of four marathons, including Yonkers, the national championship.

Soon, Corbitt found marathons too short. He entered 30-milers, 40-milers, 50-milers. At times, he did them on the track. Corbitt thrived on routines, precision, repetition. Circling a track

shoe search

In Corbitt's heyday, there were no running shoes, at least not with any support. First, he ran in tennis sneakers, then in Hush Puppies. At one time, Corbitt, who spent 2 years in the service, trained in army boots. He ran in a Riddell cross-country shoe. He tried custom-made shoes from Norway and Japan. He ran in Tigers, the forerunner to Asics, and finally Corbitt settled on New Balance, his overall favorite.

for 200 laps was his cup of tea. He traveled to England for the famed London-to-Brighton 52.5-miler on the roads, placing second twice in what was considered the world ultramarathon championship.

One of his proudest victories was the 1968 AAU national 50-miler on the roads. Corbitt was sidelined for 6 weeks leading up to the event after hurting his back while avoiding a dog. "I still won," he said, "but it was a tough recovery."

Tough? During that time, Corbitt increased his weekly mileage to 300, and a legend grew out of his occasional jaunts around the periphery of Manhattan Island—two loops at once—for 62 miles. Corbitt would not accept limits. He showed that the marathon was not the ultimate endurance test, and that people in midlife could excel in even the longest of races. Corbitt set all of his ultramarathon records past the age of 45.

In one, at 48, he ran a harrowing 100-mile race on the track in England in 13:33:06, to smash the American record by 3 hours. On the same track at 53, Corbitt competed in a 24-hour run, covering 134.7 miles to place third. Corbitt dulled the pain of these adventures with a trick he picked up from the Australian coach Percy Cerutty. With his hands closed and thumb pressed against the index finger, Corbitt squeezed hard. "This subdued the pain," he said.

Corbitt used this technique with his patients at the New York's International Center for the Disabled, where he worked for 44 years, retiring in 1993. Corbitt gradually diminished his running after collecting 199 marathons and ultras.

In recent years, he has walked the New York City Marathon, appropriately anonymous. But in 2000, at 81, Corbitt got the itch to run long again and entered his first 6-day race.

First-Timer

The 6-day race—a run, eat, and sleep endurance festival—is considered the ultimate ultramarathon. In the spring of 2000, Corbitt, 81, entered one in New York City, circling a 1-mile loop on Wards Island. His goal was 50 miles a day of walking and running. He found that "trotting" didn't work for him and ended up mostly walking a total of 240 miles, a record for his age. But then, no one his age had ever tried it before.

Citywide Tours

Corbitt routinely ran 200 miles a week and worked up to 300 for special events. At the height of his career, he maintained a Labor Day weekend tradition of running two circuits of Manhattan, 62 miles, on each of the three days. Well, it *was* Labor Day.

How did a runner with a full-time career and other interests manage to run the equivalent of almost 10 times around the circumference of the earth in his lifetime? Corbitt made efficient use of every minute of his day.

Typically, Corbitt ran 20 miles to work in the morning. He went from the Bronx up to Yonkers, reversed direction, and ran down the west side of Manhattan, around Battery Park at the southern tip, and up the east side to his office at 34th Street. Some mornings, that was not sufficient. Corbitt also did ¾-mile loops around a housing project.

After work, Corbitt might do the same course back for a 40-mile day. Other times, he would "get lazy" and take the shortest route home, 11 miles. If he knew it was going to be a lazy afternoon, Corbitt would do 30 miles before work, rising at 4:00 A.M. and running over to Van Cortlandt Park, a few miles from home. Van Cortlandt is known for its cross-country course, but it also has a track. Corbitt would do 17 miles around, 68 laps, then run down to his office, another 10 miles, arriving on the button, alert and eager, at 9:00 A.M.

On some days, just to keep himself honest, Corbitt would also run at lunch. He had only a half-hour, so he did speedwork. Corbitt was not slow by nature. In college, he ran a 50-second quarter-mile and might have stuck with short distances if blacks had been allowed into track meets in Cincinnati in the early 1940s.

no frills, just pavement

Of all the inspiring courses Corbitt ran, from Boston to Quebec, Scandinavia to the British Isles, what was his favorite? Typical of the man, he named a decidedly bland place, Clove Lakes Park, on Staten Island, New York. The park, a few miles from the Verrazano-Narrows Bridge where the New York City Marathon begins, is little more than a few spare concrete loops that total about 3 miles in a complete circuit. It's the hub of Staten Island running, but there's nothing inspiring about it. "I just like the terrain," said Corbitt.

Jim Spivey
1500 Meters, Mile, 5000 Meters

28

Lifetime Honors Point Total: 6,900

Best Times

1500 meters—3:31.01
August 28, 1988, Koblenz, West Germany (Grand Prix)

Mile—3:49.80
July 5, 1986, Oslo, Norway (Bislett Grand Prix)

2000 meters—4:52.44
September 15, 1987, Lausanne, Switzerland (international meet)

3000 meters—7:37.04
August 1, 1993, Cologne, Germany (Grand Prix)

5000 meters—13:15.86
August 30, 1994, Berlin, Germany (ISTAF Grand Prix)

Born: March 7, 1960, Oak Park, Illinois

Current Residence: Glen Ellyn, Illinois

Education: Fenton High School, Bensonville, Illinois (1978); Indiana University, Bloomington (1983)

Affiliations: Athletics West, Nike, Asics Track Club

Professions: Professional runner, college coach

Career Highlights: World Championship bronze medalist; three-time Olympian; six-time national champion; U.S. 2000-meter record holder with near-record 1500

Scaling the Peaks

Jim Spivey was a meticulous runner who found joy and significance in small details. He kept track of his workouts with finicky care in his training log and drew strength from the little things in running—like packing healthy food on a foreign trip—that can add up.

Leaving little to chance, Spivey was able to peak at the right time.

As a result, he had the best record of any American 1500 man in world and Olympic competition toward the close of the 20th century. Spivey won the bronze medal in the 1987 World Championship 1500 in Rome, the year he earned the first of four U.S. number-one rankings in the event.

In the 1993 world meet at Göteborg, Sweden, Spivey placed fifth. In his two Olympic 1500s, he made both finals, placing fifth (Los Angeles, 1984) and eighth (Atlanta, 1996).

Spivey's finest hour came in Rome in 1987. Consistent with most championship 1500s, the final was slow. No one wanted to lead; everyone wanted to rely on a kick. In a mass sprint, Spivey handled himself with panache, ripping off the last 400 in 53.54 for the bronze medal in 3:38.82, behind victorious Abdi Bile of Somalia.

"Money never motivated me during a race. I could never kick any harder knowing that the place ahead of me was worth an extra $1,000."

Few milers were more consistent than Spivey, who ran two sub-3:50 miles, earned seven top 10 world rankings, and turned in a career-marking performance almost every year. Nine days after the Rome 1500 meters, Spivey, competing in Lausanne, Switzerland, set an American record for the 2000 (4:52.44) that still stands. He promised after that season that he would only get stronger.

He did. In 1988, Spivey ran his fastest 1500, 3:31.01, to win an international race in Koblenz, West Germany. The performance made him the second fastest American to this day, behind Sydney Maree. It also helped Spivey atone for his greatest disappointment—failing to make that year's Olympic team for Seoul, South Korea. In the trials at Indianapolis, where Spivey had many fans since being an NCAA titlist at Indiana University, he did not survive the jostling in a wild 1500 finish and wound up a heartbreaking fourth. The guy who edged him for the last Olympic berth was a former Hoosier teammate, Mark Deady.

In Spivey's overall résumé, this setback was minor. He started out as a high school star from the Chicago suburbs, drawn to Indiana by the esteemed mile coach Sam Bell. Spivey

but what about me?

Spivey feels that distance runners have to be selfish at times. "My ability to focus for long periods, to put blinders on, was both a positive and a negative." It was good for his running, he says, but could present conflicts over family priorities.

ran his first sub-4:00 indoors (3:58.90) as a sophomore in 1980.

He remembers the date: February 9. And he will never forget who beat him that day: John Walker of New Zealand, the 1976 Olympic champion and Spivey's idol at the time. Every young miler adored Walker, much the rebel with long hair, beads, and a take-no-prisoners disposition.

After college, Spivey impressed his idol. In his first European tour in 1983, Spivey won the Stockholm 1500 and then, at the Oslo Games, ran a 3:50.59 mile for second behind Steve Scott. "I went from being an obscure American to Walker saying that before long I would win something big," says Spivey. "And I was only running 50 miles a week at the time."

Spivey was often linked with Scott, his friend and longtime rival, and they were quite the odd couple when sharing a hotel room on the circuit. While Scott was known as a cutup, Spivey was a hospital-corners kind of fellow. On the track, they were closely matched, and in the early 1990s, Spivey succeeded Scott as America's top miler.

In 1992, Spivey won the Olympic Trials 1500, which he considered his most rewarding victory, given his near miss in 1988. He went on to one more Olympics, in the 5000 in 1996, then phased out his career and became men's and women's track and cross-country coach at the University of Chicago. After turning 40 in 2000, Spivey hoped to compete in masters events.

Summer Vacation

At *Illinois' York High School*, a national track and cross-country power, the top runners are reputed to log a hefty 1,000 miles for base training over the summer. Spivey went to nearby Fenton High and decided he would do the same, or better. "I ran 1,013 miles before my senior year," Spivey recalls. The ambitious schedule seemed to work. In 1978, under coach John Kurtz, Spivey was the nation's top scholastic half-miler with a 1:50.3 time. He was also the second leading miler, running 4:06.2 to win the 1600 at the International Prep meet, an event held at York High.

Personal Attention

After college, Spivey continued to work with Indiana coach Sam Bell. But he realized that he needed personal attention, and Bell's first priority, of course, was the college team. In 1987, Spivey turned to a friend, Mike Durkin, an attorney who'd run for Illinois and would coach only one athlete—Spivey—in what became a close, long-term relationship. During the height of the track season, they'd confer twice a day.

Spivey had natural speed and could run a 400 in 48.9. Durkin felt Spivey needed more strength. He increased his weekly mileage to 70, still not very high. The key was a greater amount of repetition work, enabling Spivey to carry his speed over a longer distance, which is essential to the mile.

That first season with Durkin, Spivey did two track workouts a week at North Central College in Naperville, Illinois. On Mondays, he'd run 3 miles in the morning, then 6 miles of repetitions in the afternoon. This consisted of 200s, 250s, 400s, 500s, and 800s. The pace was geared to running a 3:50 mile. Spivey finished every track session with 10×100 strides. Counting the warmup and cooldown, he got in 13 miles for the day.

On Wednesdays, Spivey did less volume but faster work, such as 10×200 in 26 to 27 seconds, plus 3×600 and 2×800, for example.

Spivey's distance runs were two workouts a day totaling 60 minutes on Tuesdays, Thursdays, and Fridays. His long run was 90 minutes on Sundays. On Saturdays, he usually raced.

When he moved up to the 5000, Spivey increased his morning runs to 4 or 5 miles but still kept his weekly mileage around 70, low for an athlete at his level. Spivey's primary change, as he prepared for the 1996 Olympic 5000 at Wheaton College, was longer interval work. He did ladder sessions of 1 mile, 2×1320, 2×800, and so on.

In the early 1990s, tests by exercise physiologist David Martin showed that despite all his hard work, Spivey's maximal oxygen uptake (max VO_2)—that is, aerobic capacity—was too low. Martin suggested that Spivey do long, *slow* intervals once a week. At first, Durkin objected, saying this was not the path to a 3:49 mile. But eventually he relented, and Spivey did the slower work. It took a year before his aerobic assessment reached desired levels, and everyone agreed the effects were beneficial.

hands-on approach

It's common for top athletes to get weekly massages, which loosen tight muscles and make the body—and mind—feel better. Spivey had massages *twice a week* during the track season. Often, his hips were out of kilter "from making 2 million left turns" around the track. For the 1992 Olympics, leaving nothing to chance, Spivey flew his massage therapist to Barcelona, Spain, for the personal touch.

Pat Porter 29
10,000 Meters, Cross-Country

Lifetime Honors Point Total: 3,750

Best Times

5000 meters—13:33.91
July 2, 1988, Dedham, Massachusetts (New England TAC)

10,000 meters—27:46.80
April 23, 1988, Walnut, California (Mt. San Antonio College Relays)

Born: May 31, 1959, Wadena, Minnesota
Current Residence: Albuquerque, New Mexico
Education: Evergreen High School, Evergreen, Colorado (1977); Adams State College, Alamosa, Colorado (1982)
Affiliations: Athletics West, Nike International
Professions: Professional runner, sales manager for a construction company
Career Highlights: A record eight straight U.S. national cross-country titles; four top 10 finishes in the World Cross-Country Championships; two-time Olympian; 1985 World Cup silver medalist in the 10,000

Panther Pride

While Pat Porter was an excellent 10,000-meter runner on the track, running the event at the 1984 and 1988 Olympic Games, his forte was running the rough, hilly terrain of cross-country.

Porter's enormous strength, which he gained through rigorous training under coach Joe Vigil in the high altitude of Alamosa, Colorado, enabled him to carry his 6-foot, 135-pound body over heavy, leg-jarring turf without a hitch in his stride. You could say he ran like a panther—his nickname after he got a tattoo in 1986.

"His foot barely seems to touch the ground," said Vigil after one of Porter's many national victories. "He's real good in mud. He has great strength—mental as well as physical—to stay with high-performance workouts."

Porter was a two-time collegiate cham-

131

pion at Adams State, an NAIA power in Alamosa coached by Vigil.

After college, Porter stuck by his coach, often training at elevations above 8,000 feet in the surrounding San Juan Mountains. The union enabled Porter to win a record eight straight U.S. national cross-country titles, from 1982 through 1989.

"I started running for social reasons, but then I felt if I was putting in all this time, I might as well get it right."

From Golden Gate Park in San Francisco to Van Cortlandt Park in New York, Porter was a master of hill-and-dale events, becoming the United States's most prolific male cross-country specialist ever.

Porter competed in 10 world cross-country championships—meets that bring the best distance runners, from milers to marathoners, to the most formidable racing anywhere. He made the top 10 four times, finishing as high as fourth in 1984 when the event was held in the United States (at the New Jersey Meadowlands) for the first time.

However, Porter's most satisfying cross-country outing came at home in Colorado while he was still in college. Competing in the University of Colorado Invitational in Boulder, Porter went up against the host school's Mark Scrutton, who would later win the NCAA title, and AAU national champion Ric Rojas, also of Boulder. Just about every top gun in Boulder's noted running colony showed up for this one. Porter crushed the field, breaking the course record. "With 600 left, I put the hammer down," he recalls.

On the track, where short speed was at a premium, Porter

fat chance

Porter ate his share of pasta to replenish all the calories he burned up, but he also ate plenty of meat. Two reasons: First, he had to—he had family in the cattle-ranching business. Second, to sustain his training level, he felt that he needed sufficient fat in his diet. "When the furnace is hot," he points out, "it'll burn anything."

was humbled. At the 1984 Los Angeles Olympics, he made the 10,000 final but placed 15th.

At Seoul, South Korea, in 1988, he did not advance past the qualifying heats, even though that spring he had run his best time—27:46.80, which made him the 11th fastest American ever. That same season, Porter ran his best 5000, in 13:33.91. But his supporters kept waiting for a Porter breakthrough on the track.

When, between Olympics, Porter competed on the 1985 U.S. World Cup team in Canberra, Australia, it looked like the breakthrough might occur. Off the final curve in the 10,000, Porter led Wodajo Bulti of Ethiopia by a stride. In a nod to the fabled Bannister-Landy mile duel of 1954, Porter glanced left, while Bulti darted right and won by an eyelash.

"When my coach sees that on TV," Porter said afterward, "he's gonna kill me."

Most top U.S. distance men, focusing on road racing, ignored no-money track events like the World Cup. Porter could have made six figures a year running the roads, but he ran them only sparingly in order to focus on world and Olympic events.

Porter married high jumper Trish King in 1991 and retired after the 1994 season. They have a son, born in 1996. Porter doesn't run much anymore, but he uses PANTHER in his e-mail address.

Overcoming Asthma

Porter is afflicted with lifelong asthma and allergies that caused shortness of breath throughout his running. "Doctors always told me not to worry about it as long as I was running well," he says. "But if I could have gained another 3 percent from curbing the condition, maybe I would have never been beaten."

Hammering Wins the Day

Porter is an example of a runner who made the most of modest talent. In high school, he ran the mile in 4:29 and 2-mile in 9:51, times not even close to the national lists. But by going to Adams State and coming under coach Joe Vigil's spell, Porter trained to the utmost. There were two distinct phases to his training: college, when he trained very hard, and after college, when he trained very, very hard. Porter loved to hammer the pace, even on his easy days.

At Adams State, he ran 80 miles a week during the fall cross-country season. One day, he did fast repetitions of 100s, 200s, 400s, and 800s. This track work totaled 8 to 10 miles, high volume for a speed session. On another repetition day, at a park, Porter did 6 × mile on grass in the 4:20s and 4:30s. For hill work, the team started at Alamosa's base elevation of 7,500 feet and ran one long, sustained uphill 8-miler to about 11,000 feet. Vigil took a fairly bare-bones approach to this workout. "He just threw you out of the van and you got going," Porter recalls.

The main recovery run of the week was a Wednesday 10-miler. Porter found 5:30 mile pace easy and would sometimes lower that to 5:00, finding that his heart rate would still not exceed 75 percent of maximum. The day before Saturday meets, he'd do an easy 5 miles, and the day after, he did long runs that by his senior year had reached 18 miles at 6:40 per mile. After the long week, says Porter, "I'd go home, carbo-load, and collapse."

Physiological tests showed that Porter (despite his asthma) had an extremely high anaerobic threshold of 96, meaning that he could run to 96 percent of maximum—virtually full-tilt—before muscle-sagging waste products like lactic acid would hamper his pace.

By the mid-1980s, at the peak of his career, Porter had added morning runs and totaled 100 to 120 miles a week. In the mornings, he did 3 or 4 miles, but quickly—a pace of 5:30 to 6:00 per mile with surges down to 4:30. He continued his speed-work regimen of 8 to 10 miles' worth of short repetitions, did 6 × mile in the 4:20s, and doubled his weekly hill workouts. He ran 8 miles, past the tree line to 11,000 feet, then turned around and ran back down, for 16 miles in all.

Other innovations were weight training and plyometric drills (leaping and bounding drills), which Porter credits for preventing injury. On Sundays, he covered close to 20 miles in 2 hours, then, to refuel for the next week, "brought all my food and drink to the couch, lay down with the TV remote, and did not get up for 8 hours."

more strength, less injury

Despite his grueling program, Porter was injury-free for most of his career. He credits a year-round, 90-minute, full-body weight session, done two or three times a week, for providing the strength to withstand the intensity. He also did an hour's worth of plyometrics each week. "I didn't have enough talent to leave any stone unturned," he notes.

Brian Diemer
3000-Meter Steeplechase

Lifetime Honors Point Total:
4,800

Best Time
3000-meter steeplechase—
8:13.16
August 29, 1984, Koblenz, West
Germany (Grand Prix)

Born: October 10, 1961, Grand
Rapids, Michigan
Current Residence: Caledonia,
Michigan
Education: South Christian High
School, Grand Rapids, Michigan
(1979); University of Michigan,
Ann Arbor (1983)
Affiliations: Nike International
Professions: Professional runner,
coach, landscape designer
Career Highlights: Three-time
Olympian and 1984 bronze
medalist; 1990 Goodwill Games
champion; six-time U.S. national
champion; five-time top 10 world
ranking

Clearing the Barriers

Brian Diemer was thinking more about getting married after college than about extending his track career.

But Diemer, a 3000-meter steeplechaser, wound up becoming only the second U.S. men's Olympic distance medalist since Frank Shorter, and he made a career out of consistency on the international level.

Shortly after graduating as NCAA champion from Michigan in 1983, Diemer qualified for his first U.S. team and competed that summer in the inaugural World Track and Field Championships in Helsinki, Finland.

From that point on, he competed in at least one international event every year except two—when he was injured in 1986 and in his last season in 1996—for the duration of his distinguished career. That's 12 out of 14 years and a total of 20 American teams: 3 Olympics, 4 World Championships, 1 Goodwill Games, 1 World Cup, 1 Pan American Games, and 10 U.S. international dual meets.

Diemer's fastest times came early—a career-best 8:13.16 in a Grand Prix second-place run at Koblenz, West Germany, and 8:14.06 at the Los Angeles Olympics, both in 1984 at the age of 22. In an event overwhelmed by Kenyan power, Diemer persisted in challenging for the major medals. He ran fourth and fifth in the 1987 and 1991 world meets, respectively, and seventh at the 1992 Olympics. He picked up a silver medal at the 1995 Pan Am Games, a year before hanging up his spikes.

"It all comes down to having a dream. You have to know why you head out the door every day to run. Your purpose will motivate you in every mile you train."

It was an unlikely run of success for an athlete who'd harbored no hopes of making running a career. In the spring of his senior year at Michigan, in 1983, Diemer raced to a planned tie in the Big Ten 10,000 with teammate Gerard Donakowski, while taking second in the steeple and dropping out of the 5000.

He was not thinking much about the NCAA meet, only about proposing to his girlfriend, Jerri.

Then, Diemer went out and won the NCAA steeple in Houston. "All of a sudden," he says, "people were saying, 'Go to the U.S. Nationals.' I said, 'What are the U.S. Nationals?'" Next thing you know, Diemer was running second in the nationals to make his first American squad. When the season was over, he got married.

Instead of leaving the sport and going into his family's landscape business as he'd planned, Diemer stuck with the steeple and

college rivals

Diemer's favorite track was Stockholm's quaint Olympic Stadium, where in 1989 he ran in a world record race. It wasn't his record—Kenyan Peter Koech ran 8:05.35, while Diemer placed fifth in 8:16.92. But Diemer did get some satisfaction. Five years before, he had defeated Koech, then at Washington State, to win the NCAA title.

trained for the 1984 Olympics and beyond. At Los Angeles in 1984, he won the bronze medal. At Seoul, South Korea, in 1988, he made it to the Olympic semis. But at Barcelona, Spain, in 1992, it looked like he wouldn't make the U.S. team at all.

Two months before the 1992 trials in New Orleans, Diemer came down with a stress fracture in his sacrum. Dejected, he ran in a pool and pedaled an exercise bike for minimum fitness. "Basically," he says, "I watched my dreams of making a third Olympic team go down the tubes."

Diemer was so discouraged that he left town Memorial Day weekend for a Canadian fishing trip with his brother. They were 40 miles from the nearest phone. Diemer tried to run in the lake, but it snowed overnight and the water was too cold. He did get some exercise on his bike while being chased by bears.

But as he sat in the boat with his line out, something clicked in his mind. "When I came back," Diemer says, "everybody said I had fire in my eyes."

Diemer resumed running only 3 weeks before the trials and proceeded to capture his fourth straight national title and go on to the Games in Barcelona, where he placed seventh.

With Kenyan domination growing, it became harder for steeplers across the world to hold their ground. The family business beckoned. Diemer began his landscape career and also started coaching cross-country at Calvin College in Grand Rapids, Michigan, which won the women's NCAA Division III championship in 1999, and the men's title in 2000.

A Tall Order

As a youngster, Diemer loved sports so much that he rode his bike 2½ miles to school to arrive early and play ball. But at 5 feet 1 inch, he was the shortest kid in his ninth-grade class, and he played so hard that he'd wind up coming home with a bloody nose. "I always felt I had to make up for my size," Diemer says. Consequently, he started running to have an edge at basketball tryouts. Finally, he went out for the high school cross-country squad. And he would grow to 5 feet 9 inches, tall enough to eventually clear the steeplechase barriers.

Creating Strength

A Michigan boy through and through, Diemer rarely strayed from his Grand Rapids–Ann Arbor axis to prepare for big meets. He relied on a familiar environment and people who could help him. Diemer was creative, making something simple work to his advantage.

For the strength-building phase leading up to his bronze-medal performance at the 1984 Olympics, Diemer ran 80 to 85 miles a week. He started his week with a fartlek workout on hills, running a course that he likened to spokes on a wheel. He called it the 92nd Street Wheel. Using the main drag of Cutlerville, outside Grand Rapids, Diemer surged up hills that went in every direction from town for 75 minutes. He used hills to build his quadriceps muscles, which helped him glide over the 3-foot-high steeplechase barriers.

Four days a week, Diemer did easy distance work of 10 to 12 miles plus strides. On Saturdays, he'd either race or throw in a 6-mile tempo run. He saved Wednesdays for his hardest workout, driving 250 miles round trip to Ann Arbor to train with his college coach, Ron Warhurst of Michigan. Diemer was joined by former teammates Gerard Donakowski and Jon Scheer.

The trio proceeded with this workout: 1.5 miles in 6:45 (4:30 mile pace); 400 jog; 1320 in 3:20 (4:27 mile pace); 400 jog; 800 in 2:10 to 2:15 (4:20 to 4:30 mile pace); 400 jog; 1320 in 3:20 (4:27 mile pace); 400 jog. Diemer said the group liked to celebrate their hard workout with a Mexican dinner afterward.

To sharpen between the 1992 Olympic Trials and Games, Diemer cut his distance runs to 8 to 9 miles and generally did less mileage and more speed. He included 2 days of quality with 1 in-between day of "cruise intervals"—repeat 1000s above race pace—or a 6- to 8-mile tempo run.

Diemer's quality days were Mondays and Thursdays. On Mondays, he did the "Steve Lacy Workout," named after the miler and Olympic teammate who passed it on. This workout, used to develop a kick, calls for 3 × 800, running the first 600 in 1:30, jogging for 30 seconds, and finishing the 800 with a final 200 in 29 or 30. Then, an 800 rest-jog and repeat. Diemer feels that it's harder to take the rest and get your motor restarted than to run the full 800 distance at once.

On Thursdays, he did a more traditional session, with two sets of 400-300-200, aiming for times of 57-44-29, jogging a 400 between runs, and trying to run a little faster for the second set.

finessing the hurdles

Unlike most steeplers, Diemer rarely did repetition work on the hurdles. His rationale was that he wanted to develop his aerobic capacity like any distance runner, and if he had to train over the hurdles he wouldn't run fast enough to gain the necessary strength. He would incorporate hurdling into his post-run strides on distance days, like setting up one barrier in the course of doing 150s.

The Rest of the Best: Top 31–100 Men

(mile to the marathon, listed alphabetically)

Jon Anderson, marathon
Jack Bachelor, 10,000 meters, marathon
Arturo Barrios, marathon, road
Dick Beardsley, marathon
Bruce Bickford, 5000 meters, 10,000 meters
Garry Bjorklund, marathon
George Bonhag, 5000 meters
Bill Bonthron, 1500 meters, mile
Don Bowden, 1500 meters, mile
Keith Brantley, marathon, road
Tarzan Brown, marathon
Dick Buerkle, 1500 meters, mile, 5,000
Amby Burfoot, marathon
Matt Centrowitz, 1500 meters, 5000 meters
Mark Coogan, marathon, road
Mark Croghan, steeplechase
Paul Cummings, 1500 meters, 5000 meters, 10,000 meters
Marc Davis, steeplechase, 5000 meters
Gil Dodds, 1500 meters, mile
Benji Durden, marathon
Ed Eyestone, 10,000 meters, cross-country
Tom Fleming, marathon
Jeff Galloway, 10,000 meters, marathon
Adam Goucher, 5000 meters
John Gregorek, steeplechase
Jim Grelle, 1500 meters, mile
Tim Hacker, 1500 meters, cross-country
Ralph Hill, 5000 meters
Steve Holman, 1500 meters, mile
Thom Hunt, 10,000 meters
Don Kardong, marathon

John A. Kelley, marathon
Bob Kempainen, marathon
Khalid Khannouchi, marathon
Don Lash, cross-country
James Lightbody, 1500 meters, mile
Herb Lindsay, road
Duncan Macdonald, 5000 meters, 10,000 meters
Leslie MacMitchell, 1500 meters, mile
Ken Martin, steeplechase to marathon
Peter McArdle, cross-country, road
Bill McChesney, 5000 meters, 10,000 meters
Joe McCluskey, steeplechase
Bob McMillan, 1500 meters, mile
Greg Meyer, marathon, road
Kenny Moore, marathon
Mark Nenow, 5000 meters, 10,000 meters, road
Tom O'Hara, 1500 meters, mile
Eamon O'Reilly, marathon
Doug Padilla, 2-mile, 5000 meters
Don Paige, 1500 meters, mile
Leslie Pawson, marathon
Peter Pfitzinger, marathon
Mark Plaatjes, marathon
Joie Ray, 1500 meters to marathon
Greg Rice, 2-mile, 5000 meters
Tony Sandoval, marathon
Wes Santee, 1500 meters, mile
Steve Spence, marathon
Curt Stone, 5000 meters, 10,000 meters
Ron Tabb, marathon
Norman Taber, 1500 meters, mile
Louis Tewanina, 10,000 meters
Max Truex, 5000 meters, 10,000 meters
Gary Tuttle, marathon, road
Gene Venzke, 1500 meters, mile
Cary Weisiger, 1500 meters, mile
Jeff Wells, marathon
Todd Williams, 10,000 meters, marathon
Fred Wilt, cross-country, 5000 meters

Top 20
Women

Joan Samuelson
Marathon

1

Lifetime Honors Point Total:
23,250

Best Times: Track
3000 meters—8:53.49
June 19, 1983, Indianapolis
(TAC Nationals)

5000 meters—15:40.42
June 26, 1982, Oslo, Norway
(Bislett Games)

10,000 meters—32:07.41
June 17, 1984, Los Angeles
(Olympic Trials/exhibition)

Best Times: Road
10-K—31:44
March 27, 1983, New Orleans
(Crescent City Classic)

15-K—51:28
June 24, 1979, Portland, Oregon
(Cascade Run Off)

Half-marathon—1:08:34
September 16, 1984, Philadelphia
(Philly Half-Marathon)

Marathon—2:21:21
October 20, 1985, Chicago
(Chicago Marathon)

Born: May 16, 1957, Portland,
Maine
Current Residence: Freeport,
Maine
Education: Cape Elizabeth High
School, Cape Elizabeth, Maine
(1975); Bowdoin College,
Brunswick, Maine (1979)
Affiliations: Athletics West, Nike
Professions: Professional runner,
TV commentator, race director
Career Highlights: 1984 gold
medalist in first women's Olympic
marathon; set 26 American road
records; Boston Marathon winner
in world-record time

First for All Time

After all these years, we are still trying to figure out how Joan Samuelson did it. Did it—does it. She's still at it, still running marathons in her forties with two kids on her arm. Why? Because she can. And because, as she so aptly puts it, "It's part of who I am. If I don't run, I feel like I'm not getting anything accomplished. Running nourishes the soul."

Joanie—Joan Benoit—Joan Samuelson, the woman who has led us all with spunk and power, is an American hero of wholesome virtue who came out of Maine's central casting with her L.L. Bean sweater and *This Old House* pragmatism to knock our socks off.

She got her first taste for sports when men were men and women were cheerleaders, and of course, she was told to take a hike, kid. Is that denial what ultimately led to her Olympic Marathon victory in Los

143

Angeles in 1984 on that historic day for women? And to run, and win, the U.S. trial 17 days after knee surgery? What a time that was, a year after Samuelson won her second Boston in 2:22:43, taking 3 minutes off the world record, setting up the greatest women's field ever—Grete, Ingrid, Rosa, Joanie, and company—for Los Angeles.

"On the eve of the Olympic Marathon, I said to myself, 'Are you prepared to deal with victory?' I decided I was."

Samuelson had started out as a skier, played field hockey, fell easily into youth cross-country, and ran in high school. She went on to compete for North Carolina State but longed for Maine and returned home to finish college at Bowdoin. The coach was Bob Sevene, who would train her for the Olympics.

By 1983, Samuelson was well on her way to a collection of 26 U.S. road records and was showing the dogged versatility that marked Olympic champions. That season, in addition to her world record at Boston, she set a world half-marathon record (1:08:34) at Philadelphia, won the Pan American Games 3000-meter run in track, and took fourth in the world cross-country. Baby, she had it all.

But the Norwegian Grete Waitz, the 1983 world marathon titlist and Her Majesty of New York, was thought to be invincible. She trained in tandem with Ingrid Kristiansen—wearing double warmups for the heat, taking anti-smog inhalants, listening to psych-up tapes—for L.A.

Samuelson, still Benoit then, looked frail by comparison and had hesitation in her voice. She could also look angelic, with a touch of her French roots showing through, sweet but cunning

smelling the flowers

Influenced by three brothers, two of whom ran high school track, Samuelson loved sports in her youth in the early 1970s. "I was considered a tomboy and was embarrassed because running was not a women's sport at the time," she recalls. When she ran, Samuelson bundled up in ski clothing so people wouldn't notice a girl running. "I'd stop and walk when cars passed me. I'd pretend I was looking at the flowers."

and concealing her combativeness until the right time. L.A. was the time.

When Samuelson made her break after a mere 14 minutes into the Olympic Marathon, with TV cameras trained on her every pore, who could explain it? We knew she ran very hard. Didn't everyone? We knew she was mentally tough. Waitz was just as tough, and she had a lot more speed. What was going on?

Samuelson took off, alone, exposed, in possibly the gutsiest move the sport of running had ever seen. The Norwegians, the scientists, had to throw away their petri dishes. The race was over. Samuelson had 11 seconds by 10 kilometers and 51 seconds by 15 kilometers. It was so over it was boring. It was Tiger Woods at the Open. Wearing that goofy, oversize cap, Samuelson trucked it home in the miserable heat in 2:24:52 for the Olympic gold medal.

What about that great run, kid? "The Olympics was a relatively easy race for me," Samuelson says now without hubris.

Waitz finished 86 seconds behind, in second. Kristiansen, a year away from her first world record, took fourth, while the bronze medal went to Portugal's Rosa Mota, who would succeed Samuelson as Olympic marathon champion at Seoul, Korea, in 1988. Samuelson never made it to Seoul, but a year after L.A., she won Chicago and slashed her U.S. record to 2:21:21, coming within 15 seconds of Kristiansen's world mark.

So how did—does—Samuelson do it? She grew tired of talking about it. Maybe because she had to hide her athletics as a kid—going underground, as she once wrote—closeted strength became her most comfortable public posture. The silence was golden.

Still a Contender

At 42, Samuelson got into her best shape in years by training 80 to 90 miles a week through the Maine winter for the 2000 Women's Olympic Marathon Trial in Columbia, South Carolina. Battling snow and sub-zero cold, juggling the care of her two children (12-year-old Abby and 10-year-old Anders), combining family ski trips with last-minute workouts, Samuelson was almost like the Joanie of yore when she stepped to the line in pursuit of an Olympic berth. Don't think she didn't believe she had a chance. While the heat spoiled it, Samuelson—in her 25th career marathon—still placed ninth in 2:39:59. Then, she put her energy back into the Beach to Beacon 10-K, the road race that she founded in her hometown in 1998.

As Hard as She Could

It was Samuelson's nature to push the envelope. She ran hard, and harder. She was not big on easy days or days off. When the sun came up, Samuelson went out and belted one.

At her peak during the 1984–85 period, Samuelson ran around 90 miles a week, going over 100 several times and reaching a peak of 108. She ran twice a day. Her longest run was 20 miles.

John Babington of the Liberty Athletic Club coached her early on; Bob Sevene coached her from the end of college through her prime years. Today, she coaches herself.

Samuelson's primary track work consisted of ladders in which she ran two or three sets of 440, 660, 880, mile, mile, 880, and 440. She never ran the ladders rested, either; on those days, she did a crisp 8 to 12 miles in the morning, then went to the track in the afternoon. "I am never completely recovered for a workout," she said then.

Samuelson did not have great flat-out speed, and her fast, sustained running— even pushing the pace toward the end of a 20-miler—was an attempt to overcome that deficiency with strength. Mission accomplished.

Bearing down on the 2000 Olympic Trials at age 42, Samuelson "did more mileage at any time since the kids were born," but she ran once a day, not twice as before. She started her buildup on December 1, 1999, for the late-February event. She was on a steady diet of 10- to 15-milers and went as long as 22 miles weekly.

For track work, she went to her alma mater, Bowdoin College, and did 10×800 in 2:32 to 2:33 with a 1:45 rest. She also did a distance-ladder of 2 miles, 1.5 miles, 1 mile, 1.5 miles, and 2 miles, taking a 3-minute recovery jog after each run and maintaining a 5:10 to 5:20 mile pace. These were workouts of Olympic caliber.

on trial for 17 days

Samuelson had arthroscopic surgery on her right knee on April 25, 1984, 17 days before the women's Olympic Marathon Trial in Olympia, Washington. For 4 days after the operation, she did swimming, walking, and other cross-training. On the 5th day, she ran twice, totaling close to 2 hours, and continued running (except for 2 days spent nursing a hamstring problem) to the day of the trial, which she won in 2:31:04.

Mary Slaney

1500 Meters, 3000 Meters

Lifetime Honors Point Total: 53,900

Best Times

800 meters—1:56.90
August 16, 1985, Bern, Switzerland (international meet)

1000 meters—2:34.65
August 14, 1988, Hengelo, Netherlands (Paulen Invitational)

1500 meters—3:57.12
July 26, 1983, Stockholm, Sweden (Nordic)

Mile—4:16.71
August 21, 1985, Zurich, Switzerland (Weltklasse)

2000 meters—5:32.7
August 3, 1984, Eugene, Oregon (all-comers meet)

3000 meters—8:25.83
September 7, 1985, Rome, Italy (Grand Prix Final)

5000 meters—15:06.53
June 1, 1985, Eugene, Oregon (Prefontaine Classic)

10,000 meters—31:35.3
July 16, 1982, Eugene, Oregon (all-comers meet)

Born: August 4, 1958, Bunnvale, New Jersey
Current Residence: Eugene, Oregon
Education: Orange High School, Orange, California (1976); University of Colorado, Boulder (1978) (inc)
Affiliations: Athletics West, Nike, Foot Locker Athletic Club
Profession: Professional runner
Career Highlights: Swept 1500 and 3000 at the 1983 World Championships; set 18 world records and 32 American records

The Eternal Comeback Kid

In the 27 years since she first wowed us as an 89-pound teenage sensation in pigtails and braces, Mary Slaney has experienced running's greatest highs, and more than her share of lows, in a transcendent but star-crossed career. She is known for matching her abundant records with an almost equal number of surgeries. At last count, Slaney's operations on her feet and legs had exceeded 20, and yet, past age 40, she has not given up on continuing to run at a championship level.

Who can fathom how Slaney has endured such heartache?

Who knows how she has tolerated such pain?

She has certainly set a world record for resilience—for eternally grasping at slim hopes, surprising her doctors and coaches and overcoming injury to run faster still. As

Healthy Mary and Hurt Mary, she's a contradiction. She was strong enough to train at a superior level, but at some cellular depth, her body would crack under the stress.

Slaney, born Decker, was a fighter from the beginning. She didn't take any guff, certainly not from the Russians she tangled with in one early indoor dual-meet in 1974. That winter, Slaney, 16, had set the first of her 18 world records in the indoor 880. Pushed by a Russian woman in a relay race, Slaney pushed back and threw a baton at her opponent. She was disqualified but made a point. She was not only fast but also courageous.

"I have always felt that I need to train fast, so that when I race, it feels easy."

Slaney loved to run from the front, free and clear. Almost every American race she ran saw her a half-lap ahead while the rest of the field competed among themselves. Internationally, Slaney had to confront the Russians. They were the titleholders, and they knew how to gang up on a challenger.

In 1983, the stage was set: Slaney versus the Russians in the inaugural World Championships of track and field in Helsinki, Finland. Slaney had missed the 1976 Olympics because of injury and the 1980 Olympics because of the U.S. boycott. Now she had her chance. Despite injuries that year, she was fit and ready by summer. In what became known as the Double Decker, she proceeded to win both the 1500 and 3000 meters in dramatic fashion. She had the Soviets in her pocket.

For that achievement—and for racing undefeated in 20 events that year and holding all seven U.S. records from the 800

no waiting

I can personally attest to Slaney's relentless pace. One time in the mid-1980s, when I was editing *The Runner*, I invited Slaney to write about the women's race at the Boston Marathon. One morning, we went running "together" along the Charles River. Slaney jogged the 5 miles in 29 minutes, barely breaking a sweat, while I struggled from far behind with my tongue in the gutter. She wouldn't wait.

through the 10,000—Slaney was named *Sports Illustrated* Sportswoman of the Year. She was pictured in the magazine in the bear-hug embrace of her future husband, Richard Slaney, a 320-pound former shot-putter from England who was once dubbed "Britain's strongest man."

A year later, in Los Angeles, when Slaney's fortunes turned sour at the 1984 Olympics, Richard again had Mary in his arms, but this time he carried his weeping fiancée off the track. In the 3000, Slaney was clipped from behind by barefoot teenager Zola Budd, a Briton by way of South Africa. Slaney fell and lay sprawled on the track in anguish.

Once again, Slaney rebounded, and the next summer, 1985, she ran many of her fastest times. Despite a winter injury forcing a 12-week layoff, Slaney would train seamlessly upon her return and add to her U.S. record collection with marks in the 800 (1:56.90), the 1500 (3:57.12), the mile (4:16.71), and the 3000 (8:25.83).

The last three still stand. As in 1983, Slaney was ranked number one in the world in both the 1500 and 3000.

Married in January 1985, Slaney gave birth to a daughter, Ashley, the following year. She resumed competition in 1988, winning the Olympic Trials 1500 and 3000 while placing 8th and 10th, respectively, in the Games at Seoul, South Korea.

Her career stumbled after that, however, until the 1996 Olympic year, when, at 37, she made the U.S. squad for Atlanta in the 5000 meters.

Although Slaney did not make the Olympic final, her participation alone was a miracle because of yet another round of foot surgery. She said that she was lucky to be able to walk. But, she knew, you have to walk before you can run.

Child Prodigy

Young Slaney, known as Little Mary Decker, was so precocious that she was almost America's best female runner in junior high. At 14, when the American 800 record of 2:00.92 was held by 1968 Olympic champion Madeline Manning, Slaney ran 2:02.43. At 12, Slaney was so full of running that she raced a 440, a mile, a 2-mile, and a marathon—yes, marathon—all within a week.

Fast, Faster, Fastest

It is safe to say that Slaney trained at a pace that no other woman—or many men—could match. In 1983, before her finest hour winning the World Championship 1500 and 3000, she regularly ran 10-milers in 54 to 57 minutes, race pace for top female distance runners. She did this on the popular bike path along the Willamette River in Eugene, Oregon. "Fast 10-milers made me feel good," she says now.

For sprints, Slaney often ran 200s in 25 to 26 seconds—say, a half-dozen, twice a week—with a minute's rest between the sprints. Slaney's coach at the time, Dick Brown, gave her a long leash. She ran pretty much as she pleased, without a lot of structure, but more on instinct and "feel." With her preference for 10-milers and 200s, Brown summarized Slaney's training as "10s and 2s."

Since Slaney was often coming back from injury, she used races as training. She had to; she lacked time for a long buildup. When she was healthy, her mileage was 50 to 60 a week.

Slaney is an expert on coaching style and the athlete-coach relationship. She's had seven coaches—Don DeNoon when she was a teen; Rich Castro when she attended Colorado; world-class 5,000 man Dick Quax of New Zealand; Brown; Brazilian Luis D'Olivera; Alberto Salazar; and, most recently, Bill Dellinger. She especially likes the laid-back Dellinger because "he's not controlling and lets me be me."

Dellinger has given Slaney some of his Oregon favorites, like a combination of repeat 800s and 300s, and his tried-and-true 30-30 workout. Here, you get 60 seconds to run a 200 and rest before starting the next one. If you run 35 seconds, you get 25 seconds to rest. Slaney will do 5 to 10 repeats. She also runs sets of 300s, progressively faster, with a 100 jog between. And her longer work includes repeat 5-lappers (2000 meters).

no pregnant pause

When Slaney was pregnant in 1985 and 1986, she continued more-or-less normal training for the first 5 months. After that, she was too uncomfortable and did light walking and running a few days a week. She also lifted weights, worked out on a stationary bike and NordicTrack, and ran in a swimming pool to stay fit. She gained 28 pounds, which she lost within about 6 weeks after giving birth.

Lynn Jennings 3
10,000 Meters, Cross-Country

Lifetime Honors Point Total: 26,650

Best Times

1500 meters—4:06.4
(mile split)
July 14, 1990, Oslo, Norway
(Bislett Games)

Mile—4:24.14
July 14, 1990, Oslo, Norway
(Bislett Games)

3000 meters—8:40.45
(indoors)
February 23, 1990, New York
(USA Nationals)

3000 meters—8:43.72
(outdoors)
May 26, 1996, Eugene, Oregon
(Prefontaine Classic)

5000 meters—15:07.92
July 2, 1990, Stockholm, Sweden
(Galan Games)

10,000 meters—31:19.89
August 7, 1992, Barcelona, Spain
(Olympic Games)

Born: July 1, 1960, Princeton, New Jersey
Current Residence: Newmarket, New Hampshire
Education: Bromfield High School, Harvard, Massachusetts (1978); Princeton University (1983)
Affiliation: Nike International
Profession: Professional runner
Career Highlights: Three-time World Cross-Country champion; Olympic bronze medalist in the 10,000; winner of a record 38 U.S. national titles in track, road, and cross-country; set 10 American records

Triple Threat

Lynn Jennings is three runners in one. She's a track racer who can hammer a hard pace for the 25 laps of the 10,000 meters, winning the Olympic bronze medal at Barcelona, Spain, in 1992. She's a cross-country runner who thrives on rough-and-tumble natural terrain, dominating the U.S. nationals and winning three straight world titles from 1990 through 1992. She's a road runner, dabbling in a less demanding arena of which she once said, "It's easy to do well, win money, be lauded, and feel great."

Jennings's versatility and staying power have given her a record collection of 38 national titles in track, road, and cross-country. The distances range from 1500 meters to 10,000 meters. She's had more hits than Elvis.

And, most recently, Jennings is also an aspiring marathoner, running Boston at age 38 in 1999. The 26.2-miler is clearly a work in progress. Jennings finished 12th in 2:38:57

and passed up the women's Olympic Marathon Trial in 2000. Where is Jennings, now 40, headed? As she says, she's keeping her cards close to her chest.

Her 1998 Boston run brought Jennings full circle. As a precocious 17-year-old running on the boys' team at Bromfield High in Massachusetts, Jennings jumped into the 1978 Boston Marathon as an unofficial entrant. She ran 2:46, which would have placed her third and established a record for her age. She ran Boston against the wishes of her long-time coach, John Babington, and afterward settled back into the middle-distance events.

"Running gives me a sense of strength, power. On the way in from a run, I'm a new woman."

But Jennings's experiment showed the sense of adventure and single-mindedness that would mark her career. She's never seen fit to travel in a crowd. Jennings trains on her own, stares down her opposition at races, challenges the media, and, for a decade, remained faithful to a rare goal of her choosing: cross-country.

Visit Jennings at her home in Newmarket, New Hampshire, and you can see why. Her home is set on 4 acres and surrounded by woods. The spot is teeming with wildlife, and deer tracks line her backyard. Give Jennings a run through the brush and she couldn't be happier. "I like the way terrain dictates a race," she says. "Cross-country gives me a different aura."

It's also given her opponents fits. After a transitional college period at Princeton, Jennings won her first U.S. title, in cross-country, in 1985, and added eight more victories, six in succession. At a cross-country race, other runners would shrink in her presence. Jennings could triumph at will.

She's never missed a beat in expressing the essence of her experience, a model for female athletes. "Running has given me so many gifts: courage, responsibility, discipline, motivation—attributes that readily transfer to other areas of my life. The joy of

dog days

Jennings loves animals and has volunteered at an animal shelter, cleaning cages, walking dogs, and emptying litter boxes. She adopted one doomed dog after seeing his picture in the local paper.

being physically fit—physically clean, if you will. . . . Even on days when a run starts out with a little struggle, you come home so refreshed."

Acquiring speed and confidence from track racing, Jennings rounded out her competitive repertoire and became a contender in the world cross-country meet. She placed second, fourth, sixth, and sixth from 1986 through 1989, and in 1990, she won her first world title with a decisive victory in Aix-les-Bains, France. European reporters loved her. She answered their questions in French. Jennings was hot, and she would sustain the heat in a 3-year peak.

Garden Party

Jennings's best race of all may have been an indoor 3000 meters in New York in 1990. At the U.S. Nationals in Madison Square Garden, she ran 8:40.45 to win a magnificent duel with PattiSue Plumer and Vicki Huber, both considered superior runners at that distance. On a slow track, Jennings set an American indoor record that still stands, and to this day only seven women worldwide have ever run faster.

In track in 1990, Jennings broke records indoors and outdoors. She was ranked second in the world in the 5000. On the roads, she broke her U.S. 10-K record by 28 seconds in 31:06. In the 1991 season, Jennings repeated as world cross-country champion in Antwerp, Belgium, took fifth in the world championship 10,000 in track, and set a world 8-K record of 25:02 on the roads.

But all of that was groundwork for 1992. The world cross-country would be run in Boston, on a course that Jennings had been milk-fed, before her fans, at the peak of her powers. In a race that Jennings called "the most memorable 20 minutes of my life," she outkicked two rivals on the snowy home straight at Franklin Park for her third straight title. "I had so much in reserve, I was on extra premium gas," Jennings quipped.

That summer, Jennings crowned her streak with a bronze medal performance and American record (31:19.89) in the Olympic 10,000 meters at Barcelona. It is the only Olympic distance medal on the track won by a U.S. woman.

Jennings kept knocking off three or four U.S. championships a year, won the Olympic Trials 5000 in 1996, and placed ninth in the Atlanta Games. In 2000, Jennings continued training in seclusion, nurturing one of her favorite weapons, the element of surprise.

Four Phases, Building to a Peak

Jennings's training during 1992, her best season, was broken into four phases—endurance, strength, speed, and fine-tuning. Each segment was 1 month, as explained by her coach, John Babington. She trained for her world cross-country victory (late March) in December 1991 through March, took a 2-week vacation, then trained for her bronze-medal performance in the Olympic 10,000 (late July) in April through July.

In December 1991, Jennings emphasized volume, averaging about 80 miles a week. She was never a very high-mileage runner, getting over 100 few times in her career. "Mileage did not drive Lynn's training," Babington says.

In January 1992, Jennings ran three races—in road, track, and cross-country—not only for the results but also, in a career hallmark, for the training benefit. One interval workout on an indoor track consisted of 400, 600, mile, 400, 800, 600, 400, mile. In February, she continued racing, cut her mileage by about 20 percent, and quickened her repetition work as in this example: 400, 800, 600, 2 × 300, 2 × 200, 4 × 100.

In March, with the world meet 3 weeks away, Jennings ran a cross-country race in Europe, did a track session of 6 × 1000, and trained on the world course in Boston. Her last quality workout, on the track, came 4 days before the race.

After her break, Jennings resumed her successful training regimen. In April and May, her volume topped off at 88 miles a week. For the Olympic 10,000, the amount of her track work increased to 5 miles' worth. One workout that she did twice was 4 × 400, 1600, 4 × 400, 1600, 4 × 400. She took a 50-second recovery between 400s and a 3- to 4-minute jog before and after 1600s. She averaged 72 to 73 seconds for the 400s and 4:58 for the 1600s. The second time, in June, she averaged 70 for the 400s and did the 1600s in 4:42 and 4:43. Jennings also did drills like high skipping for strength and flexibility.

ready to blast one

Two of Jennings's workouts close to the 1992 Olympics showed that she was poised to win a medal. In one, she ran 12 laps (4800 meters) at "fast cruising" pace in 15:08 (about 75 seconds per lap). In another, she ran 400, 1600, 4 × 200, 800, 4 × 200, 400, with the 1600 in 4:43, the 800 in 2:15, and the final 400 in 63.8.

Doris Heritage
800 Meters, 1500 Meters, 3000 Meters, Cross-Country

Lifetime Honors Point Total:
35,750

Best Times

800 meters—2:02.2
July 20, 1968, London, England
(Amateur Athletic Association
Championship)

1500 meters—4:14.6
July 2, 1971, Berkeley, California
(U.S.–USSR–World All-Stars)

3000 meters—9:26.9 (en
route to 2 miles)
July 7, 1971, Bakersfield, California (AAU Nationals)

2 miles—10:07.0
July 7, 1971, Bakersfield, California (AAU Nationals)

Born: September 17, 1942,
Tacoma, Washington
Current Residence: Seattle,
Washington
Education: Peninsula High School,
Gig Harbor, Washington (1960);
Seattle Pacific University (1964)
Affiliations: Falcon Track Club
Professions: Teacher, coach, ad-
ministrator
Career Highlights: Five-time world
cross-country champion; set six
world records and 17 American
records; won 14 AAU national
titles; two-time Olympian

Inspiring Breakthroughs

Doris Heritage, whose courage paved the
way for women's track in the early years,
faced obstacles at every turn. As a youngster,
she had arthritis, which caused her feet to
swell, and in school she was not allowed to be
active or take gym. When she started running
anyway as a teenager, girls at her high school
in the late 1950s were not allowed on the
track.

There were few events anywhere for
women, and in 1960, the longest women's
Olympic distance was the 800 meters.
Women were treated shabbily by the AAU,
and Heritage had to pay her own way to the
world cross-country meet. "When you went
out running by yourself," Heritage recalls,
"people said nasty things and threw footballs
at you."

These threats moved her to tears but
didn't stop her. "The women who ran then

155

were so committed. There was no question—you just ran."

And how! Heritage (then Brown) trained hard, eventually running twice a day and clipping along at an exceedingly fast pace. She entered any race she could find, even men's races if she had to. At 18, she did the 800 meters in 2:12, then ran with the men's team at Seattle Pacific University.

"To me, running means freedom, but you need the discipline to gain the freedom. Find nice places, find people to run with. Use your runs as 'devotions,' a time to be thankful for life's beauty."

In 1966, Heritage won the first of her 14 AAU national titles and started setting world and American records left and right. Her breakthrough came that winter in Vancouver when, as an unknown, she upset the field in an indoor mile, running a world-record 4:52.0. The next year, she captured the first of a record 5 straight world cross-country titles, with victories in Wales (1967), England (1968), Scotland (1969), Maryland (1970), and Spain (1971).

By 1968, the longest women's Olympic event was still the 800, and Heritage worked toward that. In a performance that she cherishes to this day, she ran her fastest 800, 2:02.2, taking third in a world-record race that summer at London's Crystal Palace.

At the Mexico City Games, Heritage placed fifth in 2:03.9. The race was just too short for her. In Heritage's world cross-country triumphs, the distance was about 2.5 miles.

a bite of the big apple

When Heritage attempted a marathon in the early 1970s, she ran it unofficially because women were not allowed to run. Her time, she says, was "around 2:43 to 2:45," which would have been a world record at the time. Her next marathon, at New York City in 1976, was done on a whim. After a full day of teaching, she got on a plane and arrived in New York in the middle of the night with the race the following day. Heritage placed second in 2:53:02 behind Miki Gorman, whose 2:39:11 set a world record.

For the next Olympics in Munich in 1972, women at least had a 1500, and Heritage's times were coming down fast. The previous season, she had run her career-best 1500 of 4:14.6 and set a world record for the 3000, hitting 9:26.9 en route to a 10:07 2-mile. With two Pan American Games silver medals in the 800, Heritage was poised for a medal bid in the 1500.

But when she marched in the opening ceremonies, she tripped on a piece of track curbing, broke five bones in her foot, and could not compete.

After that, Heritage ran in four more world cross-country meets and won her last national title, the AAU outdoor mile, in 1974. She dabbled in the marathon and went on to run some masters (40 and up) races, breaking 5 minutes in the mile and winning age-group titles.

Heritage continues to run 5 miles a day while teaching and coaching at her alma mater, Seattle Pacific University. She is currently men's and women's cross-country coach and assistant track coach.

Never one to stand pat, Heritage has taken every opportunity to serve the sport. She has been on the coaching and administrative staff of numerous U.S. international squads including the Olympic team, she has chaired the USA Track and Field Women's Long Distance Committee, and has been a member of the U.S. Olympic Committee House of Delegates and of the IAAF Cross-Country and Road Race Committee.

Dressed for Success

Training prior to her first world cross-country title in 1967, Heritage often ran 10 to 12 miles from home in the morning to the Seattle junior high school where she taught physical education. She was not allowed to enter the school in running gear—not even in her P.E. uniform. Women had to enter the building wearing a dress. So Heritage ran with a bag carrying her dress, stopped at a student's home near the school, and changed. Once in the building, she showered and put on her P.E. suit.

An Exceptional Pace

Preparing in the late 1960s for the world cross-country meets, Heritage used every possible training method to develop a rich repertoire of racing skills. She trained by herself and also with a group of men in the Falcon Track Club, coached by Ken Foreman, also the coach at Seattle Pacific University. A former sub-4:00 miler at Oregon, Foreman would be Heritage's coach throughout her career.

Every morning, Heritage would run either 10 miles to the school where she taught, or a fast 5 miles. In the afternoons, she would either run 10 miles home from school or do sprints or hills. On Sundays, she did one long run of 60 to 90 minutes in a hilly, wooded area. At times, she ran more than 100 miles a week.

Heritage's favorite distance spot was an undulating trail along a high bluff on Whidbey Island. She took a 10-mile course that afforded breathtaking views of Puget Sound, the Olympic Mountains, and the Pacific. When she did her regular morning 5-milers, however, Heritage paid little mind to sight-seeing. Her pace was as fast as 5 minutes per mile, which, if accurate, would have made her a faster 10-K runner than almost any woman of today. "People might not believe my pace," says Heritage, "but it was accurate. And the loop had hills, too."

Her sprint work included two or three sets of 5 × 200 in under 32 seconds on a dirt track, with a short jog for rest between runs. She ran 3 miles' worth of fartlek, alternating fast surges with recovery pace. She ran muddy loops at an arboretum and pushed through heavy sand at the beach. She ran "roller coaster" hills and long repetitions like 1500s and miles.

For track, Heritage trained mostly for the 800, but her speed paid off in any event. By the early 1970s, when she was at her best, Heritage's acceleration program called for 200s on Mondays, 400s on Tuesdays, and 600s on Wednesdays. For her 400s, she would run two sets of five in 57 to 60 seconds—faster than what most stars do today. She took a lap jog for recovery. For her 200s, she did two or three sets of five in 26 to 28 seconds. For her 600s, the goal was three in 1:30. "But I never made it," she says now, still wishing she had.

if ryun could do it . . .

When Heritage read that world-record miler Jim Ryun was running twice a day, she decided to try it. "The effect was amazing," she says. "All of my performances improved, even my 100-meter times." At her early meets, Heritage ran sprints and did field events like the high jump and long jump in addition to the 800.

Francie Larrieu Smith

1500 Meters, 3000 Meters, 10,000 Meters, Marathon

5

Lifetime Honors Point Total: 46,150

Best Times

800 meters—2:00.22
August 20, 1976, West Berlin
(ISTAF meet)

1500 meters—4:05.09
August 6, 1976, College Park,
Maryland (versus USSR)

Mile—4:27.52
June 30, 1979, Philadelphia
(Brooks meet)

3000 meters—8:50.54
May 25, 1985, San Jose, California (Jenner Classic)

5000 meters—15:15.2
July 2, 1988, Eugene, Oregon
(Prefontaine Classic)

10,000 meters—31:28.92
April 4, 1991, Austin, Texas
(Texas Relays)

Marathon—2:27:35
April 21, 1991, London, England
(London Marathon)

Born: November 23, 1952, Palo Alto, California
Current Residence: Georgetown, Texas
Education: Fremont High School, Sunnyvale, California (1970); California State University, Long Beach (1977)
Affiliations: Pacific Coast Club, New Balance
Professions: Professional runner, high school and college coach
Career Highlights: Five-time Olympian; set 31 American indoor and outdoor records; ranked number one in the United States 13 times

Amateur Spirit, Professional Style

At 19, Francie Larrieu Smith—who had to sell raffle tickets to raise travel money for national meets—won the Olympic Trials 1500. Twenty years later, turning 40, she placed 12th in the 1992 Olympic Marathon at Barcelona. Her total of five Olympic teams is the most by any U.S. female runner. Smith's versatility was equaled only by her staying power.

In 27 years, Smith had three careers in one. Competing for the San Jose Cindergals, she was a teenage prodigy, winning the first of 21 national titles as a 17-year-old in the 1500 in 1970. Then, she was a professional runner, traveling the circuit with the Pacific Coast Club, setting world and American records from Austin to Athens. Finally, Smith was a supreme distance runner, placing fifth in the 1988 Olympic 10,000 meters, the first for women, and running a 2:27:35 marathon at age 38.

159

Smith is especially proud of her 1988 performance at Seoul, where her 31:35.52 was a fraction off Mary Slaney's U.S. record at the time. "It was the first time in the Olympics where I could walk off the track and know I'd given everything I had," she says.

Smith was her family's second Olympian, after older brother Ron, who ran the 10,000 in 1964. One of nine children, Smith was accustomed to persevering for a little opportunity. In school, however, she faced turmoil over her identity in an environment hostile to female athletes.

"Motivation has to come from within. I make up my mind to shoot for the moon. Even if I don't make it, I'll be among the stars."

"I used to separate myself the runner, from the feminine self, the human being," Smith recalls. "Society suggested 'athlete' and 'girl' were two different things. Eventually, I realized there was no need to separate."

In those early days, financial issues still burdened her. Smith went to UCLA for a year and won the national collegiate 800. She had no scholarship, no money and was living at home. "I was a world record holder but paying my own way," said Smith. "I didn't realize then how deprived I was."

After UCLA, Smith attended Cal-State Long Beach but competed for the Pacific Coast Club, the top club of the era. Managed by Tom Jennings, PCC pioneered payments—then under-the-table—to track and field athletes. Jennings had savvy instincts in dealing with meet promoters and knew the European track landscape inside and out.

"We were a traveling circus," says Smith. The PCC was known for kicking up some dust off the track, too. "Maybe we did play a little hard after a meet," Smith concedes.

olympic footnote

One of the toughest and most satisfying races of Smith's life was the 1500 prelims at the 1976 Olympics in Montreal. The top four and next two fastest from four heats qualified 18 women into the semis. In a blanket finish, in which a mere 1/10 of a second separated the top 6 women, Smith ran 4:07.21 in her heat to regain the American record she had held almost continuously for 4 years. Smith placed sixth but advanced on time. Then she got sick and wound up ninth and last in her semi.

Smith ran a full indoor and outdoor season plus a little cross-country. She set 13 world indoor records—in the 1000, 1500, mile, 2000, 3000, and 2-mile—and a total of 31 American records indoors and out. She collected three medals in World Cup events: 1977 silver in the 1500, 1979 bronze in the 3000, and 1991 silver in the marathon.

At her best, no American could touch Smith. "I just took the lead and ran like a wild woman," she once said. In the early 1970s, preceding her rivalry with Jan Merrill-Morin, Smith went 4 years without losing to an American. Even the vaunted Russians could not hold Smith's pace. In a 1977 U.S.-USSR-Canadian indoor meet in Toronto, Smith swept the mile and 2-mile with ease.

In the mid-1980s, Smith made a seamless transition to the longer distances, gaining top-five world rankings in the 10,000 and marathon. In April, 1991, within 17 days, she ran career bests in both events—31:28.92 in Austin, Texas, and 2:27:35 for second place at the London Marathon.

Smith's best road race may have been the 1985 L'eggs 10-K in New York. She defeated a loaded field that included 1984 Olympic gold medalists Joan Samuelson (Marathon) and Maricica Puica (3000) as well as Grete Waitz, who practically owned the Central Park course. After missing the 1984 Olympic team in the 3000, Smith's New York victory showed that longer distance would be her dish for the remainder of her career.

A charter member of the National Distance Running Hall of Fame, Smith coaches men's and women's track and cross-country at Southwestern University in Georgetown, Texas, and runs about 40 miles a week. She also promotes "Race for the Cure," which raises funds for breast cancer research.

Esteemed by Her Peers

To summarize Smith's five Olympic teams: 1972, 1500—8th in the semis; 1976, 1500—9th in the semis; 1980, 1500 (U.S. boycott); 1988, 10,000—5th; 1992, Marathon—12th. Smith was known for her integrity; in her first Olympics at age 19 in Munich, Smith was one of six Americans who volunteered to attend a memorial service for the 11 Israelis slain by Palestinian terrorists. In her last Olympics, at age 39 in Barcelona, Smith was chosen by a vote of team captains to carry the American flag during the Opening Ceremony.

Francie Larrieu Smith's Training Secret ▶▶

Short, Long, and In-Between

Smith's early training for the 1500 and 3000 consisted of a lot of speedwork and modest mileage. In the early 1970s, living at home in Sunnyvale, California, she trained at San Jose City College with coach Augie Argabright of the San Jose Cindergals. Prior to her first Olympics in 1972, she trained twice a day 3 days a week, running 30 to 40 minutes in the mornings, while doing track work almost daily. In one session, she ran 2 × 1.5 miles, then a 600 and a 200. In another, she did 10 × 400. Her longest run was 10 miles once a week.

During the 1976 Olympics, Smith was living in Long Beach while attending Cal-State Long Beach. She trained on the college track with the men's team. Her coach was former NCAA champion Preston Davis, who ordered her favorite workout: up to 4 sets of 600-400-300-200-100, with 40-yard sprints ("surge" training) between each set.

When Davis moved back to his native Texas in 1978, Smith followed. In 2 years, Davis returned to California but Smith remained and began working with Robert Vaughn. For the 1988 Olympic 10,000 meters, Smith logged 80 miles a week. For speed, she did 20 × 200. Smith also did intense speedwork with few repetitions, like 2 × 800 in 2:10 (near race pace at the time) or sets of 2 × 300, with full recovery between sets.

As a marathoner, Smith ran 85 to 90 miles a week, going up to 110 miles on occasion. She kept up the 200s and also ran ½-miles on grass as opposed to the track to keep her legs fresh and extend her career. Grass had another effect. "I became a lot stronger training on uneven surfaces," says Smith.

The linchpin of her distance emphasis was what Vaughn called B.A.E.—Best Aerobic Effort. Twice a week, Smith ran 12 to 14 miles hard, below 6-minute pace but without going so hard that it left her wiped out.

just desserts

Despite constant travel, Smith maintained a healthy diet but was not finicky about it. "Preoccupation with diet promotes eating disorders," she says, admitting, "I cannot pass up a dessert table."

Regina Jacobs 6
1500 meters, 5000 meters

Lifetime Honors Point Total:
14,350

Best Times

800 meters—1:58.08
June 24, 2000, Eugene, Oregon
(Prefontaine Classic)

1500 meters—4:00.35
August 29, 1999, Seville, Spain
(World Championships)

Mile—4:20.93
July 20, 1998, Uniondale, New
York (Goodwill Games)

3000 meters—8:39.56
July 25, 1998, Edwardsville, Illinois (U.S. Open)

5000 meters—14:45.35
July 21, 2000, Sacramento, California (Olympic Trials)

Born: August 23, 1963, Los An-
geles
Current Residence: Oakland, Cali-
fornia
Education: Episcopal Academy,
North Hollywood, California
(1981); Stanford University
(1985); University of California,
Berkeley (MBA, 1992)
Affiliations: Mizuno, New York Ath-
letic Club, New Balance, Nike
Profession: Professional runner
Career Highlights: World indoor
1500 champion; two-time World
Championship 1500 silver
medalist; 10 number-one U.S.
rankings; currently holds four
American records; two-time Fifth
Avenue Mile winner; four-time
Olympian

Daring Herself
to Succeed

Regina Jacobs is the most accomplished
American middle-distance runner since
Mary Slaney—and also the most daring. She
makes no bones about charging out at a fast
pace in pursuit of records. She challenges
the opposition to keep up. She can strike
from behind with a searing kick. And she
can muscle her way through traffic with
sharp elbows and the emotional resolve that
have led to four world championship
medals—more than any other American,
male or female, in the distance events on the
track.

Jacobs won the first of her six U.S. 1500
titles in 1987, 2 years after graduating from
Stanford, where she earned all-American
honors in track and cross-country. But she
was not effective internationally—going for
her MBA, working part-time, weakened by
an iron deficiency—until tying up loose

163

ends, finding the right coach, and training full-time. The coach, Tom Craig, would become Jacobs's husband; they married in 1995.

That was a very good year. Jacobs won the world indoor 1500 in Barcelona, capping a 12-month period in which she twice defeated the 1992 Olympic 1500 titlist, Hassiba Boulmerka of Algeria; earned her first U.S. number-one ranking; and captured the 1994 Fifth Avenue Mile. "Once I made the commitment," Jacobs says, "things took shape."

"I just love racing. I still hold with me that feeling I had as a kid, racing my cousin on the street."

Jacobs improved year by year, but even though she won her second Olympic Trials 1500 in 1996 and was ranked fourth in the world, she placed only 10th in the Atlanta Games. Jacobs began to grow impatient. When would her devotion finally pay off?

Very soon, it turned out. In 1997, Jacobs made a huge advance to the silver medal in the World Championship 1500 at Athens.

Since then, Jacobs has been the dominant American in her event—and in other events. She's moved down to the 800 and defeated the U.S. record holder, Jearl Miles-Clark, more than once. She has moved up to the 3000 and run some of the world's best times. She's tackled the 5000, setting three American records in what may ultimately be Jacobs's premier distance.

Jacobs's range has made her one of the world's most feared runners. Unlike her European rivals, Jacobs runs a full indoor season, delighting home crowds and hanging out at high school

it's okay to dog it

At one point, Jacobs ran distance with her dog, a poodle named Floyd, her best training partner. "When I'm tired," she says, "Floyd perks me up. Dogs never have a bad run. They're not judgmental. I learned from Floyd that even if a run wasn't great, we still got it in. We ran."

meets to help breathe life into track. It's also a chance for her to sharpen competitive instincts in close quarters, like the time she went elbow-to-elbow with Suzy Favor-Hamilton in the 1999 Millrose Games mile at Madison Square Garden.

Jacobs won that battle, but the war was certainly not over between these two rivals, who have given the United States perhaps the world's best 1-2 punch in the 1500.

Jacobs and Favor-Hamilton were also competing off the track—this time in the glamour sweepstakes. In a controversial photo, Jacobs appeared nude in *Runner's World* magazine. It was a graceful, shadowy image, leaving much to the imagination.

In 1999, Jacobs went on to collect her second World Championship silver medal in the 1500 at Seville, Spain. She ran brilliantly under pressure with a career best of 4:00.35, less than a second behind Russian victor Svetlana Masterkova.

With little reprieve, Jacobs jumped into a high-profile 2000 indoor season as the first step in her Olympic campaign. At 36, she never looked better. Jacobs was undefeated indoors, running a 4:21.79 mile, falling just short of Mary Slaney's U.S. record, while hitting 2:35.29 for 1000 meters, erasing Slaney's mark.

Jacobs's upward swing continued unabated at the Olympic Trials with a sweep of the 1500 and 5000. In the 1500, she defeated Favor-Hamilton. In the 5000, Jacobs improved her American record to 14:45.35, but she decided to stick with the 1500 for the Sydney Olympics.

In a devastating blow, however, Jacobs had to withdraw from the U.S. team because of a respiratory infection just a week before the Games began.

Stop Me, Please

With all her experience, Jacobs will still overdo it unless her husband and coach, Tom Craig, catches her in time. In 1999, Jacobs decided to run a half-marathon for training. She was ordered to run a reasonable 6:20 mile pace. Instead she ran 5:40 to 6:00, fatiguing herself for succeeding track events. "Half the time," Jacobs admits, "I need someone who will pull in the reins and say, 'That's enough.'"

The Perfect Balance

In 1987 and 1988, prior to her first World Championships and Olympics, Jacobs was living in Culver City, California, and training at Long Beach State with coach Ron Allice. This was her precommitment period. "I relied on my talent more than my training," says Jacobs. "I didn't have much of a base. I could run one good race, no more."

Jacobs did about 50 miles a week. She took Sundays off. Her longest run was 8 to 10 miles. She did weight work twice a week and track work twice a week. It wasn't a bad program at all but, as Jacobs says, she lacked strength. At the 1987 Worlds in Rome, she didn't make it out of her 1500 heats. Likewise for the 1988 Seoul Olympics.

On the track, Jacobs did a "whistle workout" in which she ran 2 × 1200, in a jog–run–sprint mode, depending on the coach's whistle. She also did 4 × 1000 in 3 minutes each combined with 1.5 miles of 100-meter sprints and a finishing 400 in 62 seconds. Jacobs ran hills once a week and also did a quick, 50-minute tempo run.

Currently, coached by husband Tom Craig, Jacobs's longest run is 60 to 90 minutes and she murders a track session, doing 16 × 400 in 64 or better with a mere 60-second rest between runs. Still, Jacobs is not a high-mileage runner—she totals about 60 a week. If she does more than that, she breaks down. To further guard against injury, she takes 1 day a week off from running, saving it for weights and massage. She also mixes in pool running.

But when she runs, she moves. Her distance pace averages 6:30 a mile. She does an 8-miler, going from the track to a nearby hill for repeats. For speedwork, she enlists a faster college guy to pace her. "I dig very deep in my track workouts," she says.

the american plan

While not obsessive, Jacobs is a careful eater. When she travels, she takes small cartons of rice milk with her and mixes in protein powder to fashion a high-energy drink. "It's hard to get everything you need on the road," she says.

Jan Merrill-Morin

1500 Meters, 3000 Meters, 5000 Meters, Cross-Country

7

Lifetime Honors Point Total: 27,000

Best Times

800 meters—2:02.8
August 6, 1977, Hamburg, Germany (international meet)

1500 meters—4:02.61
July 29, 1976, Montreal (Olympic Games)

3000 meters—8:42.6
July 27, 1978, Oslo, Norway (Bislett Games)

5000 meters—15:30.6
March 22, 1980, Stanford, California (King Games)

10,000 meters (road)—32:04
October 21, 1981, Boston (Bonne Bell 10-K)

Born: June 18, 1956, New London, Connecticut
Current Residence: Waterford, Connecticut
Education: Waterford High School, Waterford, Connecticut (1974); Connecticut College, New London (1980)
Affiliations: Age-Group Athletic Association
Professions: Professional runner, teacher, high school and college coach
Career Highlights: Two-time Pan American gold medalist; World Cross-Country silver medalist; set six world records and 17 American records; won 13 national titles; competed on 24 U.S. international teams

Sole Success

Jan Merrill-Morin came from a family of swimmers and first starred in high school in the breaststroke and on the field hockey team.

She developed an interest in track watching the annual U.S.-Soviet dual meet on television and was inspired by the records of Jim Ryun. "His example made me feel I could do well if I worked hard," Merrill-Morin says.

She added track to her sports menu, winning state high school titles in the 880 and mile while also doing the shot put. Merrill-Morin feels that limited opportunities for girls happened to work in her favor. "The longest girls event was the mile, which was good for me," says Merrill-Morin. "I didn't get burnt out."

Merrill-Morin started training with her longtime coach, marathoner Norm Higgins, and one year out of high school, in 1975, she won the first of two Pan American gold medals in the 1500 meters at Mexico City. The next year, at age 20, she made the Olympic 1500 final at Montreal after running 4:02.61 in the heats to break the American record by 4.6 seconds.

Each season brought her new and exciting challenges. In 1977, Merrill–Morin won the U.S. world cross–country trial, earning the first of seven straight berths in the event, highlighted by an 1981 silver medal behind five-time champion Grete Waitz in Madrid.

"I wanted to excel in running, but I was patient. I didn't feel I had to win. I could put defeat in perspective."

Merrill–Morin says her run against the indomitable Norwegian was her proudest accomplishment. "I was closing on her at the end," she recalls.

With her ponytail, high socks, and "M" on her racing jersey (for Mainz, Germany, where she sometimes trained), Merrill–Morin cut an odd figure, priding herself on her independence. She stayed in Connecticut, trained alone, and was loyal to Higgins. She attended a technical school and then a junior college before getting a math degree from Connecticut College.

Merrill–Morin's math background came in handy in keeping track of her blizzard of numbers. In 1977, she set the first of three world records in the 5000. She would also set three world indoor marks. She collected U.S. titles and U.S. records like track shoes—dozens in the 1500, mile, 3000, 2-mile, 5000, and 10,000. Indoors, outdoors, on the roads.

Her first 3000 mark lowered the American record by 8 seconds; her next, a career-best 8:42.6 in 1978, shaved another 4

roster of champions

In 1994, Merrill-Morin became a charter member of the Connecticut Sports Hall of Fame. Other inductees that year included Olympic gold medal sprinter Lindy Remigino, decathlon champion Bruce Jenner, and figure skating's Dorothy Hamill. To celebrate the occasion, her hometown of Waterford proclaimed that day Jan Merrill-Morin Day.

seconds and stood until the assault of Mary Slaney.

With Slaney in her own league, Merrill-Morin often dueled with Francie Larrieu Smith, two opposite personalities. While Smith was emotional and forthcoming in public, Merrill-Morin was dispassionate, did not mix with her competitors, and shunned reporters. "When it's running, I'm serious, I'm business. I'm not a person to talk to a competitor before or after a race," Merrill-Morin said in her college alumni magazine in 1983.

At the time, she also insisted that Higgins, who appeared overprotective, did not shield her from the press. "Francie Larrieu, who was my main competitor, liked to gab to the press. I wanted a new approach, where if I didn't feel like talking to the press, I wouldn't," says Merrill-Morin.

Merrill-Morin drew away from the running circuit in 1986 when she began coaching at her alma mater, Waterford High. Her prize athlete, Liz Mueller, the 1991 Foot Locker high school cross-country champion, seemed to inherit her independent streak. While continuing at Waterford, Merrill-Morin started coaching the women's track and cross-country squads at the U.S. Coast Guard Academy in 1992. She has produced many NCAA Division III All-Americans and continues to run 60 miles a week.

Track Attack

Merrill-Morin competed in five U.S.-Soviet dual meets that grew out of the cold war. In one, an indoor meet at Fort Worth in 1979, Merrill-Morin got a taste of the aggressive tactics the Soviet women were known for at the time. After winning the 2-mile with a meet record by 18 seconds, she was shoved off the track by a Soviet in the mile. The abusive runner was disqualified and Merrill-Morin wound up third. Afterward, Merrill was hard on herself, not the Soviets. "I must learn to deal with things like that better," she said.

Hard to Beat

Feeling that she lacked speed, Merrill-Morin concentrated on short work as she prepared for the 1976 Olympic Trials in the 1500. Five weeks before the trials, she ran only three distance runs per week, 30 to 45 minutes, and a total of 50 miles a week.

Her coach, Norm Higgins, used terms like "fresh," "good," and "hard" to indicate the desired pace. For example, Merrill-Morin said "fresh" meant 80-second 400 pace, "good" meant 72 to 75 seconds, and "hard" meant 66 to 70—all-out for her in a set of 12 × 400.

Merrill-Morin did most of her training on grass fields. Almost every workout called for some variation in speed. But her volume was moderate and she "rested tactically."

If she did 500s, she would do six of them with a 100-meter recovery, jog 10 minutes, then proceed with 2 × 150, 2 × 100, and 2 × 50, all "hard."

If she did 300s, she would do six of them in 52 to 53 with a 100-meter recovery. Then she jogged 5 minutes and proceeded with 1 × 2000 in 6:20 to 6:45, an additional 3 × 300 in 48. She would jog for another 5 minutes and finish with 3 × 150.

Or, she would do six sets of 4 × 100 in the morning; and, in the afternoon, 1 × 1000 in 2:45 to 2:50, 10 minutes' jogging, and 8 × 200 in 32 to 33 with a 200 rest between runs.

When her racing distance grew in the early 1980s, Merrill-Morin increased her repetitions and distance work. Prior to her second-place run in the 1981 world cross-country meet at 2.75 miles, she did six runs per week of 30 to 40 minutes.

On Sundays, she cruised 15 laps of a 1000-meter grass field at 4:10 per lap in the morning, and pushed 6 × 400 in 75 on a cinder track in the evening. That came the day after a simple 2000 on grass in 7 minutes.

During the week, she had 3 repetition days, all on grass. On Mondays, she ran 12 × 500, alternating hard and easy laps. In the afternoon, she did 4 × 2000 with 400 jogs in between, jogged 10 minutes, then finished with 6 × 150.

On Wednesday evenings, after morning distance work, she did 5 × 1000 in 3:30 to 3:45 with a 400 jog between runs. On Thursday evenings, Merrill-Morin did 10 × 600 in 2:00 (5:20 mile pace) with a 400 jog between runs.

second home

Merrill-Morin ran periodically in Mainz, Germany, where her coach, Norm Higgins, had trained while in the army. She ran through the area's soft forest trails prior to setting a number of her U.S. and world records.

Julie Brown
800 Meters, 1500 Meters, Marathon

8

Lifetime Honors Point Total: 15,400

Best Times

800 meters—2:00.8
July 2, 1977, Sochi, USSR
(U.S.-Soviet meet)

1500 meters—4:06.4
July 13, 1979, San Juan, Puerto
Rico (Pan American Games)

Mile—4:30.23
July 30, 1980, London, England
(international meet)

3000 meters—8:58.27
June 17, 1979, Walnut, California
(AAU Championships)

5000 meters—15:39.50
June 24, 1984, Los Angeles
(Olympic Trials)

Marathon—2:26:24
June 5, 1983, Los Angeles (Avon
Marathon)

Born: February 4, 1955, Billings,
Montana
Current Residence: San Diego
Education: Billings High School,
Billings, Montana (1973); California
State University, Northridge (1979)
Affiliations: Naturite Track Club,
Los Angeles Track Club, Team
Adidas
Professions: Professional runner,
attorney
Career Highlights: World Cross-
Country Champion; set world
10,000-meter record; set Amer-
ican marathon record; won 14
national titles; ran on 20 U.S.
international teams

Range of Abilities

Julie Brown, who increased her distance as women's opportunies grew, had the broadest range of any American runner. She competed at the championship level in every event from the 800 meters to the marathon, earning berths on 20 U.S. international teams.

It's too bad the 5000 and 10,000 were not official international events when Brown starred in the 1970s and early 1980s. She would have been an Olympic gold medal contender in both.

Brown ran anything available as she began working with coach Chuck Debus as a UCLA freshman in the fall of 1973. When Debus, a controversial figure, was fired in the fall of 1975, Brown and many teammates left UCLA to attend California State University, Northridge, where Debus had been hired.

Brown trained for the 800 and 1500, but

her distance ability was evident when she captured the 1975 world cross-country championship at 4000 meters in Rabat, Morocco. She led the U.S. women to the team title; she remains one of only three American women to capture a senior world cross-country event.

"Running should be fun. If people enjoy running, they'll do it well. That's the best advice I ever heard."

With her busy competitive schedule, the trip exhausted her. "When I got to Morocco, all I did for 4 days was eat and sleep," says Brown. "It was biggest taper of my career." Brown feels now that she raced too often. "I tried to do it all," she says. Indeed, a week after Rabat, Brown set one of the early women's world records for the 10,000, running 35:00.4 (she would run 32 and change in road 10-Ks). But the 10,000 would not make the Olympic program until 1988.

Women's marathoning was gaining popularity, however. Two months before Grete Waitz made her historic 1978 debut at New York, Brown, making a big leap in distance, won her first marathon. She ran 2:36:23, an American record, at the Nike–Oregon Track Club event in Eugene, Oregon,

At the time, the longest Olympic event for women was still the 1500, so Brown had to continue her middle-distance pursuits. She was a triple silver medalist at the 1979 Pan American Games in the 800, 1500, and 3000.

She made the 1980 Olympic team in the 800 and 1500 but missed the Moscow Games because of the boycott led by the United States.

Soon, the fight for gender equity led to a women's Olympic Marathon for Los Angeles in 1984. It looked like

peak efforts

Brown currently stays in shape by running 35 to 40 miles a week. But her most rigorous activity comes from mountain climbing. In 1999, she scaled California's Mt. Whitney, at 14,400 feet the highest peak in the contiguous 48 states.

Brown may have finally found her best event.

At New York in 1982, she ran second to Waitz in 2:28:33, becoming the third U.S. woman under 2:30, then ran the 1983 Avon Women's Marathon on the Olympic course and blew everyone away.

Avon had a top-notch field and Brown won by a mile. Literally, *a mile*. She ran a career best 2:26:24, the sixth fastest women's time to date, as former world record holder Christa Vahlensieck of West Germany took second in 2:33:22. Considering the barren road and thin spectator turnout, fifth-place finisher Joyce Smith of Britain observed that Brown's performance was "one of the greatest efforts ever."

To Brown, it felt easy. "The two most effortless races I ever ran were Avon and my world cross victory," she says. "It was almost as if I wasn't running, but standing on the sidelines watching myself."

That year, Brown had moved to Eugene, where she began training with coach Bill Dellinger of the University of Oregon. After Avon, Brown was considered a medal contender for the Los Angeles Games.

Following surgery for an injury that fall, Brown ran a comfortable second to Joan Samuelson at the 1984 U.S. trial in Olympia, Washington.

But the summer day of the Olympic Marathon was not hers. Brown lost her rhythm midway and wound up 36th in 2:47:33.

Maybe it was the heat or the pressure. "It just didn't work for me," she said after the race. Brown competed another couple of years, curtailing her career to attend law school.

Did Anyone See Julie?

Before the 1983 World Track and Field Championships in Helsinki, the U.S. team had a base outside Stockholm, where Brown ran in the forest and went longer than ever. "I got lost in the woods and ended up running 4 hours," Brown recalls.

Fast Fortunes

Working with coach Chuck Debus as a college miler, Brown focused on speed. Prior to her 1975 world cross-country triumph, Brown did three track workouts a week. When she did distance, 45 to 60 minutes, it was considered a recovery day. On Sundays, she did a long run of 2 hours, at close to 6-minute pace, 18 to 19 miles. Brown didn't know how to run slowly.

In her track work, Brown was given very short rests between hard runs. She did 4 × mile, working from 5:20 down to 5:10, with only a 400 jog for rest. She did 4 × 800, from 2:15 to sub-2:10, with a 200 jog for rest. She did 4 × 400 in 65 with only a turn of the track for rest. After that set, she ran an easy 2-mile "to get my pulse down." Then, she repeated that two more times—the 400s and the 2-mile break—for a total of three sets.

Debus also emphasized form drills. Brown did bounding and skipping exercises that were part of an hour-long warmup. Sometimes she did all-out sprints, running 12 × 165, from the middle of the turn to the finish, taking full recovery.

Debus was intense, Brown said, and when she switched to coach Bill Dellinger in 1983, she welcomed his easygoing personality. Now concentrating on the marathon, Brown did 90 to 100 miles a week and less track work. She covered 1-mile loops on a wood-chip trail, 5 to 8 repetitions, at 5:30 pace and faster—her marathon goal. Her longest run was still 2 hours. "One time I tried a 30-miler but it wasn't me," she says.

Brown's toughest quality workout was a 6:30 A.M. track session of 6 to 8 sets of 1 mile. Usually, the mile was broken down into a fast 800 and sprints interspersed with some jogging. Brown followed the same system used by men like Alberto Salazar, also coached by Dellinger at the time.

covering all bases

Preparing for the 1980 Olympic Trials, Brown lived for a period in the mountains around Lake Arrowhead, California, to do her distance runs at 5,000 feet. She still drove back to the L.A. area for track work at sea level. "I felt I'd get the best of both worlds," she says. It worked; Brown made the Olympic team in the 800 and 1500.

PattiSue Plumer

1500 Meters, 3000 Meters, 5000 Meters

Lifetime Honors Point Total:
7,150

Best Times

1500 meters—4:03.42
August 8, 1992, Barcelona, Spain
(Olympics)

Mile—4:24.90
July 6, 1991, Oslo, Norway
(Bislett Games)

Mile (road)—4:16.68
September 22, 1990, New York
(Fifth Avenue Mile)

3000 meters—8:40.98
June 22, 1992, New Orleans
(Olympic Trials)

5000 meters—15:00.00
July 3, 1989, Stockholm, Sweden
(Galan Games)

Born: April 27, 1962, Covina, California

Current Residence: Menlo Park, California

Education: Montrose High School, Montrose, Colorado (1980); Stanford University (1985)

Affiliations: Puma, Athletics West, Nike International

Professions: Professional runner, attorney

Career Highlights: Twice ranked number one in the world; seven times ranked number one in the United States; set American record for the 5000; Goodwill Games champion; Fifth Avenue Mile record holder

Born to Be Wild

In 1989, *Track and Field News* magazine put PattiSue Plumer on the cover with the headline: PLUMER RUNS WILD.

It was a crowning affirmation for Plumer, who was not offered a college scholarship (not one for running anyway) but had become a prolific track performer—an athlete respected worldwide for her teeth-gritting toughness.

At the peak of the 1989 season, Plumer won three 3000 meters in 4 days on the European circuit, defeating the reigning Olympic champion Paula Ivan of Romania in Lausanne, Switzerland. Six days after that race, Plumer set an American 5000 record, running 15 minutes flat in Stockholm to break Mary Slaney's mark by 6.53 seconds.

Plumer went on to capture the IAAF Grand Prix 3000 title that year, sustaining a high performance level despite the busiest schedule of any distance runner in the world.

And 1989 wasn't even Plumer's best season. The next year, Plumer's savvy "train-to-race" program under coach Brooks Johnson made her practically unbeatable. She won 3000s in Lille and Nice in France; Lausanne, Brussels, Belgium; and Cologne, Germany. The locale didn't matter. Plumer took the Goodwill Games 3000 in Seattle and the Grand Prix Final 5000 in Athens. Plumer's vicious kick in the last 100 was her trump card.

"I trained to race and got fit along the way. That's what distinguished me from other American distance runners."

In 1990, Plumer was ranked number one in the world in both the 3000 and 5000. Following the track campaign, Plumer won New York's Fifth Avenue Mile in a course record 4:16.68, which she considers her best performance ever. "I look back on that race and it was easy," Plumer says. "I could have run much faster."

Who would doubt her? Plumer's last quarter was 61 seconds as she rallied from behind to win a $34,000 automobile as first prize.

Fortunately, it was not a Japanese car. In 1985, Plumer suffered a broken leg when she was struck by a Japanese motorist while crossing a street in Tokyo. She missed the 1985 outdoor season, but the accident did not deter her.

A 1984 Stanford University graduate with two NCAA titles, Plumer rebounded in 1986 for the next phase of her two-pronged career—track and the law. Spurred by women's legal challenges to obtain Olympic distance events, Plumer entered

ritual slaughter

Plumer says track athletes must be adaptable and ready for anything abroad. "You can't stick with your rituals," she says. "They change schedules on you, races go off at 11 o'clock at night, you have to catch a flight early the next morning. You always have to be ready to run."

Stanford Law School. She continued training under Johnson, the Stanford coach, while moving up in the international ranks.

Plumer was known for her resiliency. In 1988, despite a bout with pneumonia shortly before the Olympic Trials, she made the U.S. team for Seoul in the 3000. In 1992, Plumer endured back problems requiring as many as 4 hours of physical therapy daily. Still, she won the trials 3000 in a career-best 8:40.98 and placed fifth in the Games despite her continuing pain.

Plumer also took 2nd in the trials 1500, and ran a career-best 4:03.42, placing 10th in the Olympic final.

Plumer wouldn't belabor a setback. She faced running pragmatically, with lively commentary on her races, and seemed to appreciate every step of her career. Unheralded in high school, Plumer had not been recruited by colleges and was lucky to get into Stanford as a track team walk-on.

Sister Act

In *high school, Plumer ran track but not cross-country because her school had no girls team. She was offered one college scholarship, for cross-country skiing. Her sister, Polly, was the family's teenage star, setting a high school record for the mile (4:35:24) in 1982 that still stands.*

At Stanford, Plumer never imagined herself in the company of Mary Slaney until her first indoor race, a 3000 in Saskatoon, Canada, as a sophomore in 1982. "I didn't even know indoor track existed," she says.

Plumer placed fourth and got a jolt from the cheering crowd in the tight arena. Soon, she was running times to match almost any college runner.

Aftr her rich success in the early 1990s, Plumer made her last Olympic bid in 1996, running ninth in the trials 5000. By then, she had two daughters and a legal career to nurture. Plumer became chairperson of the USA Track and Field Athletes Advisory Committee but would leave the law to become director of a parent resource center. She runs and walks with her dog to stay in shape.

Getting the Rhythm

In contrast to traditional high-volume base-building, maverick coach Brooks Johnson trained Plumer on speed, tempo, and strategy to race specific events like the Olympic Trials. He dissected the needs of the event—the distance, the pace, and how the race would be run—and designed a training program geared to those specifics. This method differed from the idea of first getting an athlete in great shape with a distance foundation before sharpening with speed.

"We never counted miles," says Plumer. "Brooks considered that irrelevant. My training never failed me. My injuries were not from running but from freak accidents."

In college, Plumer started the week with long intervals on Mondays. If Plumer's goal was an 8:45 3000, she ran 3 × mile in 4:40 to 4:45, the pace of an 8:45. The rest between runs was not considered important. The essence of Johnson's program was learning the rhythm of your desired race pace and having the speed to carry it out. One of Plumer's workouts was 2 × mile in 4:30 with a 10-minute rest. Plumer ran 40 to 60 miles a week.

Tuesdays were rest days. She did an easy 45 to 60 minutes plus barefoot strides on the infield of the track—"to strengthen my feet." Plumer was a great toe-runner. She could get up on the balls of her feet and sprint like mad while others strained beside her.

Wednesdays, form-and-technique days, consisted of striding with emphasis on forward lean and other aspects of good form. Thursdays were speed days. Plumer ran 12 to 16 × 200 in 28 to 29 seconds with a 200 jog between runs. Fridays were complete rest days. Saturdays were either a meet or a 10-mile run. On Sundays she did swimming or other cross-training.

At her peak, around 1990, Plumer did much the same program but with more intensity. With 8:40 as her 3000 goal, she did her 3 × mile in 4:35. For 200s, she did 2 sets of 12, the first set averaging 29, the second set in 27. She also did 16 × 400, going from 63 down to 57, with a 400 jog rest between.

Pace was everything—and finishing fast. Whatever the distance, Johnson wanted Plumer flying off the last turn. Plumer's sprint became second nature. In some of her 400s, Plumer would run the opening 100 at 70-second 400 pace, working each succeeding 100 faster. She also ran all-out 100-meter sprints, 16 of them. After each 100, she would jog 300 around the track for full recovery. Her times dipped as fast as 11.9 with the wind at her back.

It was not just Plumer's raw speed but how she timed it. "I beat a lot of people," says Plumer, "not because I was faster but because I got a jump on them and they couldn't catch me."

food for thought

In college, Plumer fussed over her food, a fixation that concerned her. But soon she saw world record holder Ingrid Kristiansen of Norway fill up her plate on the eve of a race. And Plumer will never forget one lunch she had with Eamonn Coghlan a few hours before an indoor meet in San Diego. "He sat down and ate clam chowder, a hamburger, french fries, and a milkshake," Plumer recalls. "Then he ran the mile and set a world record."

Jacqueline Hansen
Marathon

10

Lifetime Honors Point Total:
9,250

Best Times
15-K—52:15 September 29, 1974, Florence, Italy (international meet)

Marathon—2:38:19 October 12, 1975, Eugene, Oregon (Nike–Oregon Track Club Marathon)

50-mile (track)—7:14:58 September 29, 1978, Santa Monica, California (AAU Nationals)

Born: November 20, 1948, Binghamton, New York
Current Residence: Topanga, California
Education: Granada Hills High School, Granada Hills, California (1966), California State University, Northridge (1974)
Affiliations: Los Angeles Track Club, Beverly Hills Striders, San Fernando Valley Track Club, Oregon Track Club
Professions: Teacher, coach, sports administrator
Career Highlights: Twice set world marathon record; first woman under 2:40; 12 marathon wins, including Boston and Honolulu; set world 15-K record; AAU 50-mile track titlist with several records en route

World Record Catalyst

Jacqueline Hansen had no patience for the bureaucracy that limited women's running opportunities when she began to excel in the early 1970s.

She pushed for longer women's races and became involved in organizing, protesting, and shaking up the status quo. Hansen's performances spoke the loudest, and her second world record marathon in 1975—the first women's sub–2:40—stunned a running establishment that kept questioning what women could achieve.

When Hansen ran 2:38:19 at the Nike–Oregon Track Club Marathon in Eugene, Oregon, breaking the previous world mark by almost 2 minutes, *Track and Field News* magazine quaintly called her 6:05 mile pace "phenomenal."

Hansen's run was a significant piece of evidence in the dossier that would result in a women's Olympic Marathon in 1984. Hansen would head the upstart International Runners Committee that kicked the tires hard to achieve that goal.

"On my office wall," Hansen says, "there's a quote that reads, 'At the end of your days, you will say that once in your life you gave everything you had for justice.' That's how I feel about my court battles to get women's distance events in the Olympics."

"In high school I was lousy in every sport. I hated P.E. But I joined the track team and fell in love with running. This helped me find myself."

Only 10 men finished ahead of Hansen in her 2:38, prompting men's winner Jon Anderson to remark, "A lot of men would be pretty pleased with a time like hers." In fact, in the litany of favorable comparisons with men, Hansen's time would have put her on every U.S. Olympic team up to 1960.

By then, Hansen's career was 3 years in the making. In high school in Los Angeles, she had done every event she could, including the javelin, and in college, at Cal-State, Northridge, she found that "the longer I went, the better I got." In 1972, training with coach Laszlo Tabori, she won her first marathon, Western Hemisphere. She ran it on a whim and called it a fluke. In 1973, Hansen won Boston. That was no fluke. "I realized I'd found my event," she says.

Hansen still had her speed. Soon after Boston, juggling a full-time job to pay for college, Hansen won the national AIAW mile title. Hansen welcomed the discipline of Tabori's stern hand, and in 1974, she won Western Hemisphere again, setting her first world record of 2:43:55. With her 100-mile-a-

tiger on the track

Hansen's hero was pioneering Olympic hurdler Chi Cheng of Taiwan, who was based in Los Angeles. "When our club showed films of her running, I was in awe," Hansen recalls. "Then, one time when I fell in an indoor race, Chi was the first one to come up to me and see if I was okay. She used to say, 'Run like a tiger . . . Don't look back.' I hung on her every word."

week training, Hansen could string together big races. Two months after her 2:38 in 1975, she won the Honolulu Marathon in course record time.

Running two marathons in succession was perfect grounding for Hansen's greatest challenge, a 50-mile track race in September 1978. It was the AAU championship, and the 200 laps were contested at Santa Monica Community College, which still had a dirt track. Hansen's goal was a world record time of 6 hours. Forced to stop and rest after 35 miles, Hansen ran for more than 7 hours, but she still set several American records for intermediate marks en route.

After that, Hansen took a 2-year hiatus from serious competition to have a child. She resumed running to win three Catalina Marathon titles and at age 36 qualified for the 1984 Olympic Marathon Trial for women. Though her best marathon days were behind her, Hansen had to run on that momentous occasion and finished proudly in the back of the pack.

Hansen continued competing in the masters division, winning world titles in the 1500 and 5000 at Melbourne in 1987. Today, she runs recreationally, doing 5 miles a day along with swimming and weight training.

Hansen has used her charisma to charge young people. She was a teacher, department chair, coach, and athletic director at St. Monica Catholic High School in Santa Monica before taking a position in 1999 as director of coaching education at the Amateur Athletic Foundation in Los Angeles, the group handling the $94 million surplus from the 1984 Olympics. The circle was full.

What's So Hard about 200 Laps?

Hansen's 50-mile track race in 1978 was, she says, "the most profoundly depressing moment of my entire life." She meant the 35-mile point. Around then, the body uses up carbohydrate stored as energy and starts burning fat. Sinking emotions are common, and Hansen hit the wall. Her pace dropped from 7 to 9 minutes a mile. Feeling that her world record was lost, and disoriented from the ordeal, Hansen stopped and rested for 30 minutes. She resumed at a jogger's pace and still collected women's records for 20-K, 25-K, and so on. Every record was a ½-mile long, however, because an official miscounted the laps. Hansen was in such a state that no one dared tell her of the error at the time.

Sprinting for Distance

Preparing for her historic sub-2:40 world record in 1975, Hansen showed the importance of speed in marathon training. She did a Sunday long run that reached 20 to 22 miles and two other 10-milers in a week that totaled 85 to 100, but Hansen's bread-and-butter workouts emphasized speed on a dirt track at Los Angeles Valley College in Valley Glen, California.

Speed was what her coach, Laszlo Tabori, was known for. Hansen's favorite workout consisted of a 5-lap jog followed by 20 laps of in-and-out sprints, tearing down the straightaways and cruising the turns. This is common stock for high school teams, but rare for marathoners. Hansen also ran sets of everything: 200s, 300s, 400s, 600s, 800s, and 1000s. She improved her threshold for running long and fast.

Tabori had great flair for spicing up the workouts, making them different, challenging, intriguing, each night. When Tabori called for a fast mile, he had the runners do five laps and wouldn't tell them which of the four laps—the first four or last four—he would time, so they had to go hard for all five. "It was perfect for me," says Hansen, who thrived on Tabori's mischievous approach. "At the end of a workout, Laszlo would put his arms around you and say, 'You're ready.'"

Three years later, for her 50-miler, Hansen increased her mileage to 120 a week and more. She lengthened her track work to repeat miles. Her long run went to 35 to 40 miles. To get in the long run and have some company, Hansen would run a few miles, jump into a marathon unofficially, run the 26, and do a few miles more.

getting out the wrinkles

In 1974, traveling to Tunisia after running a marathon in Germany, Hansen stopped in Florence, Italy, and saw a poster for a 15-K race in a gelato shop. She figured that a 15-K would be a good workout and showed up to run. And even though she was forced to stop at the 5-K and 10-K so that an official could stamp her race number, Hansen set a world record of 52:15. One Italian man whom she outran told her afterward, "Now that I've been beaten by a woman, I will never run again." Hansen's prize for winning? An iron.

Suzy Favor-Hamilton
800 meters, 1500 meters

Lifetime Honors Point Total:
5,650

Best Times

800 meters—1:58.10
August 1, 2000, Stockholm,
Sweden (Galan Games)

1000 meters—2:33.93
June 4, 1995, Eugene, Oregon
(Prefontaine Classic)

1500 meters—3:57.40
July 28, 2000, Oslo, Norway
(Bislett Games)

Mile—4:22.93
July 20, 1998, Uniondale, New
York (Goodwill Games)

3000 meters—8:46.16
May 6, 2000, Madison, Wisconsin
(Twilight Invitational)

5000 meters—15:06.48
March 18, 2000, Long Beach, California (Long Beach State Classic)

Born: August 8, 1968, Stevens
Point, Wisconsin
Current Residence: New Glarus,
Wisconsin
Education: Stevens Point High
School, Stevens Point, Wisconsin
(1986); University of
Wisconsin–Madison (1990)
Affiliations: Reebok, Nike
Profession: Professional runner
Career Highlights: Winner of 17
national titles, including record
nine NCAA championships;
second fastest American 1500
runner with first sub-4:00
women's 1500 in 13 years; two-
time Olympian

Track's Darling Speeds Up

With her scrubbed Midwestern good looks
and personalized, sexy pinup calendar, Suzy
Favor-Hamilton has been track's darling since
her college days as a record-breaking nine-
time NCAA champion at the University of
Wisconsin.

She's promoted both the sport and herself, and she has made fans from Madison to
Monaco. "I want to sell myself as a great athlete first, but I see nothing wrong with being
sexy," she's said.

Favor-Hamilton has lived up to her bill-
ing at every stage of her career. At Stevens
Point High, she won 11 state titles, 3 U.S.
junior 1500 titles, and 2 Pan American junior 1500 titles. A life-size blowup of her
hangs in the school gym. But small-town
life offered little recreation, and Favor-
Hamilton got her kicks skinny-dipping with
friends in a nearby lake.

"I have a wild side," she says. "I'm adventurous."

Favor-Hamilton's excellent adventure continued in her Wisconsin years when she captured 40 straight finals under innovative coach Peter Tegen and was probably the greatest female college runner ever. As a pro, she's won five U.S. championships—three outdoor and two indoor—and competed in two Olympics and three World Championships.

"I want to wear jewelry and makeup when I run. I want to be feminine. It's part of who I am."

If international success has thus far been fleeting for Favor-Hamilton, she has shown flashes of brilliance that suggest future world stardom. At Monaco in August 1998, Favor-Hamilton ended the American sub-4:00 1500 drought with a 3:58.38, becoming the fastest U.S. woman since Mary Slaney in 1985. The mark even exceeded her license plate, which reads 4FLAT. "We wanted 'sub-4,' but somebody had it," she says.

After the race, which occurred on her thirtieth birthday, Favor-Hamilton and her husband Mark raced down to the Mediterranean surf with Tegen, the coach, to celebrate in the altogether. But Favor-Hamilton stopped short at the last moment, observing the first rule of big-time track: "It's not good to go skinny-dipping with your coach."

Favor-Hamilton is like the prom queen who gets caught smoking in the girls' bathroom. She gives off a hint of danger, of risk. And that's how she competes: running tall, elbows out, frequently on the edge. She can take a punch and dish it out.

Her shoulder-brushing duels with American rival Regina Jacobs have been beauties. However, there's American Tough

getting her fingernails dirty

You would think that someone like Favor-Hamilton would have had a summer job as a lifeguard in her youth. Or maybe, being from Wisconsin, farm work. Nope. She says that she's never milked a cow, but she did get down and dirty one summer as a lab assistant at the University. Her job: cultivating worms.

and European Tough, which is more brazen, the rules be damned. A month before her 3:58, in Oslo, Favor-Hamilton fell victim to Russian Svetlana Masterkova, the 1996 Olympic 800 and 1500 champion. Masterkova was leading when Favor-Hamilton, feeling fitter than ever, came up on her shoulder with 300 to go. A strapping 5'8", Masterkova walloped Favor-Hamilton out of her space. Favor-Hamilton stumbled, lost ground, regained the chase, grazed Masterkova's heel, fell, splattered to the track, and did not get up.

"If I'm going to beat Masterkova," she said at the time, "I'm going to have to swing wide."

She's also going to need more strength, and as the 2000 season unfolded, Favor-Hamilton seemed to have it. She had her best spring ever and looked like an Olympic medal contender for Sydney.

After a year in which Achilles tendon surgery waylaid her career, Favor-Hamilton came back to run early-season career bests in the 3000 (8:46.16) and the 5000 (15:06.48). In both races, the opposition was a half-lap behind.

Favor-Hamilton said that her 1999 injury was a blessing in disguise, forcing her into more long mileage for 1500 strength. She used San Diego as a winter training base and felt that her time had finally arrived.

After taking second to Jacobs in the Olympic Trials 1500, Favor-Hamilton prepped for Sydney with a career-best 3:57.40 in Oslo to defeat several Olympic contenders, including Masterkova.

However, Favor-Hamilton collapsed on the home straight of the Olympic 1500 final and barely finished the race. She attributed the crash to dehydration from anti-inflammatory medicine she'd been taking for an injury.

Making Gains from a Loss

Favor-Hamilton suffered a family tragedy in the fall of 1999 when her brother, Dan, 37, a manic-depressive, committed suicide. Favor-Hamilton talks openly about the impact her brother's death had on her. "It gave me a different way of looking at the world," she says. "In my career, I had lost sight of the big picture. Now I realize how short life can be. I try to be kinder to people. I feel empowered by what happened. Dan's death was a reawakening."

Big-Time Tough

Peter Tegen, who's coached Favor-Hamilton since her college days, brings a European flavor to his training system. A German, Tegen has coached in many countries and started the Wisconsin women's program in 1973. He emphasizes abundant speed drills and calisthenics against resistance—like pulling a sled with a 50-pound weight on it—in almost every practice. The warmups are workouts in themselves.

Every step in Favor-Hamilton's training has a purpose in bolstering the body and mind for racing. Tegen calls his system dynamic running-systematic surge training. "I want to make sure my athletes are always ready to surge or kick, and not get left in the dust," he explains.

In 1998, when Favor-Hamilton ran her first sub-4:00 1500, she trained during the winter on an indoor track three times a week with the Wisconsin women. These were speed days, and each time, she did a warmup consisting of a 2-mile run, 6 × 75-meter strides, stretching and calisthenics, 6 to 8 × 100-meter sprints ("diagonals" across the football practice field), and a 1-mile run. This routine took close to an hour.

Favor-Hamilton's main speed running ranges from repeat 150s and 200s to 800s to a 1000-meter time trial. Afterward, she'll stand in a tub of ice-cold water to soothe her muscles. A couple of times a week, she goes to a gym for additional weight training. Her recovery days are 45- to 60-minute runs. On Sundays, she does a long run of about 11 miles. Sometimes, she switches her long run to Saturday and takes it easy on Sunday to be fresh for Monday's speedwork.

Training in close quarters with the college women helps prepare Favor-Hamilton for the elbows of the track circuit. "We have 'Triple-P' training," says Tegen. "Pacing, passing, and pushing. I always say, 'An athlete should never get boxed in on the track.'"

grilled cheese and a shower

Peer pressure is monumental in high school, but Favor-Hamilton didn't care. Instead of gossiping with her buddies at the Stevens Point lunch table, she went out and ran 2 miles. Later, she did the team practice, running fast 200s or 400s or a 6-miler. Including weekend runs, Favor-Hamilton totaled about 40 miles a week and says her coach, Mike Olsen, "made sure we had a lot of fun."

Patti Catalano Dillon
Marathon

12

Lifetime Honors Point Total:
14,450

Best Times

10-K—32:09, April 5, 1981
New Orleans (Crescent City Classic)

15-K—49:34
May 14, 1981, Jacksonville, Florida (River Run)

10 miles—53:40
August 23, 1980, Flint, Michigan (Bobby Crim)

20-K—1:09:27
May 23, 1981, Wheeling, West Virginia (Elby's)

Half-marathon—1:14:04
September 23, 1979, Manchester, Vermont (Maple Leaf)

Marathon—2:27:52
April 20, 1981, Boston (Boston Marathon)

Born: April 6, 1953, Chelsea, Massachusetts
Current Residence: Hyde Park, Massachusetts
Education: Sacred Heart High School, Kingston, Massachusetts (1971)
Affiliations: Boston Athletic Association, Athletics West, Nike
Profession: Professional runner
Career Highlights: Three-time Honolulu Marathon champion; three-time Boston Marathon runner-up; three-time American record holder in the marathon; set 12 U.S. road records and world records in the 20-K and half-marathon

Running for Her Life

Patti Dillon, who sparked American women's road racing in the late 1970s, unearthed her running talent after a troubled youth. The oldest of nine children—she is Native American (Micmac) on her mother's side—her parents were migrant farm workers picking potatoes and blueberries in the fields around Bangor, Maine. "I had to scrub floors. I had a lot of responsibility," she says.

When her family moved to the Boston area, Dillon joined the high school swim team. But, insecure, she smoked and drank, and once out of school, hung out in bars, got fat and depressed, and felt sorry for herself. Finally, at 23, she realized, "I wanted to do something that made me happy, and that was physical fitness."

She started running in 1976 (she remembers the date, March 28), quit smoking, lost 45 pounds, broke off a brief marriage,

187

joined the Quincy YMCA, and began training with some male runners.

In an approach that would remain her signature style, Dillon obsessively ran herself to exhaustion as an outlet of aggression stemming from her checkered life. "I'd been supporting myself since I was 17," she says.

Dillon, then working as nurse's aide, ran with the guys, trying desperately to keep up. Gradually she did; each run was like a race for her. When the guys said that they were running a marathon in the fall, Dillon said that she would, too.

"As a kid, I was shy. I would never speak up. My mother called me Stillmouth. But once I started running, all my emotions came out."

First, she tried something shorter, the Brockton 5-miler. She was the first woman in 28:53 and won a pewter plate. When she proudly showed her award to a nurse from work, the woman scolded her, saying, "What are you doing taking trophies away from little kids?" Initially crushed, Dillon didn't run for 2 weeks. But she rebounded and set her quest to excel.

There was no stopping her. Dillon won her first marathon, Rhode Island's Ocean State, that fall in 2:53:40. She won it again in 1977 and kept rolling, racing often and piling up victories and records without letup. She acquired a coach, Joe Catalano, whom she married in what would become a tempestuous relationship.

Catalano taught her speedwork, and Dillon trained 150 miles a week and up, new ground for a woman. Demons still swirled in her mind and Dillon developed bulimia, an eating disorder that would plague her for years.

In 1980, despite her affliction, Dillon collected 12 victories, five second-place finishes, and two third places in 19 major races, earning women's Runner of the Year honors from *The Runner* magazine.

That year, in four marathons, Dillon won her third title at

a clean getaway

Dillon was superstitious about never washing the Athletics West racing singlet she wore in her fastest marathons. She would try to keep the shirt clean by throwing water on it in races. She dried the shirt by placing it over a lighted lamp.

Honolulu, won Bermuda, and set two American records while winning Montreal and taking second at New York in the first U.S. women's sub-2:30 (2:29:33) ever. Other victories included the Peachtree 10-K in Atlanta, the Cascade Run Off 15-K in Portland, Oregon, the Bobby Crim 10-miler in Flint, Michigan, Elby's 20-K in Wheeling, West Virginia, and the Maple Leaf Half-Marathon in Manchester, Vermont, where her 1:14:04 set a world record.

The next year, Dillon lowered her U.S. record marathon to 2:27:51 in her third straight runner-up performance at Boston. At one point, Dillon held just about every women's road record. "Each record was like a gift," she says. "I was still unsure, skittish, putting pressure on myself. I never thought I was genuinely liked."

Injuries took Dillon away from marathons for 2 years and prevented her from doing better than 16th in the 1984 Olympic Trial. In 1985, she ran two more marathons, winning Rio, then drifted away from competition. Dillon says that she regrets not testing her talents on the track but that her sponsors preferred that she stick with the roads.

Early on, in 1977, Dillon did run one indoor track 2-mile in about 10 minutes even, defeating a field of men at the Coast Guard Academy. Around then, Dillon also outran a teenage Lynn Jennings to win the New England cross-country title.

In time, Dillon's priorities shifted to motherhood and, in her forties, she had two children with her fourth husband, runner Dan Dillon. Currently, Dillon runs 30 to 40 miles a week, some of it while pushing her kids in a baby jogger.

Toeing the Line

Before her next-to-last marathon at Rio de Janeiro in 1985, Dillon was hit with a severe stomach ailment from drinking the local water. Even though, as she said, "I'd gone to the bathroom 19 times and was a wreck," Dillon felt obliged to run. She started slowly, ducking behind cars to make periodic pit stops as spectators watched in amusement; and she had to change her running form to take pressure off her stomach muscles. Still, Dillon won in 2:38:44, a course record. But altering her form battered her toes, and when Dillon took off her shoes, all 10 toenails fell off.

Pushing the Limits

At her peak, Dillon ran 150 miles a week, and occasionally went higher, reaching a limit of 210 in 1981, when then-husband Joe Catalano was coaching her. Her training focused on dissecting the marathon's 26 miles and running at a pace geared to sub-2:30 performances. A typical week in 1981 went like this.

MONDAY: A.M.—70 to 75 minutes on roads. P.M.—70 to 75 minutes on roads.

TUESDAY: A.M.—60 minutes on roads. P.M.—At the track, 2.5-mile warmup. 8 × mile in 5:10, with 2:30 rest between runs. 2.5-mile cooldown.

WEDNESDAY: A.M.—2-hour "run how you feel," close to 6-minute-mile pace. P.M.—45 to 60 minutes on roads.

THURSDAY: Ladder workout on track or hills. If on a track, do three sets of 440-660-880-1320, then finish with 1 mile. If on hills, do the same workout on Heartbreak Hill of the Boston Marathon course, finishing with a mile in 5:10 on the track. "The 5:10 felt really easy," says Dillon.

FRIDAY: A.M.—Easy 60 to 70 minutes on roads. P.M.—Easy 60 to 70 minutes on roads.

SATURDAY: Occasional race. "Believe me, racing was easier than training. And I got cheers."

SUNDAY: A.M.—2½-hour run, with the first hour consisting of 45 minutes at 6:10 pace, 5 minutes hard at 5:40 pace, 10 minutes at 6:30 pace. Repeat for the second hour, then finish the last 30 minutes easy, as long as it's under 7-minute pace. P.M.—30 to 45 minutes "just to shake out the crud."

a 5-hour flight

Personal conflicts can cause a runner of any level to "run out" his or her feelings. It happened in Dillon's case, when she would periodically split from Catalano, unable to bear the relationship. "Whenever I left Joe," Dillon recalls, "all I did was run. Two hours in the morning, then 3 hours at night."

Kim Merritt
Marathon

13

Lifetime Honors Point Total:
4,750

Best Times

20-K—1:11:38
July 2, 1976, Chicago (Distance
Classic)

Marathon—2:37:57
September 11, 1977, Eugene,
Oregon (Nike–Oregon Track Club
Marathon)

Born: May 22, 1955, Racine,
Wisconsin
Current Residence: Racine,
Wisconsin
Education: Case High School,
Racine, Wisconsin (1973); University of Wisconsin–Parkside (1977)
Affiliations: None
Professions: Professional runner,
factory worker
Career Highlights: Only woman to
win New York City, Boston, and
Honolulu marathons; set American marathon record; won numerous road races at many
distances

Onion Farmer Peels Off

Growing up on a farm in Racine, Wisconsin, Kim Merritt saw that the men in her family were accorded privilege—including the privilege of hard work. "My dad never liked me working on the farm," she recalls. "I said, 'I'm sorry, my brothers are working the farm, I'm working the farm!' I was raised seeing that men got treated better, so I was determined to do whatever men did."

Merritt's spirit brought her out for high school track. There was no girls' team at first so the coach had Merritt train with the boys somewhat clandestinely until the athletic director put a stop to it. She managed to win two state titles in the mile and went to college at nearby University of Wisconsin–Parkside.

Same deal: There was no women's team at Parkside, so Merritt ran with the men. "Guys always respected me. I was right there with them," says Merritt. Sometimes, she was ahead of them. While the college men shirked weekend workouts, Merritt never missed a run.

Young women in Merritt's day capitalized on a wonderful irony. Forced to train with men, they worked harder and improved dramatically. Without a full women's program, they gravitated to long distances and the marathon, which was gaining recognition.

"Rest days? What the heck is a rest day? A rest day—that's when you collapse."

When Merritt, shy and sheltered, left the onion fields of Wisconsin to stake her claim in the big city—New York was first—she was overwhelmed by the attention and acquired the reputation of a recluse. In 1975, the New York City Marathon, still contested on the suffocatingly hilly course within Central Park, was the AAU women's national championship. Everyone turned out: defending champ Kathrine Switzer, 1973 New York champion Nina Kuscsik, 1974 Boston winner Miki Gorman, American record holder Jacki Hansen, and rising stars like Gayle Barron.

Merritt, 20, had some fast times but had run only one marathon, 3:03:27, more than a year before in Illinois. In New York, she showed up on the starting line at the last moment and proceeded to run 2:46:14 in the field of 44 women and triumphed by more than 6 minutes. Afterward, Merritt eluded reporters, sat pensively on a park bench, discarded the laurel wreath placed on her head, and had to be dragged to the awards ceremony. "I didn't like people making a fuss," she says.

Like it or not, Merritt went back to Wisconsin a celebrity. Her coach, Vic Godfrey, helped her raise money to run

inner wisdom

"You have to love running," advises Merritt. "On days when you feel good, pick up the pace. If you feel poopy, back off. Use your inner wisdom. Go with the flow."

Boston in 1976. She won that, too, running 2:47:10 in "the run for the hoses" to defeat Gorman by 5 minutes. After training in 30°F weather, Merritt confronted Boston's 100°F heat that year. Unaccustomed to drinking in races, she took little fluids, and even in victory, practically walked the last mile and was hospitalized with dehydration. It was another badge of honor for the onion farmer.

In 1976, Merritt also captured Honolulu, becoming the first and only woman to win New York, Boston, and Honolulu. But her times were stuck in the 2:40s and Merritt pined for a breakthrough. A year later, she was virtually unbeatable, winning the Falmouth 7.1-miler and Charleston 15-miler leading into the fall marathon season.

Merritt put it all together at the 1977 Nike–Oregon Track Club Marathon in Eugene. She won by 11 minutes in 2:37:57, a U.S. record and the third fastest worldwide. Afterward, Merritt berated herself for being "lazy" and not running faster. "I don't feel as tired as I should," she told the press.

Merritt knew only one pace: hard. One week after Eugene, she won the Lynchburg, West Virginia, 10-miler. "Then I crashed," says Merritt. "I found a tree, laid down, and wanted to die." Still, a month later, she took second at New York in 2:46:03 and was named Road Runners Club of America Runner of the Year for 1977. And twice Merritt placed second in the women's international marathon in Waldniel, West Germany.

Eventually, she would crash. Merritt had gotten married at 18 and did not finish college. Injuries caught up with her and she became despondent. She went through a divorce, developed an eating disorder, and did little running for a decade. But Merritt has reclaimed her health, is running every day again, and hopes to obtain a teaching degree.

Back Door Policy

Before girls' track became an official sport at Case High School, the boys coach, Bill Greiten, was not allowed to include girls in his program. He figured out a way to encourage Merritt by having her come to the back door of the school and run unnoticed with boys who were injured and not doing the regular workouts. "Bill helped me and inspired me," says Merritt.

Kim Merritt's Training Secret ▶▶

College Paves the Way

Merritt averaged 95 miles a week during the height of her career. She used a college men's program as a springboard to marathon success. "Not 'men's' training," Merritt instructs, "people training."

Merritt did 20 miles on Sundays, 10 to 15 miles three times a week, and speedwork at least twice a week. For speed, she ran a standard set of 10 to 12 400s, but with a very short 90-second rest between runs. Merritt's toughest workout was 10 × 1 mile on the college cross-country course. "Our coaches worked us to death," she says with pride.

Today, Merritt's favorite place to run is still the college trails. She lives nearby and runs there with her dogs, a Rottweiler and a golden retriever.

heavy lifting

Now in her forties and balancing 8- to 10-mile runs each day with working two jobs to pay for her teenage daughter's gymnastics program, Merritt gets up at 3 o'clock in the morning. She goes to her first job from 3:30 to 5:00 A.M. She runs from 5:00 to 6:00 A.M., then works her main job in a factory doing heavy lifting. After work, she runs home because her daughter has the car.

Kim Jones 14
Marathon

Lifetime Honors Point Total:
4,750

Best Times

10-K—32:23
March 11, 1989, Orlando, Florida
(Red Lobster)

Half-marathon—1:11:34,
September 18, 1988, Philadelphia
(Philly Half-Marathon)

30-K—1:47:41
October 12, 1986, St. Paul, Minnesota (en route, Twin Cities Marathon)

Marathon—2:26:40
April 15, 1991, Boston (Boston Marathon)

Born: May 2, 1958, Sonoma, California
Current Residence: Boulder, Colorado
Education: Port Townsend High School, Port Townsend, Washington (1976); Eastern Washington University, Cheney (1979) (inc)
Affiliations: Reebok, Nike International
Profession: Professional runner
Career Highlights: 10 second-place finishes in major marathons, including two each at New York and Boston; fastest U.S. marathoner of the 1990s; set American record for 30-K; three-time World Championship team member

The Long and Winding Road

Inspired by Joan Samuelson's Olympic gold medal in 1984, Kim Jones decided she wanted to run the marathon. She'd just started jogging 3 miles a day after being away from the sport.

Jones knew she had speed: In high school, she was state champion in the 400 and the 800. Now, for 26.2 miles, she had to work on endurance.

Within a year, Jones had a coach, Benji Durden, a 1980 Olympic marathoner who would counsel her for most of her career. Jones advanced to 50 miles a week and took second in her first marathon, the 1985 Twin Cities, in 2:35:59, an excellent debut. She went on to win Twin Cities the next year and again in 1989, the year she made a big breakthrough by running under 2:30 while earning the second of her four number-one U.S. rankings.

Two-thirty is considered the world-class dividing line for female marathoners. Jones has had three sub-2:30s, two of them in 1989. She ran 2:29:34 for third at Boston, then 2:27:54 for second at New York, where she was fortunate not to lose time because of a freak occurrence. Jones is superstitious about running under a train trestle when a train is coming through. "At 20 miles," said Jones, "a train was coming over a bridge on the course and I paused, thinking, 'What am I going to do?' Fortunately, when I got to the trestle, the train had passed."

"People are amazed at how much food I consume. I eat red meat three times a week, and close to 4,000 calories a day."

That was about the only good luck Jones has had in her career. At the 1987 World Championship marathon in Rome, she dropped out at 5-K after twisting an ankle on the cobblestone road, and was sidelined for a month. Jones ran her career best of 2:26:40 while taking second at the 1991 Berlin Marathon, but she couldn't really savor the effort. The winning woman, Renata Kokowska of Poland, had two male pacesetters who blocked Jones's path and prevented her from getting drinks. "I was very dehydrated," she said.

The Olympic years have not been kind to her. Jones had to drop out of two Olympic Trials Marathons, in 1992 and 1996, because of illness and injury. In 1992, in particular, Jones was in tremendous shape and, on the heels of her 1991 personal best, considered an Olympic medal threat for Barcelona. But 3 weeks before the Trial, Jones sprained an ankle running in the snow.

She had to train in a pool to stay fit. Jones ran the trial in

marathon mentality

If it's true that being a risk taker makes for successful marathoning, Jones, as a teenager, was an ideal candidate to eventually tackle 26.2 miles. "In high school, on a dare during the winter," Jones recalls, "I climbed a 20-foot crane at a dock and jumped over the boats and into the water."

Houston with a good-luck ring made by her daughter, Jamie, but her ankle didn't hold up and she had to drop out.

Worst of all, Jones, who is still competing at a high level past age 40, suffers from asthma.

"The harder I trained," she said, referring to her early running, "the more prone I was to have an asthma attack." In time, Jones was able to somewhat control the condition with medication, but she still has had to race with an emergency inhaler secured in her shorts or Jogbra. "At times," she said, "it can be a life-or-death situation."

After her 1992 disappointment, Jones rebounded to run 2:30:00 the next year, when she was again ranked number one in the United States.

She continued her world-class running through 1997. That season, she raced to a thrilling victory in her hometown of Spokane, capturing the Bloomsday 12-K run, in a field of 60,000, at age 38.

Soon after that, Jones's personal life went into a tailspin. She went through a divorce and, with all the stress, got sick, lost her motivation, and quit running for 6 months. She moved from Spokane to Boulder, where in 1999 she got back on her feet and resumed training and racing, still feeling that she could run a fast marathon.

Running on the Edge

Jones's life-threatening asthma almost ended her career for good at the 1992 New York City Marathon. "I was on the edge of an attack, but I kept pushing," she recalls. At 17 miles, Jones couldn't breathe; she stopped and was rushed to the hospital. It took an agonizing 3 minutes or so for her airway to function properly. "After that," said Jones, "I was afraid to race for a while."

Distance Destiny

Long runs of up to 3 hours have been essential to Jones's résumé, which includes more than 30 marathons. She has regularly run the marathon distance in training, and her resting pulse hovers around 30. But even with natural speed, she has not neglected short, fast work—the "final ingredient," she says—which has helped her control her asthma.

Before her first marathon victory at Twin Cities in 1986, Jones did a weekly 2½- to 3-hour run, and it wasn't pure LSD, either. In the middle hour, she threw in six combinations of 3 minutes at 10-K race pace with 7 minutes at marathon race pace. On another long day, she ran 90 minutes in the morning, including 30 to 40 minutes at an accelerated tempo. Most days, Jones did a second workout of 30 minutes easy in the afternoon.

Her weekly speed workout, done on the roads, consisted of alternating 3 minutes hard (about a half-mile) with 2 minutes easy. She worked up to 10 repetitions. On her three recovery days a week, Jones ran 40 minutes and lifted weights. She put in 70 to 80 miles a week.

Five years later, when she ran her career-best 2:26:40, Jones advanced to a peak of 100 miles a week. She would do 3 weeks of 100, then taper for a short race, using it for speed, then go back to the higher mileage. She increased her second workout from 30 to 60 minutes, logging at least 30 miles on her long day. And she kept up the fast middle hour in her long run, sometimes done on a treadmill in bad weather.

In another change, Jones switched her speedwork from the roads to the track, where the workout could be more easily monitored and diversified. For example, Jones would do 6 to 8 × 1000 in 3:10 (5:04 mile pace).

going nowhere fast

Because of inclement weather or just because she feels like it, Jones does periodic runs of up to 3 hours on a treadmill. While listening to music, Jones puts her mind on automatic pilot. "It helps condition me not to think about anything, which is how you have to run a marathon," said Jones, adding, "I have more mileage on my treadmill than on my car."

Nina Kuscsik
Marathon

Lifetime Honors Point Total: 13,700

Best Times

10-mile (track)—1:03:24
July 11, 1971, Bronx (Road Runners Club of America event)

Half-marathon—1:23:50
December 3, 1977, Dallas (White Rock Half-Marathon)

Marathon—2:50:22
October 23, 1977, Minneapolis (AAU women's championship)

50-mile—6:35:54
November 5, 1977, New York City (New York Road Runners Club event)

Born: January 3, 1939, Brooklyn
Current Residence: Huntington Station, New York
Education: Midwood High School, Brooklyn (1955); Brooklyn College (2-year degree, 1957)
Affiliations: Long Island Cinderbelles, Greater New York Athletic Association
Profession: Hospital patient representative
Career Highlights: 15 marathon victories, including two New Yorks, one Boston, and seven Yonkers; set world record for 50 miles and U.S. record for 10 miles (track)

Leader of the Pack

With her embracing vigor, behind-the-scenes determination, and courageous performances, Nina Kuscsik has been one of most influential figures in women's running. If you said, "Why?" she said, "Why not?" In her native Brooklyn, she started moving on skates and wheels—winning national events in speed skating, ice skating, and bicycling—and fell into running quite by accident.

"I started running in the spring of 1967," Kuscsik recalls. "I had a flat tire on my bike and had to mail away for a new tire." Without wheels, she started running out of curiosity.

Kuscsik read somewhere "that if a high school runner could do a 7-minute mile, she was worth training." She went out to a track and ran a 7:05. "I figured I was worth training," she said.

Running in ordinary sneakers, Kuscsik

worked up to 5 miles. But she was also pregnant with her third child. While the doctor allowed her to run, Kuscsik felt discomfort, stopped after 3 months, and went back to speed skating. But she'd caught the running bug.

In 1969, on 30 miles a week, she decided to run the Boston Marathon. Women were not yet allowed, but that didn't worry Kuscsik. She jumped out of the bushes near the start and went on to the finish in 3:46. Kuscsik was not one for fanfare. She analyzed a problem and developed a professorial strategy to bust chops.

"I've always felt running is a form of meditation. Running enables us to stop our lives, to go out and find a safe place for ourselves."

She jumped into Boston again in 1970 and 1971 and, lo and behold, women became official in 1972. Kuscsik was the women's winner by 10 minutes in 3:10:26.

At the same time, Kuscsik gained fans at New York, where women were readily accepted by the progressive New York Road Runners Club. The only woman among 127 starters, she ran the first New York in 1970 and, along with 61 others, did not finish on a hot day. In 1971, she took second to Beth Bonner, and their times of 2:55:22 and 2:56:04 made them the first women under 3 hours. Kuscsik won in 1972 and 1973, the latter in 2:57:07 to defeat Kathrine Switzer by 19 minutes in a field of 12 women.

Kuscsik was not above raising hell. In 1972, there was an AAU rule that required women to start the marathon 10 minutes before the men. Only 2 weeks before, Frank Shorter had won the Olympic Marathon in Munich, and there was excitement in the air.

the kennedy touch

In the early 1960s, President John F. Kennedy's touch football on the White House lawn and long hikes captivated a nation and inspired some people, like Kuscsik, to run. "I always believed exercise was good for you," she said. "And if the President took time for a 50-mile hike, I could run."

Disdaining their separate-but-equal status, the women, with Kuscsik in the forefront, staged a sit-down protest on the starting line in Central Park. Officials gave in, and the field ran as one small happy family.

Kuscsik did some training in the early 1970s with a team near her home called the Long Island Cinderbelles, coached by Art Spear, who helped her with speedwork.

One time, she whipped off 20 × 440 the day after running the Yonkers Marathon. Kuscsik won Yonkers seven times. She won other marathons, at least 15 in all, from the Bronx to Indiana to Minnesota, where she posted her career best, 2:50:22 in 1977, taking third in the AAU women's championship.

Kuscsik was at her best that year. Negotiating the hilly, 6-mile loops of Central Park, she set a women's world record for 50 miles, 6:35:54, in November. Altogether, Kuscsik has run "over 80" marathons and ultras as well as the Empire State Run-Up, the annual winter jaunt up 86 flights of the Empire State Building. She won for 3 straight years in the 1980s.

One-Armed Bandit

Kuscsik's Achilles' heel is her shoulder. She has congenital shallow shoulder joints and had to have surgery on both shoulders in the early 1960s. A speed skating fall caused her shoulder to come out of place, and before her first "unofficial" marathon in 1969, she had to train with a cast on her arm.

All along, Kuscsik pressed for women's rights. She held various positions at the New York Road Runners Club and was women's long-distance running chair of The Athletics Congress, the national governing body. Kuscsik played a key role in creating a women's Olympic Marathon in 1984. In 1999, she was named a charter member in the National Distance Running Hall of Fame.

Amid the hustle and bustle, Kuscsik, who currently runs 5 hours a week, was always most content running along the beach at Fire Island, where she had a summer place. "It was 15 miles up and down the surf," she said. "I had it timed for low tide."

The Segment System

In her prime, Kuscsik took an innovative, systematic approach to training. She ran about 70 miles a week, but every 4 or 5 weeks she took a break and lowered it to 40. A couple of times, she hit 100. But, again, she knew to ease up, always taking the whole month of December off before revving up for the new year.

She was a stickler for weekly long runs, 20 to 26 miles, setting drinks along her route and running in a way that enabled her to stimulate "recall" in competition. If Kuscsik went out for 3 hours, she thought of it as twelve 15-minute segments.

"It was a way of marking time. I would observe how I felt during the various segments, if I had an energy lapse and how I worked through it," she said. Kuscsik committed her feelings to memory for races. "It enabled me to assess energy expenditure," she adds. "In my PR marathon in Minnesota, I could say, 'I have five segments to go . . .' "

Kuscsik balanced distance with rigorous speed training. Five days before her first sub-3:00 marathon in 1971, she ran 5 × mile in under 6:00 with a mere 440 jog between runs. She also did a mix of fast 220s and 440s.

Leading up to her 2:50:22 PR in 1977, Kuscsik ran four sets of 5 × 440 in 88 seconds. She jogged a 110 between each run, and a 440 between each set. She also did hill repetitions in Central Park, doing eight climbs of the notorious ascent on the north end. And her 20-miler at the time also had plenty of hills.

When Kuscsik set her mind to run, there was no stopping her. One year, she got caught in traffic and missed the start of a half-marathon on Staten Island. She turned around, drove 3 hours home, and decided to run a full marathon on her own.

before baby joggers

In the 1970s, it was not easy for a single mom to meet her running goals. Kuscsik missed one marathon she was keen on because her kids had the chickenpox. Oftentimes, her babysitter's availability dictated Kuscsik's training plan. "She could only come for a half-hour," said Kuscsik. "I couldn't do distance. So I rushed to a nearby track for speedwork."

Miki Gorman 16
Marathon

Lifetime Honors Point Total: 6,500

Best Times

5-K (track)—17:39.2
July 31, 1979, Hannover, Germany
(World Masters Championship)

10-K—35:23
September 17, 1978, Beverly
Hills, California (Perrier 10-K)

Half-marathon—1:15:58
November 19, 1978, Pasadena,
California (Rose Bowl Half-
Marathon)

Marathon—2:39:11
October 24, 1976, New York City
(New York City Marathon)

Born: August 9, 1935, Chingtau,
China
Current Residence: Los Angeles
Education: Asaka High School,
Fukushima, Japan, 1952
Affiliations: San Fernando Valley
Track Club
Professions: Professional runner,
secretary
Career Highlights: Two-time
winner of both the New York City
and Boston Marathons; set U.S.
marathon record; greatest
achievements at age 40 and up

Forty and Flying

Michiko "Miki" Gorman, one of the few runners worldwide ever to win major open events past age 40, is a Chinese émigré who lived in Japan for many years and came to the United States in 1964. Soon after, she started running for health purposes at the Los Angeles Athletic Club.

Gorman had no idea she had endurance until she ventured into a crazy event in which participants circled the club's small indoor track for up to 24 hours. The goal was to cover 100 miles within that time. The track was 10.7 laps to the mile, and so 100 miles added up to a dizzying 1,076 laps.

The runners were allowed to stop for food, drink, rest, whatever. Total distance was all that mattered.

The first time Gorman tried it, in 1968, she ran 84 miles. The next year, Gorman succeeded with room to spare. The only woman in the field, she did 100 miles in 21 hours. "It was a great feeling of accomplishment," she recalls.

A coach took notice of her and invited her to train and compete outside the club. "I still didn't think I was a good runner. I was very scared," said Gorman.

"Sometimes, if I still felt good after training 18 to 20 miles, I came home and cleaned the house."

But Gorman had a runner's instinct for adventure and left the club to train with other runners in a coached setting. She joined the AAU in 1973, and that year ran her first two marathons, both local, in Culver City. Gorman did not finish the first one, but in December, at age 38, she clocked 2:46:36 for an American record.

Organized women's distance running was still in its infancy, and Gorman was among those setting the pace. She was also noticeable for her size—a tiny 89 pounds. In 1974, Gorman won the Boston Marathon by almost 6 minutes, running 2:47:11 to become the first woman under 3 hours at that event. The victory led Gorman to her first New York City Marathon in 1975. She might have challenged course record breaker Kim Merritt, but Gorman had given birth to her daughter, Danielle, earlier in the year—by Caesarean section after 20 hours' labor—and was still regaining fitness as she placed second in 2:53:03.

Back at Boston in 1976, Gorman, 40, was engaged in a friendly rivalry with the 21-year-old Merritt. On an unbearable, freak 100°F day in which more than 40 percent of the field dropped out, Gorman was again second to Merritt, 2:47:10 to 2:52:27.

That season, Gorman won the women's title in almost every

photo op
Gorman and Kim Merritt, a college student from Wisconsin, became rivals while trading marathon victories. Like a college kid herself, Gorman kept Merritt's picture on her wall for motivation. "I was not very talented," she explains. "Just very competitive."

other event she entered, from the Beverly Hills 10-K to the Ohme, Japan, 30-K, and she carried her hot streak into New York in the fall. Elevating her training with 100-mile weeks, Gorman breezed through the exciting, new 5-borough course in 2:39:11 to triumph by nearly 14 minutes in a course record and career-best time. Her prerace carbohydrate-loading meal apparently played a role. "I ate for two people," Gorman said.

Helping Hand?

After her 1977 Boston Marathon victory, a Runner's World *magazine story included a picture of Gorman holding hands with a male competitor as they neared the finish. "We ran side-by-side from the beginning. He helped me, giving me water and encouragement,"* said Gorman.

Gorman diversified into track and cross-country events, enhancing her racing skills and developing her speed. She was either the first woman, or the first masters woman, in every one of a dozen races in 1977 that flanked her two big marathons. Gorman won Boston again (2:48:33) on another hot day, finally defeating Merritt, who dropped out at 5 miles. Merritt was back at New York to challenge, but Gorman again prevailed, outrunning her by 3 minutes in 2:43:10.

With that victory, Gorman became the only runner, male or female, to capture Boston and New York in the same year; and to this day she's the only runner other than Bill Rodgers to win both races at least twice. Gorman was also victorious abroad. She captured four events—the 1500 meters, the 3000 meters, the 10-K cross-country, and the marathon—in the 40–44 age group at the 1977 World Masters Championships in Göteborg, Sweden.

With her pluck and humility, Gorman became an international ambassador for women. In 1979, at age 44, she enjoyed 1 more year in the world-class ranks, running three sub-3-hour marathons in four months. The last was a 2:54:09 in the first Tokyo Women's Marathon. "Then," said Gorman, "I was ready to retire."

Gorman still ran masters events for awhile and currently does 30 miles a week to stay in shape, with an occasional race for fun.

Tracking Her Speed

Oddly for a marathoner, Gorman loved to train on the track. Maybe it stemmed from her incessant laps as a jogger at the L.A. Athletic Club facility. Even in a 10-mile run, Gorman preferred doing 40 laps at the Beverly Hills High School track to striding some nice trail.

This preference made her ideal raw material for Mihaly Igloi and Laszlo Tabori, the speed-oriented Hungarian coaches she worked under for a period. Pushed by training partners including her husband Michael, a handball player, she sprinted 300s and 400s once a week prior to her 1973 U.S. record 2:46:36 marathon. Gorman also did a weekly 10-miler on the track in a sizzling 62–63 minutes. For a third quality workout per week, Gorman ran hills at Griffith Park. Other days, she did easy distance, going long, 20 to 22 miles, on Sundays. Her mileage totaled 70 to 80 a week.

By 1977, the year she swept both the Boston and New York City marathons, Gorman had intensified her training. Now she was running short speed twice weekly like this: 3 × 300, 5 × 200, and 3 × 400, anchored by a 2.5-mile warmup and a 2.5-mile cooldown. She was still doing her 20 to 22 miler on Sundays, but also picking up close to 20 miles on weekdays with 6 miles in the morning and 10 to 13 at night. At her peak, Gorman logged up to 140 miles a week. And she rarely got injured.

did the alarm go off?

With her ambitious program, Gorman needed an extra push to get up and train every day. "I'm not a morning person," she said. "My husband Michael [now her ex] had to drag me out to run every morning. Otherwise, I would have stayed in bed."

Vicki Huber
3000 Meters

17

Lifetime Honors Point Total: 2,550

Best Times

1500 meters—4:07.40
June 18, 1988, Tampa (TAC Nationals)

3000 meters—8:37.25
September 25, 1988, Seoul, South Korea (Olympic Games)

5000 meters—15:34.94
April 20, 1996, Walnut, California (Mt. Sac Relays)

5-K (road)—15:14
March 29, 1992, Carlsbad, California (Carlsbad 5-K)

Born: May 29, 1967, Wilmington, Delaware
Current Residence: Wilmington, Delaware
Education: Concord High School, Wilmington, Delaware (1985); Villanova University, Villanova, Pennsylvania (1989)
Affiliations: Nike International, Asics Track Club
Career: Professional runner, receptionist in a doctor's office
Career Highlights: Sixth in the 1988 Olympic 3000 meters; eight-time NCAA champion; second-fastest U.S. 3000 runner ever; fourth in the 1992 World Cross-Country Championships; former American record holder in the 5-K on the roads

Surpassing Expectations

Vicki Huber, a world-class performer in track, road, and cross-country, always had the drive to exceed her own expectations. Of her greatest international success, a sixth-place in the 1988 Olympic 3000 final, she says today: "I ran over my head."

Speaking of her other Olympic appearance, in Atlanta in 1996, Huber says, "I should not have made the U.S. team in the 1500 in 1996. But after dropping out of the 5000 [at the Olympic Trials], I was driven."

This pattern of surpassing expectations began in high school in Wilmington, Delaware, where Huber started running to get in shape for field hockey. Discovered by her longtime coach, Joe McNichol, much like a Hollywood star at a drugstore lunch counter, Huber went on to win five state titles.

McNichol likened Huber's long stride to

that of Cuba's 1976 Olympic champion of the 400 and the 800, Alberto Juantorena. "She ran like a thoroughbred," said coach McNichol.

But initially at Villanova, Huber had trouble adjusting to the accelerated college training. The workouts were so intense that Huber was running some of her best times in practice. She questioned whether she could hack it.

"As a runner, you never feel that what you're doing is good enough. You always feel you can work harder. My main tool is my ability to focus. When I'm focused, I'm on."

Huber found a groove in her sophomore year and began collecting NCAA titles. She swept the indoor and outdoor 3000-meter crowns in 1987, 1988, and 1989, won the indoor mile in 1988, and captured the cross-country title in 1989.

Huber's total of eight was one short of the NCAA women's record held by Suzy Favor-Hamilton of Wisconsin.

In 1989, Huber's cross-country victory came in her final collegiate race and sparked a new era in Villanova women's running. Competing at the Naval Academy, Villanova won the first of six straight NCAA cross-country team titles, a record for any men's or women's squad. Huber ran 15:59 on the Annapolis 5000-meter course to triumph by 27 seconds.

Few distance runners make it to the Olympics while still in college. Huber followed her junior season at Villanova by placing second to Mary Slaney in the 1988 Olympic Trials 3000. Amid battering heat in Indianapolis, Huber was the only athlete in the race to set a personal best, running 8:46.68 to break her own collegiate record.

Huber went on to the Seoul Games that summer lacking in-

my hero, my coach

Huber credits her success to her greatest inspiration—her coach Joe McNichol, who has counseled her almost continuously throughout her career. "He's a brilliant, wonderful man, very nurturing, with a great sense of humor," says Huber. McNichol is now living in York, Pennsylvania, and coaches Huber by phone. McNichol feels that Huber has a lot of life left in her legs and championship potential.

ternational experience. All three American women made the 3000 final, but it was Huber who led the trio in sixth place, running a career best of 8:37.25. "I think I handled myself pretty well," Huber said, in typical understatement.

In the next Olympic year, 1992, Huber started out like a potential medalist with a fourth place in the World Cross-Country Championship (6300 meters) held in Boston, and a U.S. record road 5-K (15:14) at the Carlsbad race in California. But Huber would struggle with injury and personal issues, finally regaining decent form when the Games came to the United States in 1996.

By the 1996 Trials, held in Atlanta's Olympic Stadium, Huber had a 1-year-old daughter, Alyssa, the product of a turbulent 3-year marriage to runner Shannon Butler that had ended the previous year.

Beaming with the baby in her arms between races, Huber was not strong enough to finish the 5000 but made the U.S. team in the 1500, placing third on guts alone after a long period of ups and downs. Huber did not advance beyond the qualifying heats at the Games.

After Achilles tendon surgery in 1998, Huber gradually resumed running and launched an exciting comeback in 2000. It was a rebirth, on and off the track. Huber was remarried, back in her hometown of Wilmington, and working with McNichol again. Her daughter was 5, and Huber was balancing family and athletic needs. She felt that she still had some unfinished business on the track and was planning to run the 5000 meters with hopes of exceeding expectations one more time.

Making the Right Moves

Huber's favorite track is the University of Oregon's Hayward Field in Eugene, site of many championship meets and known for its vocal, trackwise fans. It was there, at the 1988 NCAA meet, that Huber ran "the one race that will stick in my mind forever." It was the 3000 against hometown favorite Annette Peters of Oregon. Villanova coach Marty Stern had instructed Huber to make her move late in the race. "Annette was leading and I decided after three laps to go," says Huber. "Marty was saying 'Oh, no,' like I made a mistake. But I knew myself well and I ran a personal best to win. The victory lap in front of the Oregon fans was a great thrill."

Vicki Huber's Training Secret ▶▶

Groomed for Speed

Groomed on the Villanova program of short, fast workouts, Huber has never been a high-mileage runner. Like most college runners, Huber did a few miles every morning at Villanova to loosen up. Her road runs, serving as rest days between track workouts, were 6 miles. During cross-country, the team did fast-paced 8-mile trail runs. Huber's longest runs rarely exceeded an hour, and her weekly mileage was about 40.

Coach Marty Stern gave the squad three track workouts a week. The first one, on Mondays, served as a "prep" for Tuesdays, when the women ran their hardest. On Mondays, Huber ran 3 × 600 or 6 × 400, but slower than race pace. She got her legs moving but did not tax her body. She was fresh for Tuesday; she had to be.

On Tuesdays, Huber would do sets of 400s, 600s, 800s, or 1000s at much faster than race pace. Stern dished out few repetitions but required near-peak effort and allowed full recovery. For example, Huber would run 5 × 400 in 61 seconds. Or she would run a 1500-meter in 4:13, rest, then run an 800-meter in 2:08. Stern was no fan of aimless jogging. On Thursdays, with Saturday meets coming up, Huber would run a set of eight 200s, but slowish—37 to 40 seconds each—to remain limber for competition.

Once on her own, Huber increased her mileage to 65 a week to prepare for the 1992 world cross-country meet in Boston. The race distance was 6300 meters, just short of 4 miles. She increased her long run to 11 miles and did a lot of work on hilly trails at Brandywine Creek State Park in Wilmington. Training mostly by herself, she would run hard for 3 to 4 minutes, take a short rest, and repeat that several times. Or Huber would run a mile hard, slow down, and repeat that three times. In another workout, she did half-mile loops on uphills and downhills on terrain similar to what she would find in Boston.

In her current comeback, Huber trains cautiously in the aftermath of Achilles tendon surgery. "My foot tends to get sore," she says. "No more two runs a day." In other concessions, she has cross-trained with pool running and bicycling. But she hasn't forgotten the money workouts she learned at Villanova. Huber does track work twice a week. One day, it's short repetitions like 200s or 400s; another day, it's long repetitions like 3 × 1200. Her longest run is a Sunday 12-miler, and she does 50 miles a week.

gimme a dozen plain

Huber did her best running in her college years, when her routines were most rigid. "The night before a meet I had to eat pizza, and on race day, 5 hours before my event, I had to eat a plain bagel." Problem was, Huber could never find a bagel when she competed abroad.

Cathy O'Brien
Marathon

18

Lifetime Honors Point Total: 2,300

Best Times

10,000 meters—32:05.40, July 26, 1990, Seattle (Goodwill Games)

15-K—48:56, March 11, 1995, Jacksonville, Florida (River Run)

10 miles—51:47, August 26, 1989, Flint, Michigan (Bobby Crim)

Half-marathon—1:09:39, September 16, 1990, Philadelphia (Philly Half-Marathon)

Marathon—2:29:38, March 3, 1991, Los Angeles (L.A. Marathon)

Born: July 19, 1967, Janesville, Wisconsin

Current Residence: Durham, New Hampshire

Education: Dover High School, Dover, New Hampshire (1985); University of New Hampshire, Durham (2000)

Affiliations: New Balance

Professions: Professional runner, high school coach

Career Highlights: Two-time Olympic marathoner who placed 10th at Barcelona in 1992; set a 10-mile world road record; Goodwill Games silver medalist in the 10,000 meters

Prodigy Fulfills Hope

Like a musical prodigy playing Carnegie Hall, Cathy O'Brien, at age 16, was the youngest competitor in the first Olympic Marathon Trial for women in 1984. Then a junior at Dover High in New Hampshire, O'Brien (née Schiro) had a lighter-than-air stride, easy comfort with long distances, and a New England sensibility rooted in running. The trial, held in Olympia, Washington, was a historic occasion with the debut of the women's marathon coming up that summer at the Los Angeles Olympics.

O'Brien ran 2:34:24 to place ninth, and it was obvious she had a great future in the marathon. That time set a high school record that still stands, and before O'Brien was finished at Dover High, she set many other records, collected 10 state and New England cross-country titles, and won the Foot Locker high school cross-country championship.

She was the talk of track and her precocity caused quite a stir. One parent of a girl O'Brien defeated in the eighth grade went to the school board to try and ban eighth-graders from high school meets. When her coaches, Tom and Marcia Dowling, moved to Kansas City but continued to work with her, some coaches in New Hampshire objected. Other people wondered if perhaps the young kid was doing too much too soon.

"Be consistent, take easy days, establish a good base as opposed to worrying about speed. A good base lasts a lifetime."

But O'Brien was a natural. Nevertheless, when she left home in the fall of 1985 to attend the University of Oregon on an athletic scholarship, she felt out of place. "I was not comfortable competing on a collegiate schedule. And being so far away from home, I missed family," she says now.

O'Brien gave up her scholarship, left Oregon after one semester, and returned home to New Hampshire. She went through a period of readjustment, got away from the running circuit for awhile, and resurfaced to focus on the 1988 Olympic year.

Early in 1988, O'Brien, 20, ventured to New Zealand for training, where she met a New York runner, Mike O'Brien. They got married that February. With stability in her personal life and her best training yet behind her, O'Brien went on to run 2:30:18 for third in the women's Olympic Trial in Pittsburgh, making the U.S. team for Seoul. In her first Olympics, she finished 40th in 2:41:04, nothing to shout about, but a good springboard for next time.

coaching colleagues

How often is the same high school coached at separate times by two of running's most celebrated citizens? O'Brien coached boys' and girls' track at Oyster River High in 1999. Years before, the school's coach was Jeff Johnson, who in the early 1970s came up with the name for a fledgling shoe company he helped get off the ground: Nike.

After that, O'Brien broadened her résumé with road victories in events like the Peachtree 10-K, the Jacksonville 15-K, the Philadelphia Half-Marathon, and the Bobby Crim 10-miler. At the Crim, held in Flint, Michigan, O'Brien ran a world record 51:47 in 1989. Her time still stands as the American record.

She added to her international experience with marathons in Paris and Osaka. Back home, O'Brien took third in the 1989 Chicago Marathon, won the 10,000-meter silver medal (32:05.40) at the 1990 Goodwill Games in Seattle, and earned her biggest victory ever—and fastest time—winning the 1991 Los Angeles Marathon in 2:29:38. O'Brien became the sixth U.S. woman to break 2:30. But her momentum was slowed by a hamstring injury and she couldn't compete for months.

O'Brien recovered in time to get ready for the 1992 Olympic Marathon Trial, held in Houston, where she led for most of the way until those same hamstring muscles tightened up. She eased up to finish second, making the Olympic squad for Barcelona. Despite some training lost to a foot injury, O'Brien placed tenth in the Games to lead the three U.S. women.

O'Brien made one more Olympic bid, in the 10,000 in 1996, running ninth in the Trials.

After that, she got away from competition to devote time to coaching, studying for a college degree in psychology, and starting a family. She gave birth to a son in 1999 and continues to run for up to an hour almost every day.

The Odd Couple

Housing officials at the 1984 U.S. Women's Olympic Marathon Trial in Olympia, Washington, had an intriguing idea when deciding who should room with 16-year-old O'Brien (then Schiro), the youngest runner in the field. There was no other teenager in the race who might share the same anxieties, not to mention taste in music. So the rooming gendarmes chose the oldest woman in the field—54-year-old Sister Marion Irvine, known as "The Flying Nun." How did it work out? "She was fun," said O'Brien.

Going Long

O'Brien's stock-in-trade was always the long run, balanced by long repetitions. Everything else was an easy day. Even in high school, she ran 20 to 22 miles on a Sunday, doing 60 miles a week as she launched her marathon career. She added a midweek medium-long workout of 12 to 15 miles. And she always did repeat miles or 2-miles, like 3 × 2-miles in 10:40 to 11:00, with a half-mile jog-rest.

Training in New Zealand for the 1988 Olympics, O'Brien ran on hallowed terrain made famous by Kiwi legends like Peter Snell and John Walker. She put in several 90-mile weeks in the ultra-hilly Waitakere mountains outside Auckland. On occasion, she'd extend her long run to the full marathon distance of 26 miles. She intensified her repetitions, doing 4 to 6 × mile in 5:15 with a 3–4 minute rest between runs. O'Brien was clearly in 2:30 shape (5:44 pace), or even better.

O'Brien made a big shift in venue for her 1992 Olympic training, going to San Diego, where she had good weather but few hills. Now coached by Bob Sevene, who had worked with Joan Samuelson a decade before, O'Brien increased her mileage to 100 a week. She continued her two long runs and one long repetition workout per week. But she quickened her overall pace, making one of her easy runs more of a tempo workout.

O'Brien did not enjoy running on the track and stayed away from speedwork. Sticking to the roads, her temperament was in sync with her environment.

local color

With all her worldwide travels, O'Brien's favorite training route has always been right at her doorstep in New Hampshire. She could take Bay Road, run along Great Bay, and go as far as 22 miles in the Durham-Newmarket area.

Lifetime Honors Point Total:
4,250

Best Times

Marathon—2:51:37
April 21, 1975, Boston (Boston
Marathon)

Born: January 5, 1947, Amberg,
Germany
Current Residence: New York City
Education: Marshall High School,
Falls Church, Virginia (1964);
Syracuse University, Syracuse,
New York (1968)
Affiliations: Syracuse Track Club,
Central Park Track Club
Professions: Director of Avon
Women's Running Circuit, author,
TV commentator
Career Highlights: New York City
Marathon winner by 27 minutes;
Boston Marathon runner-up; top-
five eight times at New York and
Boston; ran 35 marathons; noto-
rious women's "intruder" at
Boston in 1967

Egads, It's a Woman!

Kathrine Switzer didn't set out to break barriers, shock the running establishment, or
make headlines. Those goals came later. At
first, she just wanted to feel like an athlete.
Growing up in Virginia, Switzer played high
school field hockey and then lacrosse at
Lynchburg College. Her mother, a college administrator with a Ph.D. in English, taught her
the value of education; her father, a big, strapping military man, taught her to be aggressive.

Consequently, young Switzer formed a
worldview that stressed unity of body and
mind and a willingness to buck the system.
"The Greek ideal of the scholar-athlete,"
Switzer states. "I started running because of
what that meant. I have a lot of disdain, even
now, for top athletes who are just jocks."

As Switzer encountered resistance, it was
time to starting shocking people. She told the
college lacrosse coach that she was quitting to
join the men's track squad. She told her

boyfriend, a midshipman from Navy who frowned on her running, to take a hike. The track coach accepted her and entered Switzer in a mile race with men. Switzer ran fourth and last in 5:59, her first race.

No 5:59 mile ever got more media coverage. But college guys still shouted nasty things to Switzer from their dorm windows. That's the way it was: the more high-profile Switzer became, the more vocal the objection.

"My greatest heroine was always Margot Fontayne, the ballerina. Ballet seemed like torture. She made it look beautiful and was a great athlete."

When she left Lynchburg after 2 years for the journalism program at Syracuse, she connected with a crazy guy who'd run the Boston Marathon, Arnie Briggs. They ran through the bitter upstate–New York winter. But Switzer was still scorned by some and had to fend off crap tossed at her through car windows.

Switzer toughed it out, going as far as 20 miles, and told Arnie she wanted to run Boston, too. Switzer knew Roberta Gibb had already run it unofficially, finishing in 3:21. Arnie told her that if she could do a trial run of 26 miles in training, he'd give her his blessing.

In March 1967, a month before Boston, they ran the 26-mile test together. Arnie collapsed in exhaustion. Kathy came through the finish dancing. Arnie said okay, you win, run Boston.

It was 5 years before women were allowed into the race. Switzer signed her entry, "K.V. Switzer," because that's how she'd signed her papers in class—to diminish the chance of her grades being influenced by gender. While that was a savvy act for the 20-year-old, Switzer was still worried that as a runner her femininity was suspect.

For Boston, she put a ribbon in her hair, wore jewelry, and wore contact lenses instead of glasses. She was given number 261 in the field of 601 starters. Switzer never imagined that being a woman would cause such a ruckus. But at 4 miles, Switzer was

cheering squad

In high school, Switzer, a gangly youth, wanted to be a cheerleader—or thought she did—because of the cachet. But her parents discouraged it because they didn't want her "getting a reputation" for hanging around boys. Switzer was secretly glad and had an excuse for her girlfriends: "My parents won't let me." Instead, she went into sports.

picked out, and—as preserved in classic wirephotos—an irate Jock Semple, the old coach and Boston official, charged after her and tried to snatch the number off her back.

Switzer was protected by Arnie and her running fiancé, Tom Miller, who body-blocked Semple into the air. Spectator reaction went along gender lines. Men called her a stupid broad. Women said, go get 'em, baby. Switzer went on to finish in 4:20, and reporters asked, "Are you a suffragette?" Switzer told them, "I just like running."

The "Syracuse coed" was an instant star who went on *The Tonight Show* with Johnny Carson and was suspended by the AAU for breaking every rule in the book, including "traveling without a chaperone." Being cast as a villain, said Switzer, "radicalized" her.

Switzer lived up to the *New York Times*'s estimation that "despite her soft brown hair and winsome look, she can be more than peaches and cream." She trained harder, raced faster, got her bachelor's and master's degrees from Syracuse, and won the 1974 New York City Marathon (3:07:29) by 27 minutes. The next year, running 100 miles a week, Switzer ran Boston in a career-best 2:51:37 (taking second behind Liane Winter's world record 2:42:24), making her the eighth fastest American at the time.

In 1977, Switzer started doing promotional work for Avon and soon created the Avon women's international marathon and running circuit, which helped create a women's Olympic marathon in 1984. The Avon program lasted 8 years and was recreated by Switzer in 1998 with events throughout the United States and other countries. Today, Switzer runs 20 miles a week and says, "I still feel better after a run than after anything else I do."

Avon's Calling

Switzer compromised her own running career to stimulate women's running excellence around the world. Switzer's first Avon marathon was held in Atlanta in 1978 and was won by Marty Cooksey. The 1983 event was held on the Los Angeles Olympics course and won by Julie Brown. When Switzer brought back the Avon program in 1998, it featured 10-K runs and 5-K walk/runs with a global championship. All along, Switzer did broadcasting work, covering the Olympics and more than 50 marathons for the major networks. In 1997, she received an Emmy Award for her work on the Los Angeles Marathon. In 1998, she was a charter inductee in the National Distance Running Hall of Fame.

The Road Came to Her

As a college student aiming for her first, infamous Boston Marathon of 1967, Switzer ran 70 miles a week. Every night after classes, she ran 6 to 10 miles. On Saturdays, she did 10 miles. On Sundays, she ran with a group from the Syracuse Track Club, reaching 20 to 22 miles. It was nothing fancy, just mileage.

Once on her own, Switzer did 10-Ks and other races for speed and increased her long run to 28 miles so that the marathon would seem easier, mentally as well as physically. Before one marathon, she did seven weekly 28-milers in a row.

By the mid-1970s, Switzer was living in the New York City suburbs and training on residential streets and at the local high school track in White Plains. Committed to breaking 3 hours with room to spare, she ran 80 to 110 miles a week for the 12 months leading to the 1975 Boston Marathon. Her training was structured, combining speed with distance, with no days off.

Every morning, Monday through Saturday, Switzer ran 6 miles at 7:45 pace per mile. Every evening, she did another 4 miles, plus occasional speedwork, finishing with a 3-mile cooldown. Her speedwork consisted of either 880s in 2:45–2:50, 440s in 82 seconds, 220s in 37.5 seconds, or repeat 2-milers in 12:20—an ambitious, ideal complement to her long, slow distance. On Sundays, Switzer ran 20 miles with negative splits, starting at 8-minute pace and working down to 7:15. Reflecting on her 2:51 marathon best, she says now, "I found the perfect wave. The road was coming to me. . . ."

just a coke, please

Before the Boston Marathon, Switzer would abstain from alcohol for a month. "Discipline," she said.

Cindy Bremser
1500 Meters, 3000 Meters, 5000 Meters

Lifetime Honors Point Total:
2,150

Best Times

1500 meters—4:04.09
August 30, 1985, Brussels, Belgium (Van Damme)

3000 meters—8:38.60
August 22, 1984, Zurich, Switzerland (Weltklasse)

5000 meters—15:11.78
July 8, 1986, Moscow, U.S.S.R. (Goodwill Games)

Born: May 5, 1953, Milwaukee
Current Residence: Middleton, Wisconsin
Education: Community High School, Mishicot, Wisconsin (1971); University of Wisconsin–Madison (1975)
Affiliations: Wisconsin United, Nike North Track Club
Professions: Professional runner, nurse, health administrator
Career Highlights: Pan American Games, World Cup, and Goodwill Games medalist; third fastest American 3000-meter runner ever

The Leader of the Track

When Cindy Bremser started running in the early 1970s, she was practically an adult and knew little about the sport. It was a time when the federal Title IX legislation that mandated funding of women's educational athletics programs was brewing, and Peter Tegen, a German coach, started a women's squad at the University of Wisconsin, where Bremser was a student. As a result, Bremser discovered a latent talent that led her to nip at the heels of superstardom.

"It was 1973, and they were looking for people to run for the team. I was already 20, mature, and goal-oriented," Bremser recalls.

"There was no scholarship money available. I considered myself good at sports. I needed the exercise. So I went out, starting from scratch," she says.

Like many a novice, Bremser picked up stress fractures in both shins and took a while to find her rhythm. But soon enough, Bremser began to win, make breakthroughs, and run with the consistency that would mark her 15-year career. In her senior year, she defeated collegiate stars like Kim Merritt and Peg Neppel in the mile indoors, running 4:54, fast for the day. "People were excited about me," she said. "Peter told me I could be really good."

"I thrived on hard work. When I got done with a grueling workout, it made me feel really proud."

Indeed she was, but with Mary Slaney around, Bremser ran second a lot. She collected 10 seconds and 7 thirds in U.S. national championships, winning the indoor 2-mile in 1980. Bremser was sturdy, strong, a plugger. She competed on the European circuit every summer and ran on at least 15 U.S. international teams.

In 1983, Bremser won the Pan American Games 1500 silver medal in Venezuela. In 1985, she won the World Cup 3000 bronze medal in Australia. In 1986, she won the Goodwill Games 5000 bronze medal in Moscow, running a career-best 15:11.78 to outleg PattiSue Plumer and gain the number-one U.S. ranking (and number five worldwide) for the year.

Bremser's best season was 1984, and her best event was the 3000. At the Olympic Trials, she ran 8:41.19, her fastest to date, for second behind Slaney. Then, Bremser was a bit player in the Slaney–Zola Budd drama of the 1984 Olympics in Los Angeles. While Slaney and Budd collided in controversy, Bremser placed fourth in 8:42.78, missing a medal by a half-stride.

shower power

Before heading to the track for a meet, Bremser packed her bag, reviewed her strategy, and always took a shower. Why? "I wanted to get rid of dirt, any extra weight," she said. "I think I was pretty normal."

Soon after, in Zurich, Bremser ran what she called the perfect race. She improved her best time to 8:38.60, second by inches to Ulrike Bruns of Germany. Bremser's performance was second only to Slaney's string of marks on the American listings; and even in the year 2000, 16 years later, Bremser stood third (behind Vicki Huber) in the all-time American 3000 annals.

Bremser loved running in Zurich, where "the knowledgeable crowd made every athlete feel important." Groomed by Tegen, a street-smart, globe-trotting coach, Bremser traveled well.

The next season, in Brussels, Bremser ran her fastest 1500, 4:04.09, but it got her only sixth in a race won by Slaney. Bremser's last big year was 1987, when she made her second world championship team. She competed in the 3000 in Rome but did not make the finals.

Bremser went into nursing and currently teaches CPR and works in health promotions.

She has two children, one adopted from China. Bremser runs 40 miles a week, and at 47, dares to do weekly track work with the young Wisconsin women, still coached by Tegen. After all, Bremser was the runner who started it all.

Drake's Cake

With all her fastest times abroad, it was an American meet in the Midwest where Bremser found her greatest kicks. She won the Drake Relays 1500 in Des Moines, Iowa, 5 straight years, from 1981 through 1985, and her 4:10.89 in 1985 stood as the meet record until 2000.

Bound for Speed

Bremser's coach throughout her career, Peter Tegen of Wisconsin, was big on sprints, drills, and calisthenics to develop the speed, strength, and stride that went into track racing. Starting in college, Bremser worked on her form with sets of 50s and 100s. "I used to let my hands hang down," she said, "and accentuate knee lift."

Tegen required track sessions 3 days a week. In her senior year, Bremser mixed 400s for speed with 800s and 1000s, pace work for the 1500. Her distance runs were 45 to 60 minutes, weekly mileage 30 to 40, and she took 1 day off a week.

By the 1984 Olympics, Bremser had doubled her mileage to around 80 a week and was a more complete runner. On the days when she trained on the track, she did 4 miles easy in the mornings. Her three distance runs per week consisted of a 90-minute long run, controlled fartlek with a lot of speed changes, and a tempo run at near race pace for 10 to 20 minutes.

Tegen emphasized race-specific drills that grew to workouts in themselves. Bremser ran up bleacher steps with a weighted vest; year by year, the weight increased. She ran sideways and backward. She did lunges with heavy weights. She used a stretch cord for additional strength and flexibility work.

On the track, Bremser ran sets of 200s in the low 30s with 60-second rests between runs and 400s in the low 60s with 2- to 3-minute rests. Her longer work included 3 × 1000 in under 2:50. Bremser got so fit that she could run a 1500 in under 4:20, take 10 minutes of rest, and do another one in under 4:20. By sustaining good training habits, she enjoyed a long career of peak efforts.

guilt-free diet

As a nurse, Bremser knew that fad diets didn't work. She ate well and also enjoyed the benefits of her labor. "I always figured if I did all that running," said Bremser, "I could have a hot fudge sundae and not feel guilty."

The Rest of the Best: Top 21–50 Women

(mile to the marathon, listed alphabetically)

Gayle Barron, marathon
Sara Mae Berman, marathon
Laurie Binder, marathon
Lynn Bjorklund, 3000 meters, cross-country
Beth Bonner, marathon
Cheryl Bridges, marathon
Nancy Conz, marathon, road
Marty Cooksey, marathon
Marianne Dickerson, marathon
Nancy Ditz, marathon
Deena Drossin, 5000 meters, 10,000 meters
Betty Springs Geiger, 5000 meters, 10,000 meters
Roberta Gibb, marathon
Margaret Groos, 10,000 meters, marathon
Joan Hansen, 3000 meters, 5000 meters
Libbie Hickman, 10,000 meters, marathon
Julie Isphording, marathon, road
Janis Klecker, marathon
Anne Marie Lauck, 10,000 meters, marathon
Peg Neppel, 5000 meters, 10,000 meters
Annette Peters, 5000 meters, 10,000 meters
Sue Peterson, marathon
Amy Rudolph, 3000 meters, 5000 meters
Marla Runyan, 1500 meters, 5000 meters
Judi St. Hilaire, 5000 meters, 10,000, marathon
Julie Shea, 5000 meters, 10,000 meters, marathon
Mary Shea, 5000 meters, 10,000 meters, marathon
Joan Ullyot, marathon
Lisa Weidenbach, 10,000 meters, marathon
Ruth Wysocki, 1500 meters, mile, 3000 meters

▶▶

Train the
Champions'
Way

Training Rundown:
Your Guide to Greatness

The training methods used by the 50 greatest American runners show that there are at least 50 different paths to running excellence. Some athletes did most of their training on the roads. Others preferred the track or grass fields or the mountains. Some ran with partners; others trained alone. Some devoured long mileage while others focused on sprints. Whatever the approach, two qualities are emphatic in the roster of the 50 that deliver a message to all runners: To fulfill your potential—and to derive the most enjoyment from running—you have to work hard and on occasion train fast.

Whether your goal is the 5-K, 10-K, or marathon, pure jogging is not sufficient for ultimate fitness. You'll improve only if you spice up your running a bit. Even if you're not a competitor, variety and a little speed will give both your stride and your mind a lift. Most people, racers included, run for weight control and stress relief, and also because running gives them a feeling of health and well-being.

That feeling can be enriched by applying some methods of the elite to your own program. For faster running, greater endurance, less injury, and more fun, take the champions' challenge and see how you can gain from their success.

Lynn Jennings's Four-Stage Buildup System

The method: Jennings prepares for a big event 4 months in advance. Each month features specific elements, as follows: first month—endurance (high mileage); second month—strength (long repetitions); third month—speed (shorter repetitions); fourth month—fine-tuning (racing and final refinements).

How you do it: If you want to key in on a 5-K race in September, run your highest weekly mileage in May, then gradually drop your volume in June while adding long repetitions like a few miles or 1200s. July is for shorter and faster repeats like 200s or 400s. In August, pick a couple of races and run them to sharpen up, not for performance goals. If your 5-K has hills, run a hilly 5-miler about 3 weeks before. Try to work in a mile race on the track for quickness and focus.

How you benefit: A 4-month program gives your running structure and definition and motivates you to proceed step-by-step in a progressive manner. You'll look forward to accelerating into each new stage. Your body will adapt to each new training dose. Your running will always have a purpose, and once you get some speedwork under your belt, you'll have the confidence to run stronger and faster than ever.

Jim Beatty's Easy Swing Tempo

The method: It's not a dance step but a training pace—the language of Beatty's coach, Mihaly Igloi. "Easy swing tempo," "middle swing tempo," and "hard swing tempo" were among Igloi's training designations for the workout of the day.

How you do it: A coach helps, but you can come up with terminology of your own that suggests the pace and style of training sessions. "Hard," "middle," and "easy" are obvious choices. Make it more personal, something particular to your approach and goals. An easy run can be a "quiet" day. A hard run can be a "challenge" day. A long run can be a "patient" day, or, to pick up on Beatty's usage, "patient tempo," suggesting a deliberate pace that conserves energy and keeps you going.

How you benefit: These terms personalize your training and offer familiar, comfortable cues as motivation. They also soften the perceived difficulty of hard running. Terms like "hard" and "tough" are not swallowed as readily as other labels. Keep your internal dialogue spinning with a language you enjoy.

Francie Larrieu Smith's Best Aerobic Effort

The method: Smith and her coach had their own language, and they termed one regular workout Best Aerobic Effort, or BAE. At least once a week, Smith ran 12 to 14 miles hard, but not so hard that it wiped her out. The pace was aerobic but did not approach racing speed. She used instinct to determine the intensity.

How you do it: Some people call these hard-but-not-too-hard runs FCRs for fast, continuous runs. Take one run per week and pick up the pace to about 80 percent of maximum. You can use a heart rate monitor to figure the effort. Or you can take your fastest pace for a given distance, say an 8-minute pace for 10-K, and run at an 8:40 to 8:45 pace, to give you the necessary effort without generating undue fatigue. "Uncomfortably sustainable" is how one coach describes these 80-percent efforts.

How you benefit: An occasional change of speed prevents you from getting into a running rut. The faster pace improves your conditioning, and you'll run better in training and racing. A BAE is a run to look forward to. It develops concentration because you have to pay close attention to your pace.

Dyrol Burleson's Birthday Run

The method: After miler Burleson's world-class career ended, he continued running an all-out 5-miler on his birthday as motivation to stay fit. With his talent, he was able to hold the 5-minute pace for many years. After that, he slowed and switched goals to 10 miles at 6 minutes a mile.

How you do it: Some runners try to run their age in miles on their birthday, but that can prove to be too daunting for anyone over 30. Burleson's approach is more realistic. Choose a distance and go for it on your special day. Cut yourself some slack and allow a range of time or a few seconds' slowdown per year. For example, if you ran a 5-K and your best was 22:00, you could aim for no worse than a 1-percent slowdown, or 22:13, the next year.

How you benefit: Can you think of a better birthday party, a better way to approach aging, than a fast, validating run? Do it on a favorite course, wear your favorite T-shirt, reward yourself with a good meal after. Make running a celebration of your maturing fitness. Enlist friends and family to join. Don't be too hard on yourself. If you miss your goal, there's always next year.

Kathrine Switzer's Marathon-Plus Training Plan

The method: For her important marathons, Switzer trained longer than the marathon distance, logging 28 miles weekly for 7 straight weeks at one stretch. Switzer did it smartly. When she did her "shorter" 20-milers, she would start at 8:00 per mile and work down to 7:15. After that, her longer runs at a slower pace felt manageable. Mainly, she had to train her mind to spend that much time on the road.

How you do it: If you're a marathoner, start running the second half of your 20-milers a little faster. Do it gradually with small accelerations. Eventually increase your distance, but at a slower pace. Ultimately, you can have the best of both worlds, running a slow 26- to 28-miler one week; then, a couple of weeks later, doing 20 with a faster second half. Experiment with the variables, and don't rush it.

How you benefit: The longer runs will add to your strength and confidence for marathon day. Going 26.2 miles won't seem nearly as intimidating. It'll feel like another long-run weekend with some excitement thrown in. The main point is that you should not assume that 20 miles is your training limit. It's just a number. Don't let artificial barriers hold you back.

Bob Kennedy's 1000 Meters of Speed

The method: Repetition workouts are often done in increments of 400 meters, one lap around the track. Kennedy's pivotal workout is repeat 1000s (2½ laps) and when he's humming, he'll do 5 × 1000 in 2:31 to 2:32 with a short rest. That's practically a 4-minute mile pace, but then, Kennedy's 13-minute goal for the 5000 is about 4:10 per mile.

How you do it: Kennedy runs five repeats because it adds up

to his race distance. If you run the 5-K, do the same: five repeats at 10 seconds faster than your race pace, preferably on a
track. If you run an 8-minute mile pace for a 5-K, that's 5:00
per 1000, so run your repeats at 4:45 to 4:50. Start out taking
the same amount of jog-rest between runs: 5 minutes. Each
time, reduce the rest by 30 seconds until you get down to about
3 minutes.

How you benefit: Running fast on a track requires concentration and courage, and makes road racing seem like a breeze. Your
5-K will feel like a snap. This is a powerful workout that improves stamina, smooths out your stride, builds confidence, and
sharpens your sense of pace. Try it monthly and let the pride last.

Nina Kuscsik's Marathon Segment System

The method: Kuscsik's longest runs, 20 to 26 miles, kept her
on the road for upward of 3 hours. To manage the time, she did
not encounter the workout psychologically in one big swallow.
Instead, she thought of the run as 12 segments of 15 minutes
each. She used mental imagery to commit the route to memory,
so that when she raced a marathon she could use recall to think
of where she trained and tackle each 15-minute segment with
the confidence of the previous experience.

How you do it: Copy Kuscsik. Use 15-minute segments. Or
10 or 20 minutes—whatever works. Never think of a long distance all at once. Even Frank Shorter would break up his
marathons into "intermediate" steps. Run on courses with
enough variation and landmarks so that you can easily separate
the segments in your mind. The segment that passes your old
school, the segment that goes through a park, the segment that
passes the Starbucks, and so on. Write the segments in your
training log.

How you benefit: Any imposing task should be confronted in
small pieces; otherwise, it can be overwhelming. Consider long
runs as small bites of a meal. Digest one bite and proceed.
When you apply your training recall to a race, the results
should prove effective. Visualization is an essential training tool.
The process of cataloguing segments and changing them will
be fun, like a game unto itself.

Bill Dellinger's Finger Method

The method: When Dellinger was in the army, he was stationed at a remote oceanfront base in Washington State, far from a track. Without any distance markers, he counted his strides, calculating the number of strides per quarter-mile, based on his customary pace. In his runs, Dellinger would raise a finger when he knew he'd covered a quarter-mile. He could use the finger-counting system wherever he ran and continue his preferred workouts.

How you do it: Go to a track (or any site with a precise distance) and count your strides for a quarter-mile lap. An average runner does 160 to 170 strides per minute. Apply your finding to any terrain or running environment.

How you benefit: You can use this distance guideline as needed. When you travel and find a new path, you can calculate distance and pace this way. The method gives you greater control over your training. If you find yourself running on a golf course, you can create a workout instead of running indiscriminately. You become a shrewd self-coach.

Jan Merrill-Morin's Home Field Advantage

The method: Merrill-Morin did a lot of training on a grass field. The soft footing helped her minimize injury, and the site was her personal home court. The field had a running path measured at an odd distance of 500 meters. Merrill-Morin used that distance and multiples of it, running 500s, 1000s, and 2000s. She had her times down pat for the various distances and knew what they meant when applied to her events like the 1500, the 3000, and the 5000.

How you do it: Most communities have grass fields for soccer, football, and other recreation, and they're often underutilized. Carve your own path, give it a name, and develop different routes. You can cut a wide berth, doing long loops, or run some fast repeats around one field. These sites often have bathrooms and water fountains.

How you benefit: The soft ground is much easier on the body than concrete roads and also facilitates stretching exercises. Different distances and terrain give your running variety, lessen the tedium, and prevent staleness. A home court is excellent motivation. Having a place for yourself promotes a sense of responsibility and gives your running a boost.

Jim Ryun's Two-Runner Relay

The method: One way Ryun did speed training was to team up with a partner and run a two-person "relay," alternating fast laps of the track. When one man ran, the other one rested. The faster you run, the less rest your partner gets, and that's part of the fun. The idea is to run fast, but not too fast, so you can complete your workout goals and hold an even pace throughout.

How you do it: Grab a partner and go for it. You can run any distance. You can even find two partners and get extra rest between runs. If you proceed with one partner—hopefully someone whose pace matches yours—try doing Ryun's workout of one-lappers (400s). Aim for a pace slightly faster than 5-K race pace. If you run a 6-minute pace for 5-Ks, run the 400s around 85 seconds. Since your rest will be very short (hypothetically, 85 seconds), attempt to do no more than 4 × 400. If that's too rigorous, you'll need more rest or will have to find two partners the next time.

How you benefit: You get all the benefits of speedwork—improved heart function and oxygen transport at a fast pace, and greater tolerance of race conditions—with the camaraderie of one or more training partners. Cheer one another, motivate one another, poke fun, whoop it up. Time each other—the slower person buys dinner—and you'll rise to a level that might surprise you.

Joan Samuelson's Climb-the-Ladder Workout

The method: For fast work and gear changes needed for racing, Samuelson favored ladder training in which she did two or three sets of a 400, 600, 800, mile, mile, 800, 600, and 400. Each change in distance calls for a change in tempo, to mirror race conditions. Samuelson was never considered a particularly fast runner among the elite, but these workouts made up for that lacking and gave her the power to sustain a fast pace.

How you do it: You're not an Olympic champion, so stick with one set. Cut the 2 × mile to one mile and try this: 400, 600, 800, mile, 800, 600, 400. Run each distance at 10-K race pace, except for the mile, which should be done at 5-K race pace. Take a jog-recovery at the same distance of each fast run. The whole workout will be about a 10-K.

How you benefit: If, like Samuelson, you're not a speed demon, ladders won't necessarily make a sprinter out of you. But they will give you the power to hold your desired pace in competition. Ladders are tough, but they're very rewarding. On the back end, after the mile, you should find yourself moving with spirit in the final repeats.

Billy Mills's Tee-to-Greens Golf Course Training

The method: Mills liked to train weekly on the cushiony terrain of a golf course. He would run close to 4 miles hard, dashing from the tee to the green at each hole, taking a brief rest, and repeating the cycle. The hard runs were 300-plus yards, the jogs about 150 yards. Mills did 18 repetitions, covering 18 holes.

How you do it: Find a golf course when it's not busy so that you can be free to roam without being chased away or hit by a ball. Winter may be the best time. Check the course layout ahead of time so you know the distances for each hole. You don't have to be as structured as Mills. Run from each tee down the fairway, but avoid stomping all over the green. Just make sure your fast runs are at least a minute. Jog it off, and go to the next hole. Nine holes are enough. You can always return and do the back nine.

How you benefit: This is a repetition workout on a leg-friendly course. The turf is excellent for generating speed without pounding the body. The pretty surroundings are inspiring and there are new things to see everywhere to keep your mind active. Even while tired, you feel refreshed to the end, and there might even be hoses going to cool you off. Take advantage of it.

Patti Catalano Dillon's Mixed-Pace Marathon Workout

The method: Dillon's long run was 2½ hours, roughly the same time as she would race the marathon, and it was structured with varied paces. She ran the first 45 minutes at 6:10 per mile (30 seconds slower than race pace), the next 5 minutes at 5:40 mile pace (race pace), and the next 10 minutes at 6:30 pace (50 seconds slower than race). That gave her an hour. She repeated that cycle for the next hour, and for the final 30 minutes she ran at about 7 minutes per mile (1:20 slower than race pace).

How you do it: Whatever your pace or distance, you can also intersperse quality training into a long run. Say you're a 4-hour marathoner (about 9-minutes per mile). Divide your 20-mile run, which will take you more than 3 hours, into 1-hour cycles. Run each hour in Dillon's 45-5-10 manner: 45 minutes at 9:30 pace, 5 minutes at 8:30 pace, 10 minutes at 9:50 pace. If there's any time left, finish up easily at over 10 minutes a mile.

How you benefit: Long marathon runs can drag on, and this system gives you a lot to think about and act upon, making the run feel less tedious. The brief faster pace will enable you to improve your pace for racing, and you'll have the confidence of knowing you've done it. The quicker tempo also forces you to change your stride pattern so that you won't get stuck in the same gait for hours on end, which can tighten the body and cause injury. Also, you'll have to consider the distance in smaller pieces—the best way to mentally tackle a long run.

Marty Liquori's KISS System

The method: Liquori's Villanova coach, Jumbo Elliott, mocked the overthinking of training that he felt was in vogue with a no-frills approach: Keep It Simple Stupid (KISS). His workouts were basic sets of fast laps of the track, and Liquori found that he could sharpen up for a race by running hard 3 days in a row, as long as the runs were short—and simple. He would run 4 × 400 one day, 2 × 200 the next, and finally a mile's worth of 100s the 3rd day in fine-tuning for a race.

How you do it: Experiment with 3 straight days of quality work the week before a race. Do the 400s, 200s, and 100s at faster than race pace. If you want to vary it, get off from the track and do the 100s on grass or trail. Remember to do at least a mile warmup and cooldown.

How you benefit: You'll get your body into a consistent racing groove without overdoing it. A few 400s and 200s are easy to tolerate, especially if you're pretty fit. Coaches have been saying that too much tapering off before a race is counterproductive, and that you need to keep moving at a good pace to keep your body primed.

References

Periodicals

Track and Field News
Runner's World
The Runner
The Harrier

Books

A Cold Clear Day by Frank Murphy (Wind Sprint, Kansas City, 1992).

Always Young by Frank Dolson (World, Mountain View, CA, 1975).

The American Marathon by Pamela Cooper (Syracuse University Press, 1998).

Best Efforts by Kenny Moore (Doubleday, New York, 1982).

Corbitt by John Chodes (Tafnews Press, Los Altos, CA, 1974).

In Quest of Gold by Jim Ryun with Mike Phillips (Harper and Row, New York, 1984).

The Jim Ryun Story by Cordner Nelson (Tafnews, Los Altos, CA, 1967).

Marathon by Clarence DeMar (New England Press, Shelburne, VT, 1981).

Marathoning by Bill Rodgers with Joe Concannon (Simon and Schuster, New York, 1980).

Marty Liquori's Guide for the Elite Runner by Marty Liquori and John L. Parker (Playboy Press, Chicago, 1980).

The Miler by Steve Scott with Marc Bloom (Macmillan, New York, 1997).

Never Quit by Glenn Cunningam with George X. Sand (Chosen, Lincoln, VA, 1981).

Olympic Gold by Frank Shorter with Marc Bloom (Houghton Mifflin, Boston, 1984).

The Olympic Marathon by David E. Martin and Roger W. H. Gynn (Human Kinetics, Champaign, IL, 2000).

Olympic Track and Field by Bert Nelson (Tafnews, Los Altos, CA, 1979).

Pre by Tom Jordan (Tafnews, Los Altos, CA, 1977).

Runners and Races: 1500/mile by Cordner Nelson and Roberto Quercetani (Tafnews, Los Altos, CA, 1973).

Running Tide by Joan Samuelson (Knopf, New York, 1987).

Running with the Legends by Michael Sandrock (Human Kinetics, Champaign, IL, 1996).

Tales of Gold by Lewis H. Carlson and John J. Fogarty (Contemporary, Chicago, 1987).

USA Track and Field Media Guides, Record Books, and Annuals

Photo Credits

Horace Ashenfelter: Courtesy of Horace Ashenfelter
Jim Beatty: Courtesy of Jim Beatty
Cindy Bremser: © Diane Johnson/Allsport
Julie Brown: © Paul J. Sutton/DUOMO, 1980
Dyrol Burleson: © Bettmann/CORBIS
Ted Corbitt: Courtesy of Ted Corbitt
Glenn Cunningham: © CORBIS
Bill Dellinger: © Bettmann/CORBIS
Clarence DeMar: © AP/Wide World Photos
Brian Diemer: © Simon Bruty/Allsport
Patti Catalano Dillon: ©Paul J. Sutton/DUOMO
Buddy Edelen: © Bettmann/CORBIS
Suzy Favor-Hamilton: © Andy Lyons/Allsport 1997
Miki Gorman: © 1979 Steven E. Sutton/DUOMO
Jacqueline Hansen: Courtesy of Jacqueline Hansen
Johnny Hayes: Courtesy of Johnny Hayes Estate
Doris Heritage: Courtesy of Doris Heritage
Vicki Huber: © David H. Wells/CORBIS
Regina Jacobs: © Donald Miralle/Allsport
Lynn Jennings: © Tony Duffy/Allsport
Kim Jones: Courtesy of Kim Jones
John J. Kelley: Courtesy of John J. Kelley
Bob Kennedy: Courtesy of Bob Kennedy
Abel Kiviat: © Bettmann/CORBIS
Nina Kuscsik: Courtesy of Nina Kuscsik
Gerry Lindgren: © AP Wide World Photos
Marty Liquori: © Paul J. Sutton/DUOMO, 1980
Sydney Maree: © DUOMO, 1987

Henry Marsh: Courtesy of Henry Marsh
Jan Merrill-Morin: © Steven E. Sutton/DUOMO
Kim Merritt: © Paul J. Sutton/DUOMO, 1978
Billy Mills: © UPI/Bettmann
Cathy O'Brien: Courtesy of Cathy O'Brien
PattiSue Plumer: © Mike Powell/Allsport
Steve Prefontaine: Courtesy of the University of Oregon and the Prefontaine Family
Pat Porter: © Paul J. Sutton/DUOMO, 1984
Bill Rodgers: Courtesy of Bill Rodgers
Jim Ryun: © Bettmann/CORBIS
Alberto Salazar: © Alvin Chung/Allsport
Joan Samuelson: Courtesy of Joan Samuelson
Bob Schul: © Bettmann/CORBIS
Steve Scott: © Diane Johnson/Allsport
Mel Sheppard: © Bettmann/CORBIS
Frank Shorter: © CORBIS/Bettmann-UPI
Mary Slaney: © Gary Mortimore/Allsport
Francie Larrieu Smith: © Mike Powell/Allsport
Jim Spivey: © Steven E. Sutton/DUOMO
Kathrine Switzer: Courtesy of Kathrine Switzer/Avon Marathon
Craig Virgin: © Warren Morgan, courtesy of Craig Virgin
George Young: Courtesy of George Young

Index